Innovatives Markenmanagement

Band 55

HHL LEIPZIG GRADUATE SCHOOL OF MANAGEMENT

Herausgegeben von

Ch. Burmann, Bremen, Deutschland
M. Kirchgeorg, Leipzig, Deutschland

Marken sind in vielen Unternehmen mittlerweile zu wichtigen Vermögenswerten geworden, die zukünftig immer häufiger auch in der Bilanz erfasst werden können. Insbesondere in reiferen Märkten ist die Marke heute oft das einzig nachhaltige Differenzierungsmerkmal im Wettbewerb. Vor diesem Hintergrund kommt der professionellen Führung von Marken eine sehr hohe Bedeutung für den Unternehmenserfolg zu. Dabei müssen zukünftig innovative Wege beschritten werden. Die Schriftenreihe will durch die Veröffentlichung neuester Forschungserkenntnisse Anstöße für eine solche Neuausrichtung der Markenführung liefern.

Herausgegeben von
Professor Dr. Christoph Burmann
Universität Bremen,
Lehrstuhl für innovatives
Markenmanagement (LiM®)

Professor Dr. Manfred Kirchgeorg
HHL Leipzig Graduate School
of Management,
SVI-Stiftungslehrstuhl für Marketing

Barbara Kleine-Kalmer

Brand Page Attachment

An Empirical Study on Facebook Users' Attachment to Brand Pages

Foreword by Prof. Dr. Christoph Burmann

Springer Gabler

Barbara Kleine-Kalmer
Bremen, Germany

Dissertation Universität Bremen, 2015

Innovatives Markenmanagement
ISBN 978-3-658-12438-0 ISBN 978-3-658-12439-7 (eBook)
DOI 10.1007/978-3-658-12439-7

Library of Congress Control Number: 2016930288

Springer Gabler

Printed on acid-free paper

Springer Gabler is a brand of Springer Fachmedien Wiesbaden
Springer Fachmedien Wiesbaden is part of Springer Science+Business Media
(www.springer.com)

Foreword

Brands evoke emotions. That is a known fact. Emotions become even more important for the success of brands in the current market situation. As a result of globalization, product and process technologies nowadays are diffusing faster and the internet accelerates the widespread availability particularly of technological know-how. As a consequence of both developments, functional benefits of brands (based on technology) can be imitated easier than ever.

Another reason for the importance of emotions is that today most needs of buyers are satisfied, especially in highly industrialised countries. Hence, the wish for emotional benefits and special experiences becomes more important for buyer behaviour. Therefore differentiation and competitive advantages of brands today and in the future are based primarily on emotions rather than functional benefits.

The emotionality of a brand depends on the extent to which a brand reflects the buyer's identity. The more it does, the more attractive a brand becomes and the feeling of emotional connectedness towards a brand grows. This connection is called brand attachment. Research e.g. from Park and his colleagues shows, that brand attachment has high predictive power for future purchase behaviour. Further, studies revealed that brand attachment is influenced highly by emotions. In other words, in every emotional brand attachment and purchase decision, rational justification is implicit.

Dr. Barbara Kleine-Kalmer transfers this state of the art research on brand attachment into the context of Facebook brand pages. Thus, she introduces the concept of brand *page* attachment. On the basis of a comprehensive quantitative study Dr. Kleine-Kalmer validates the new construct as relevant for buyer behaviour. She further investigates which instruments and antecedents influence brand page attachment. Through these conceptually and empirically profound analyses, the author detects highly interesting implications for the management of brands in the context of social media.

The PhD thesis at hand represents Volume 55 of the edited book series entitle "Innovative Brand Management" published by Springer Gabler. These book series document research projects conducted by Germany's first and only Chair of innovative Brand Management (LiM) at the University of Bremen and the Chair of Marketing Management at Leipzig Graduate School of Management (HHL). My co-editor Prof. Dr. Manfred Kirchgeorg and I are looking forward to getting feedback (please e-mail to burmann@uni-bremen.de or mkirchgeorg@t-online.de). We will go on to publish at least five PhD thesis projects per annum within these book series in order to vitalize the growing interest in innovative brand management. This growing interest is also represented through the translation of the book "Identity-based Brand Management" into the Chinese (March 2015), English (December 2015) and French language (January 2016).

Finally, I wish the thesis of Dr. Barbara Kleine-Kalmer a very broad distribution in theory and practice given the excellent conceptual and empiric quality of this study.

Univ.-Prof. Dr. Christoph Burmann

Preface

Rapid development and fast adoption of digital devices into everyday life has changed perspectives. When I grew up, I used to call friends from a landline telephone and we would agree on a fixed time and place where we would meet. Today, such a routine seems almost impossible without communication via smartphones and immediate response from friends. When we went on holidays, we studied a map and planned the route before the trip started. I do not know how we ever found any place without satellite navigation and google maps. Going to a different country meant being disconnected because there was no wireless LAN, no skype, facetime, facebook or what's app. I might sound like a dinosaur but I actually just turned 33.

Digital technology entered our lives and changed the way we communicate, travel, research, work and manage our everyday lives. It also altered the way we manage brands. The rise of social media fostered the transformation from one-way mass communication to a dialogue between users and brands and between users about brands. Being fascinated from these phenomena, the aim of my doctoral thesis is to contribute to closing one of the many knowledge gaps about brand management in digital media.

The focus of this work is to research the role of connection in social media. Though many studies have been published about social media by now, the discussion about measuring engagement and the effects of branding is still evolving. Quantitative measures as likes, shares and comments are challenged to be the right diagnostics. Hence, the intent of this thesis is to consider the emotional connection to brand pages and correspondingly investigate the antecedents and consequences. For this purpose the conceptual framework was developed by a thorough investigation of state of the art research. The concept of brand attachment could be identified as most suitable for the measurement of emotional connection and was therefore transferred to the context of brand pages. Consequently, the construct of brand *page* attachment was developed.

Through a comprehensive quantitative study, the impact of brand page attachment on consumer behaviour in social networks could be validated. Furthermore, insights on antecedents and determinants for impacting and controlling brand page attachment could be generated and hence implications for practitioners were deducted.

This document was accepted as doctoral thesis by the Faculty of Business Studies & Economics at the University of Bremen, Germany in early 2015. The thesis was written during my time as Research Associate at the Chair of Innovative Brand Management (LiM).

The successful completion of this work was only possible thanks to the great support of many people. First, I would like to thank my PhD advisor Prof. Dr. Christoph Burmann for giving me the opportunity to pursue my doctoral education and for supporting my wish to study a field of research that was rather unexplored at the time. Further, I would like to thank Prof. Dr. Martin Missong for taking over the role of second reviewer. Many thanks also to Prof. Dr. Georg Müller-Christ and Prof. Dr. André W. Heinemann for joining the Examination Committee.

To my friends and colleagues at the Faculty:

Michael Schade, Rico Piehler, Frank Hemmann, Heidi Schröder, Maleen Ulbricht, Daniela Eilers, Fabian Stichnoth, Sabrina Hegner, Christopher Kanitz, Andreas Müller, Stephan Hanisch, Ines Nee, Florian Horstmann, Corinna Beckmann, Uwe Schnetzer, Tanja Koppen, Tilo Halaszovich and Julia Feddersen

thank you for the team spirit, for great memories, for sharing your knowledge, for your support, for the great time we spent together. You really made these three years a very special and unforgettable time.

Without the support of my family, this thesis would have never been possible. To my parents Maria and Achim Kleine-Kalmer and my siblings Ruth and Joachim thank you for being the greatest and for supporting me in every phase of my life.

Finally, I would like to express my deepest gratitude to my husband Oskar, for your love and patience, your encouragement and for caring. To you, I dedicate this work.

Barbara Kleine-Kalmer

Contents

Figures

Tables

Abbreviations

AVE	average variance extracted
CB-SEM	covariance-based structural equation modelling
cf.	confer (compare)
ed.	editor
e.g.	exempli gratia (for example)
et al.	et alii (and others)
et seq.	et sequens (and the following one)
et seqq.	et sequentes (and the following ones)
eWOM	electronic word-of-mouth
FMCG	fast moving consumer goods
i.e.	id est (that is)
KPI	key performance indicator
p.	page
pp.	pages
PLS-SEM	partial least squares structural equation modelling
ROI	return on investment
RSVP	répondez s'il vous plaît
SEM	structural equation modelling
U&G	uses and gratifications
VIF	variance inflation factor
WOM	word-of-mouth

A Relevance of social networks for brand management

1 How new media challenge brand management

Due to innovations in technology, numerous social media platforms have been launched in the past decade.[1] The term social media embraces all kinds of digital media that provide platforms for users to interact.[2] Social media can be characterised as a "group of internet-based applications that build on the ideological and technological foundations of web 2.0[3], and that allow the creation and exchange of user generated content[4]."[5]

The advent of new media[6] has led to a communication shift.[7] While traditional mass media are typified through sender-receiver relationships, social media are characterised through their interactivity[8].[9] Consumers are commenting, sharing and creating various materials including brand related content.[10] They are becoming co-producers

---

[1] Cf. MUNTINGA/MOORMAN/SMIT (2011), p. 13, cf. SASHI (2012), p. 254, cf. MARKETING SCIENCE INSTITUTE (2010), p. 7, cf. JAHN/KUNZ (2014), p. 2.

[2] Cf. JAHN/KUNZ (2014), p. 5.

[3] KAPLAN/HAENLEIN (2010) define web 2.0 "as a platform whereby content and applications are no longer created and published by individuals, but instead are continuously modified by all users in a participatory and collaborative fashion." KAPLAN/HAENLEIN (2010), p. 61.

[4] KAPLAN/HAENLEIN (2010) define user generated content "as the sum of all ways in which people make use of Social Media. The term [..] is usually applied to describe the various forms of media content that are publicly available and created by end-users." KAPLAN/HAENLEIN (2010), p. 61.

[5] KAPLAN/HAENLEIN (2010), p. 61.

[6] "New media are websites and other digital communication and information channels in which active consumers engage in behaviors that can be consumed by others both in real time and long afterwards regardless of their spatial location." HENNIG-THURAU ET AL. (2010), p. 312. New media allow "real- time information exchange" HENNIG-THURAU ET AL. (2010), p. 311.

[7] Cf. HENNIG-THURAU ET AL. (2010), p. 311, cf. JAHN/KUNZ (2012), p. 344.

[8] EILERS (2014) defines brand related interaction as communication between a brand and one or more consumers or among consumers in social media, that contains brand related content and is characterized through reciprocity. EILERS (2014), p. 64. More detail on the subject of interaction is provided in chapter B 1.4. For review on the relevant literature on interaction, please read EILERS (2014).

[9] Cf. WALLACE/BUIL/DE CHERNATONY (2012), p. 129.

[10] Cf. JAHN/KUNZ (2014), p. 2.

of marketing messages[11], rather than consuming one-directional corporate communication. Therefore the professional management of social media communication is imperative for brands.[12] Companies act in response by hiring social media specialists. In 2013, 16% of German businesses employ at least one person for the management of social media. Another 7% are planning to establish such a role.[13]

Numerous platforms can be subsumed under the umbrella of social media. To reduce complexity, TUTEN/SOLOMON (2013) organise the social media universe into four zones: **social networks** which include platforms that focus on relationships among people with shared interests, **social publishing** sites like blogs or media sharing sites support distributing content, **social entertainment** platforms include gaming sites or virtual worlds and **social commerce** sites assist in buying and selling products.[14] An overview of characteristic platforms is provided in Figure 1.

[11] Cf. KOZINETS ET AL. (2010), p. 72.

[12] Cf. WALLACE/BUIL/DE CHERNATONY (2012), p. 129.

[13] The high-tech network BITKOM appointed the market research institute Aris to survey 854 chief executives and human resources managers of German companies. The sample is representative for the German economy. The results of the study were published in March 2013. Cf. IHNENFELDT (2013), cf. MOZART (2013).

[14] Cf. TUTEN/SOLOMON (2013), p. 7.

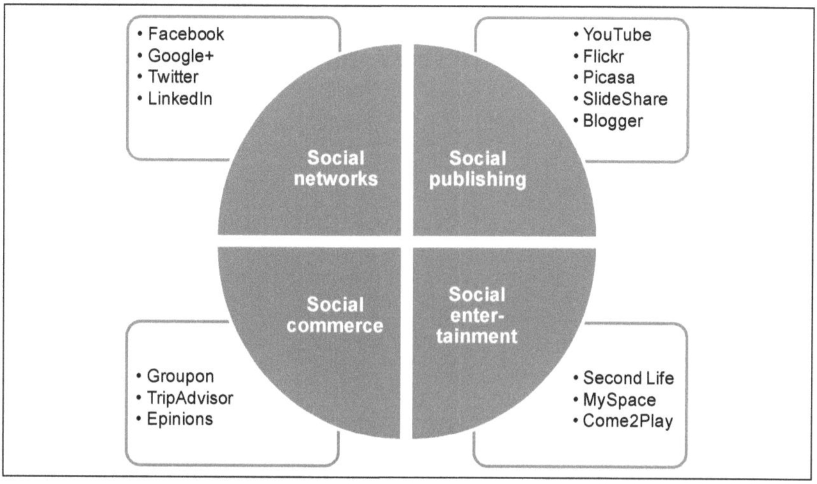

Figure 1: **Social media zones and characteristic sites**
Source: Own illustration based on TUTEN/SOLOMON (2013), p. 7.

Because of their immense reach[15], social networks (e.g. Facebook) play a significant role amongst social media. Social networks offer virtual space where people, companies and organisations have the possibility to establish relations.[16] Depending on the technology, those networks enable users to create profiles, set up groups, interact, discuss, send messages, exchange pictures, upload videos or make video calls.[17] An overview of social networks ranked by the number of users in Germany is provided in Figure 2.

[15] Cf. NELSON-FIELD/RIEBE/SHARP (2012), p. 262.

[16] Cf. ZAGLIA (2013), p. 217.

[17] Cf. JAHN/KUNZ (2014), p. 2.

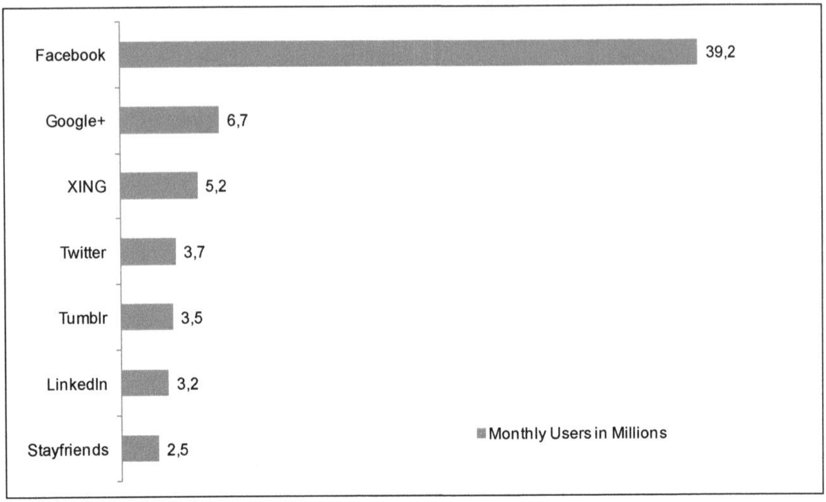

Figure 2: **Number of monthly users in social networks in Germany**
Source: Cf. COMSCORE (2013).

Facebook – the number one social networking site in most countries[18] – claims to have exceeded the mark of one billion monthly active users worldwide.[19] The main reason to join social networks is to connect with family and friends.[20] Users can set up a profile, become "friends" with other users, inform their network with status updates and read information that their friends post.

Due to the ubiquity of the network, people can connect and keep in touch all over the world. Communication between friends has shifted away from traditional emails towards the network.[21] Especially among people under the age of 30, "not to be on Facebook, is not to exist, so it seems."[22] In a study dedicated to explore consumers'

---

[18] Cf. PATTERSON (2012), p. 528.

[19] Cf. FACEBOOK (2013).

[20] In an international study conducted by IBM (n=1.056), 70% of respondents said they use social networks to connect to friends and family. Cf. IBM INSTITUTE FOR BUSINESS AND VALUE ANALYSIS (2011)

[21] Cf. PATTERSON (2012), p. 528.

[22] PATTERSON (2012), p. 528.

fascination for Facebook, 134 US-American undergraduate students were asked to write essays about their experiences with Facebook. Applying a meta-introspective approach[23], the author got access to insights into the thoughts and behaviours of the students. Those were published in the Journal of Business Research.[24] He summarised his findings about "facebooking" into four sections. First, Facebook can become *addictive*. Some students are constantly checking their accounts for updates and messages, increasingly when the mobile app was launched. The second characteristic of "facebooking" is *personal branding* which means the creation of the individual's desired personality on the network. Third comes the "*stalking*" which ranges from looking up people's activities and pictures to spying on friends and "enemies". And the fourth section is about *brand relationships*. Over half of the students are connected to at least one brand on Facebook.[25]

In Germany, **nearly one quarter of all internet users like at least one brand page** in a social network, a representative study conducted by BITKOM (2013) shows. This equals around 13 million internet users. Among the 14-29-year-olds nearly half of the internet users are "fan" of a brand page in a social network (see Figure 3).[26] Because of the high reach, the impact of brand pages on consumer perception needs to be evaluated thoroughly.[27]

---

[23] A meta-introspective approach is a meta-analysis of insights. In this case here, students were asked to write essays about their experiences with Facebook. The researcher clusters the thoughts and extracts important insights. Cf. PATTERSON (2012), p. 529.

[24] Cf. PATTERSON (2012), pp. 527-534.

[25] Cf. PATTERSON (2012), pp. 530-532.

[26] Cf. BITKOM (2013).

[27] Cf. GUMMERUS ET AL. (2012), pp. 857 et seqq.

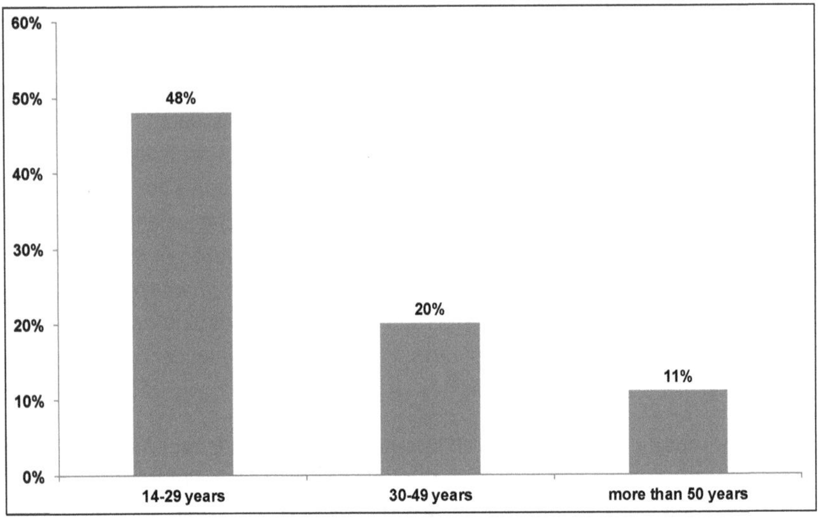

Figure 3: **Internet users that are "fan" of a brand in social networks in percent by age**
Source: Own illustration based on BITKOM (2013).

Brand managers soon realised the importance of communicating with consumers via social networks. It opens up opportunities for building substantial bonds with actual customers and potential customers.[28] Social activities should be seen as long-term investments, according to STEPHEN/GALAK (2012).[29] Today, social networks are an integral part of the day-to-day business in brand management.[30] In a survey executed by the Chair of innovative Brand Management at the University of Bremen, the top 100 "best global brands"[31] were examined in view of the existence of a Facebook

[28] Cf. JAHN/KUNZ (2012), p. 345.

[29] In their study comparing traditional versus social earned media's effect on sales, STEPHEN/GALAK (2012) found that due to their immense reach, traditional media had a higher per-event effect on sales. While those events were scarce, the accumulation of smaller but more frequent social media events was found to have a substantial long-term effect on sales. Cf. STEPHEN/GALAK (2012), p. 636.

[30] Cf. NAYLOR/LAMBERTON/WEST (2012), p. 105.

[31] The top 100 "best global brands" are summarised in a report provided by Interbrand who rank brands in terms of their brand value on an annual basis. Only brands that are truly global with a

(Continued on next page)

brand page. The high relevance managers ascribe to brand pages was evident: 90 out of the 100 brands had at least one Facebook profile.[32]

But there are also critical aspects that need to be considered. Trust in Facebook regarding the management of confidential personal data is very low.[33] Facebook is criticized for storing user data and for the lack of respect for privacy.[34] Young people are therefore intensifying their usage of chat services (e.g. Snapchat, threema) instead, because they delete messages or pictures right after delivery to the recipient.[35] So far, most studies neglect the raising issue of privacy concerns[36].

Another critical perspective on Facebook brand pages opens up the discussion whether relevant target groups are going to be reached through brand pages.[37] NELSON-FIELD/RIEBE/SHARP (2012) analysed the Facebook "fan"base of a chocolate brand and found that 57% of the "fans" are heavy buyers. 42% are light or moderate buyers and the remaining 1% are non-buyers.[38] This distribution is the opposite of a typical distribution of chocolate category shoppers. This implies that the majority of users "liking" the brand page are already loyal customers of the brand.[39] The authors are cautious towards Facebook as a marketing instrument and recommend targeting the light and moderate buyers.[40] If the brand page is the right channel remains unclear and requires further investigation.

---

presence in at least three continents, visible in public and whose financial results are accessible are included in the evaluation. Cf. INTERBRAND (2012).

[32] Cf. LIM (2013).

[33] Cf. BURMANN/KLEINE-KALMER/HEMMANN (2014), pp. 62 et seq.

[34] Cf. MUI (2011), cf. CBS (2013), cf. THE GUARDIAN (2013), cf. STÖCKER (2014).

[35] Cf. SCHMUNDT (2013), p. 122.

[36] For more details on the subject of privacy concerns regarding the storage of personal data, please read chapter B 5.2 and BURMANN/KLEINE-KALMER/HEMMANN (2013).

[37] Cf. NELSON-FIELD/RIEBE/SHARP (2012), p. 263.

[38] The buying intensity was self-reported and organised in the following categorisation: non-buyers: never; light buyers: once; moderate buyers: two–three times; heavy buyers: four or more times in three months. Cf. NELSON-FIELD/RIEBE/SHARP (2012), pp. 264 et seq.

[39] Cf. NELSON-FIELD/RIEBE/SHARP (2012), pp. 263 et seqq.

[40] Cf. NELSON-FIELD/RIEBE/SHARP (2012), pp. 264 et seqq.

Due to the hype on social media among practitioners and because of its high reach among existing and potential customers[41], the topic gained more attention in research. However, the subject of brand (fan) pages in social networks is still a young research field in academia.[42] Studies on brand pages in Facebook have focused on motives for brand page usage[43], brand post popularity[44], comparing traditional and social media advertising in social networks[45], gaining consumer insights[46], determining influential users[47], and fostering participation[48].

So far, the value of brand pages and their impact on consumer behaviour in favour of the brand could not be specified further. Researchers are trying to evaluate the impact of brand pages through measuring the degree of user participation[49] also referred to as engagement[50]. Often, the terms engagement, participation and interaction are used synonymously. They commonly measure the level of activity on a brand page.[51] But their meanings are slightly different. These will be illustrated briefly and further explained in subsequent chapters. Interaction always includes a minimum of two people; central element to interaction is reciprocity.[52] It describes the process of *mutual* exchange; i.e. two or more people exchanging content (in social networks

---

[41] Cf. JAHN/KUNZ (2012), p. 345.

[42] Cf. SMITH/FISCHER/YONGJIAN (2012), p. 104.

[43] Cf. JOINSON (2008), pp. 1027 et seqq., cf. MUNTINGA/MOORMAN/SMIT (2011), pp. 13 et seqq., cf. TAYLOR/LEWIN/STRUTTON (2011), pp. 258 et seqq., cf. KLEINE-KALMER/BURMANN (2013a).

[44] Cf. DEVRIES/GENSLER/LEEFLANG (2012), pp. 83 et seqq., cf. SMITH/FISCHER/YONGJIAN (2012), pp. 102 et seqq., cf. EILERS (2014).

[45] Cf. BRUHN ET AL. (2011), pp. 40 et seqq., cf. BRUHN/SCHOENMUELLER/SCHÄFER (2012), pp. 770 et seqq., cf. ARNHOLD (2010), cf. CHU (2011), pp. 30 et seqq.

[46] Cf. PATTERSON (2012), pp. 527 et seqq., CASTELEYN/MOTTART/RUTTEN (2009), pp. 439 et seqq.

[47] Cf. TRUSOV/BODAPATI/BUCKLIN (2010), pp. 643 et seqq.

[48] Cf. JAHN/KUNZ (2012), pp. 344 et seqq., cf. GUMMERUS ET AL. (2012), pp. 857 et seqq., cf. SASHI (2012), pp. 253 et seqq., cf. ZAGLIA (2013), pp. 216 et seqq.

[49] Cf. PARENT/PLANGGER/BAL (2011), pp. 219 et seqq.

[50] Cf. GUMMERUS ET AL. (2012), pp. 857 et seqq.

[51] Cf. SCHOENFELD (2012).

[52] The meaning of interaction will be further specified in chapter B 1.4. Cf. TROPP (2011), pp. 47 et seq, cf. EILERS (2014), p. 60.

these are typically brand and user).[53] For measurement of *user* behaviour (only includes one party involved in the interaction), the concepts participation and engagement are preferred. Participation in the context of social networks is seen as active user behaviour in the form of posting, liking, sharing, and commenting.[54] It is the degree to which a user is contributing.[55] The meaning of engagement is discussed controversially in academia (chapter A 2.1). While JAHN/KUNZ (2012) highlight the behavioural aspect and define it similar to participation as "an interactive and integrative participation in the fan-page community"[56]; BRODIE ET AL. (2013) see engagement as a multidimensional construct and define it as "a context-dependent, psychological state characterized by fluctuating intensity levels that occur within dynamic, iterative engagement processes."[57]

Typically, participation and engagement are measured through constructs or formulas that reflect the level of activity on a brand page which has been identified as crucial indicator for brand page performance.[58]

However, **in social networks only very few people actively participate on brand pages**.[59] In fact, only 1.3% of users that follow a brand page are participating according to a study[60] conducted by the Ehrenberg-Bass Institute.[61] This raises the issue whether those behavioural constructs should be seen as key for brand page evaluation. In summary, the evaluation of **brand page performance and its impact on consumer behaviour** requires further attention in research.[62] The routes of meas-

---

[53] Cf. TROPP (2011), pp. 47 et seq.

[54] More information on the concept of participation is provided in chapter A 2.2. Cf. ZAGLIA (2013), p. 220, cf. GUMMERUS ET AL. (2012), p. 876.

[55] Cf. PARENT/PLANGGER/BAL (2011), p. 219 et seqq.

[56] JAHN/KUNZ (2012), p. 349.

[57] Cf. BRODIE ET AL. (2013), p. 107.

[58] Cf. SOCIALBAKERS (2013a), cf. PARENT/PLANGGER/BAL (2011), pp. 219 et seqq.

[59] Cf. GUMMERUS ET AL. (2012), p. 870.

[60] The study analysed the user engagement of 200 brand pages on Facebook during a time span of six weeks. To measure engagement, they used the publicly available metric "people talking about this" cf. HEDEMANN (2012), cf. FACEBOOK (2012), cf. DARWELL (2012).

[61] Cf. HEDEMANN (2012), cf. EILERS (2014), p. 72. Further detail is provided in chapter B 1.4.

[62] Cf. MUNTINGA/MOORMAN/SMIT (2011), p. 13, cf. SMITH/FISCHER/YONGJIAN (2012), pp. 102 et seqq.

urement attempts that have been taken so far will be exploited next. The focus of this thesis will be laid on brand pages in Facebook because of its high dispersion and level of implementation in marketing management.[63]

2 Approaches evaluating brand pages

Managers are under pressure to provide evidence for the success of their marketing activities.[64] Systematic evaluation leads to a better performance of the marketing mix activities.[65] Establishing scales and metrics not only secures rationality in management; their evaluation also guarantees efficiency and effectiveness of the measures undertaken.

Marketing specialists believe that up to 40% of marketing budgets are not allocated sufficiently. In a questionnaire carried out with online marketing experts in Germany, 61% shared the opinion that this is due to a lack of proficient digital performance measurement.[66] This theory can be verified by a study accomplished by the University of St. Gallen. From the 186 interviewees, 64% criticise that the impact of digital communication is not calculable and there are no standardised scales available. The existing methods are neither trusted to be valid nor reliable, affirm 46% of the respondents.[67]

The majority of existing approaches for evaluation of social media activities is considered to be insufficient.[68] As a result, researchers call for new scales and metrics.[69] SMIT/NEIJENS (2011) review traditional measures that have been applied to television

---

[63] Cf. WALLACE/BUIL/DE CHERNATONY (2012), p. 130.

[64] Cf. ROSSMANN (2013), p. 7.

[65] Cf. HOMBURG/ARTZ/WIESEKE (2012), pp. 70 et seqq.

[66] The performance agency eprofessional published a survey asking 123 Online-Marketing-Experts on their opinion on marketing budget allocation. The survey was executed in August 2013 in Germany. Cf. EPROFESSIONAL (2013).

[67] The University of St. Gallen interviewed 186 executives, communication experts and researchers in Germany, Austria and Switzerland regarding their view on social media performance measurement. Cf. ROSSMANN (2013), p. 27.

[68] Cf. ROSSMANN (2013), p. 10.

[69] Cf. SMIT/NEIJENS (2011), p. 131.

and print and conclude that the complexities of the media landscape forces the development of cross-media data, hybrid methods and new metrics. Due to the interactivity of digital media, scales that measure the audience's appreciation should be elaborated, according to the researchers.[70]

The same summons is made by WILCOX/KIM (2012) who stress the necessity of adding another component to the traditional advertising effectiveness measurement.[71]

There are various measurement efforts that attempt to evaluate brand page performance. Those approaches can be subsumed into four categories:

- Brand page monitoring

  Different research agencies and consultancies offer monitoring tools that evaluate the sentiment of the chatter about a brand in social networks (and social media in general).[72] These tools review the content of messages that are posted digitally and summarise them into positive, negative and neutral posts.[73] Further, they are clustered regarding the topics they contain.[74] Information about the source, the diffusion and the relevance of different topics can also be provided.[75] These listening services provide rich information regarding the content. But on the other hand, they also carry the risk of misinterpretation. In the case of sarcasm for example, words might be coded inappropriately. Further, in most cases they are based on a pure content analysis and are rarely related to any performance indicators.

---

[70] Cf. SMIT/NEIJENS (2011), pp. 131 et seq.

[71] Cf. WILCOX/KIM (2012), p. 99.

[72] Cf. TUTEN/SOLOMON (2013), p. 196.

[73] Cf. LANGE (2008), p. 657.

[74] Cf. TUTEN/SOLOMON (2013), p. 192.

[75] Cf. CORSTJENS/UMBLIJS (2013), pp. 437 et seq.

A study that interviewed communication experts showed that 80% of the agencies and companies surveyed use one or more monitoring tools.[76] The frustration with the performance of these tools was confirmed in the study. 55% were of the opinion that the tools were too complicated to operate. Further, 34% of the respondents stated that they could not comprehend the results visualised in the reports. Detailed background information was only rarely available and difficult to extract.[77]

- Return on brand page investment

There are several attempts to measure the return on investment (ROI) of digital activities.[78] As FISHER (2009) cynically states "new ROI calculators are being created almost as fast as new social networking sites."[79] In academia, it is agreed that traditional measurement systems do not meet the requirements of the interactivity of social networks.[80] HOFFMAN/FODOR (2010) argue that rather than measuring the financial return on their investment, companies should analyse the investment a consumer makes.[81] In their view, measurement models to date focus too much on frequency and reach.[82] Instead, the authors support the measurement of consumer engagement and word-of-mouth metrics.[83] The existing methods are not proficient, so none of the developed formulas or methods for ROI measurement has been established among practitioners or

---

[76] The survey was carried out by Talkwalker, a company that offers social media monitoring and analysis tools. The interviews were based on an online-questionnaire that was answered by 110 communication experts from agencies and companies. The study took place in November 2013. Cf. GOEBEL (2014), cf. TALKWALKER (2014).

[77] Cf. GOEBEL (2014).

[78] Cf. GILFOIL/JOBS (2012), p. 639, cf. DUBOFF/WILKERSON (2010), p. 33, cf. FISHER (2009), p. 189, cf. BLANCHARD (2009).

[79] FISHER (2009), p. 189.

[80] Cf. HOFFMAN/FODOR (2010), p. 42.

[81] Cf. HOFFMAN/FODOR (2010), p. 42.

[82] Cf. HOFFMAN/FODOR (2010), pp. 41 et seqq.

[83] Cf. HOFFMAN/FODOR (2010), pp. 41 et seqq.

researchers so far.[84] Further, the evaluation of a brand's performance assessing only one "silver metric" is not compulsory.[85]

- Impact of social networks: longitudinal studies

When longitudinal data is available there is a possibility of running multivariate time series analysis, quantifying the impact of digital activity on sales[86], website traffic[87] or new customer acquisition[88]. HOFFMAN/FODOR (2010) criticise the short-term thinking of this method. According to them, the narrow focus neglects qualitative measures.[89] Another issue with this method is the isolation of effects.[90] Though the analysis allows controlling for other marketing stimuli, traditional and new media are known to cross-fertilise each other which contradicts segregating the two.[91]

Longitudinal studies are able to verify the existence and strength of effects.[92] There is no insight into consumer's attitudes. Thus, psychographic measures are necessary to understand the processes that happen between confrontation with brand page stimuli and ensuing consumer behaviour.

- Impact of social networks: cross-sectional studies

First attempts in measuring brand page performance have ranked brand pages by the number of people that liked the page.[93] By benchmarking the num-

---

[84] Cf. ROSSMANN (2013), p. 26.
[85] Cf. AMBLER/ROBERTS (2008), p. 745, cf. FILISKO (2011), p. 2.
[86] Cf. STEPHEN/GALAK (2012) or KELLER/FAY (2013).
[87] Cf. WILCOX/KIM (2012).
[88] Cf. KELLER/FAY (2013).
[89] Cf. HOFFMAN/FODOR (2010), pp. 41 et seqq.
[90] Cf. MEFFERT/BURMANN/KIRCHGEORG (2012), p. 861.
[91] Cf. MEFFERT/BURMANN/KIRCHGEORG (2012), p. 861.
[92] Cf. TABACHNICK/FIDELL (2013), pp. 926 et seqq.
[93] Cf. SOCIALBAKERS (2012).

ber of likes against those of competitors, managers get a rough idea about the performance of their site.

Soon, social media experts realised that those quantitative evaluations were not sufficient for a dependable statement.[94] Hence, measures were developed that focus on the level of activity[95] on a brand page.

Consequently, researchers as well as practitioners were interested in studying the triggers for engaging with brands in social networks.[96] Several studies on uses and gratifications for digital media usage have been launched subsequently.[97] Their common goal is to explain user activity. To measure this, the term *engagement*[98] was coined, sometimes also phrased as participation[99]. The concept of engagement was transferred from community research where it plays an important role.[100] However, **in social networks only very few people actively engage with brands**.[101] The reasons for low participation have not been elucidated so far and are an important field of research.

---

[94] Cf. SMIT/NEIJENS (2011), pp. 124 et seqq.

[95] The brand community research identifies consumer activity as the key to success. In this context, the concept of customer engagement was introduced. The Marketing Science Institute put customer engagement on their list of research priorities for 2010-2012 within the research area "understanding customer experience and behaviour". Cf. MARKETING SCIENCE INSTITUTE (2010), p. 4. The concept of customer engagement will be further explored in chapter A 2.1.

[96] Cf. JOINSON (2008), pp. 1027 et seqq., cf. MUNTINGA/MOORMAN/SMIT (2011), pp. 13 et seqq., cf. TAYLOR/LEWIN/STRUTTON (2011), pp. 258 et seqq., cf. KLEINE-KALMER/BURMANN (2013a).

[97] Cf. HENNIG-THURAU ET AL. (2004), cf. HUANG ET AL. (2007), cf. PARK/KEE/VALENZUELA (2009), cf. MUNTINGA/MOORMAN/SMIT (2011), cf. TAYLOR/LEWIN/STRUTTON (2011).

[98] Cf. WIRTZ ET AL. (2013), p. 229.

[99] Cf. WIRTZ ET AL. (2013), p. 229.

[100] Cf. ALGESHEIMER/DHOLAKIA/HERRMANN (2005).

[101] Cf. GUMMERUS ET AL. (2012), p. 870.

Approach	Short description	Advantages	Disadvantages
Brand page monitoring	Evaluate the sentiment and topics of content that is published about brand	- Content analysis - Sentiment analysis	- Risk of misinterpretation - Only works in categories that are discussed intensively
Return on brand page investment	Invent formulas or thumb rules that calculate the return on investment for brand pages	- Attempt to elaborate economic value	- Neglects qualitative measures - No formula could be established so far
Longitudinal studies on the impact of social networks	Link website traffic or traffic generated from social media campaigns to sales data	- Attempt to quantify impact - Try to link activities to sales performance	- Effect of marketing or sales activities cannot be isolated - Neglect qualitative measures - No management implications, just deliver proof for effect
Cross-sectional studies on the impact of social networks	Establish metrics that measure consumer engagement	- Integrate qualitative measures - Try to explain consumer perspective - Deliver management implications	- Focus on behavioural components - Neglect moderators and passive consumption

Table 1: Approaches assessing brand pages
Source: Own illustration.

Table 1 summarises the four measurement approaches advantages and disadvantages. The cross-sectional studies establish the engagement construct which attempts to explain consumer behaviour in social networks.[102] Measuring *engagement* is currently highly in fashion within social media research.[103] But establishing engagement as central construct to measure brand page performance bears several

[102] Cf. MALHOTRA/MALHOTRA/SEE (2013), p. 18, cf. CHAUHAN/PILLAI (2013), pp. 41 et seq.

[103] Cf. BERRY (2014), cf. SCHULTZ ET AL. (2009), p. SCHULTZ ET AL. (2009), pp. 206 et seqq.

issues.[104] Before those issues will be further exploited in chapter A 2.3, the state of the art research on engagement will be reviewed.

2.1 State of the art research on engagement

Consumer engagement has been identified as crucial for customer retention.[105] Especially with the forthcoming of new media that allow dialogue between firms and their customers, the subject of engagement has developed into a new research area.[106] Academics and practitioners make efforts to measure engagement, establish scales and investigate its determinants and outcomes.[107] The Marketing Science Institute put engagement on the list of research priorities for 2010-2012 under the headline "understanding customer experience and behaviour."[108] Hence, engagement has become a frequently used term within marketing research and it is still on the raise. A search in EBSCOhost® on the term „customer engagement" shows that the number of scholarly peer reviewed articles in academic journals published on the subject of customer engagement has constantly gone up (see Figure 4).

---

[104] Cf. ALLARD (2012).

[105] Cf. BRODIE ET AL. (2011), p. 253.

[106] Cf. STONE/WOODCOCK (2013), p. 394.

[107] Cf. VAN DOORN (2011), p. 280.

[108] Cf. MARKETING SCIENCE INSTITUTE (2010), p. 4.

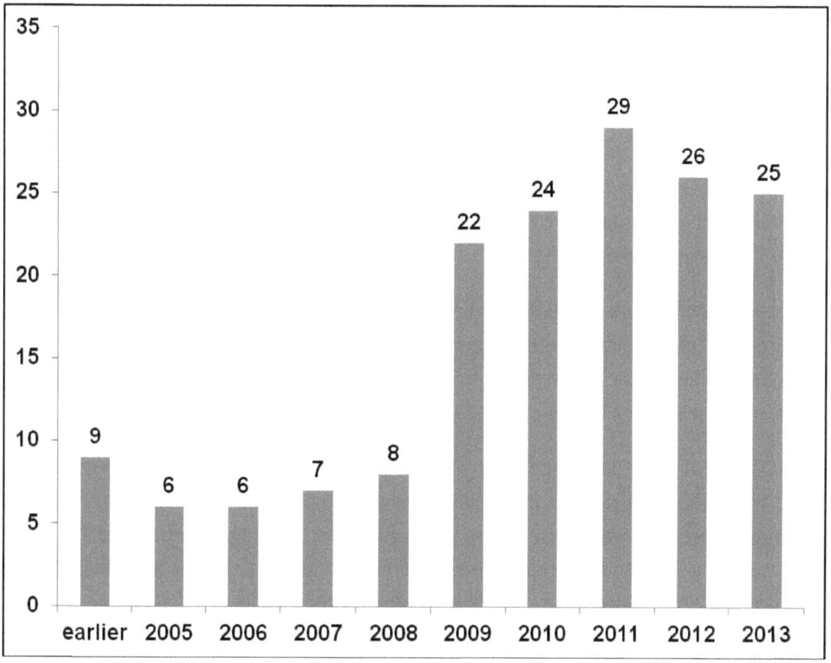

Figure 4: **Number of scholarly peer reviewed articles published in academic journals on the subject of customer engagement, November 2013**

Source: Own illustration.

As different academic disciplines address the concept, attitudes about definition and conceptualisation have been discussed diversely.[109] Academics are discordant whether engagement is an attitudinal, motivational or behavioural concept.[110] The next passages will give a succinct overview on the discussion in academic literature.[111] Plus, engagement and its use in practice will also be illuminated.

---

[109] Cf. VAN DOORN (2011), p. 280.

[110] Cf. BRODIE ET AL. (2011), p. 255.

[111] A detailed review on customer engagement and its assessment in academic disciplines like marketing, sociology, politics, psychology, and organizational theory is provided in BRODIE ET AL. (2011).

ALGESHEIMER/DHOLAKIA/HERRMANN (2005) introduced the concept to the community research by establishing a scale for community engagement. Their perception is that "community engagement refers to the positive influences of identifying with the brand community, which are defined as the consumer's intrinsic motivation to interact and cooperate with community members. Community engagement suggests that members are interested in helping other members, participating in joint activities, and otherwise acting volitionally in ways that the community endorses and that enhance its value for themselves and others."[112]

ALGESHEIMER/DHOLAKIA/HERRMANN (2005) develop a new scale for community engagement.[113] They discern engagement as a motivation to participate in the community. So the construct is not solely of attitudinal components but implicitly inherits a behavioural intention. This is also reflected in their operationalisation.

VAN DOORN ET AL. (2010) point out that in former studies consumer behaviour like word of mouth, referrals, or transactions have been looked at in isolation. The authors strive for a comprehensive view on such brand related behaviour and introduce their concept of customer engagement behaviour in a special issue published by the Journal of Service Research.[114] In their definition they state that "*customer engagement behaviours go beyond transactions, and may be specifically defined as a customer's behavioural manifestations that have a brand or firm focus, beyond purchase, resulting from motivational drivers.*"[115] Those behaviours can be positive like a recommendation on a community platform or negative in form of a shitstorm and may also involve cocreation.

The authors come up with five dimensions of customer engagement[116]:

---

[112] ALGESHEIMER/DHOLAKIA/HERRMANN (2005), p. 21.

[113] Cf. ALGESHEIMER/DHOLAKIA/HERRMANN (2005), p. 24.

[114] The Journal of Service Research launched a special issue on customer engagement (Vol. 13 No. 3, 2010) due to the high relevance of the subject. Several studies relating to the subject have been published in this issue.

[115] VAN DOORN ET AL. (2010), p. 254.

[116] Cf. VAN DOORN ET AL. (2010), pp. 255 et seq.

- Valence

  Consumer engagement can have positive or negative impact for the brand. If a user comments about a brand in a social network or writes about it in a blog, the tonality can be either positive or negative. So the valence expresses the manner in which a consumer campaigns about a brand.[117]

- Form or modality

  The form or modality stands for the type of interaction a consumer chooses for the dialogue with the brand. This can be a complaint, a suggestion, a recommendation etc. and can be placed through different ways reaching from face-to-face contact with an employee of the company to anonymous online platforms.[118]

- Scope

  The scope determines time and place of customer engagement. Regarding the time, customer engagement can happen only once, be sporadic, or ongoing. Especially the latter is important for companies to observe and act in response. The geographical scope correlates with the form and modality and decides whether the engagement is global or local[119].

- Nature of its impact

  This dimension describes how the engagement of a customer affects the brand. At first, the impact can be immediate or occur with a time-lag. So the time span of the influence on the brand is of relevance. Second, the impact can be either strong or weak. Third, it is a matter of how many people are af-

[117] Cf. VAN DOORN ET AL. (2010), p. 255.
[118] Cf. VAN DOORN ET AL. (2010), p. 255.
[119] Cf. VAN DOORN ET AL. (2010), p. 255.

fected. And last, brands have to account for the longevity of the impact, which means how long the engagement is conservable.[120]

- Customer goals

  The customers purpose of engaging should be considered. If there is a fit between the customer's and the brand's goals, the consequence of the engagement is likely to be positive for the brand.[121]

BIJMOLT ET AL. (2010) agree with the behavioural conceptualisation of the construct customer engagement. They start from the premise that the key behavioural manifestations of customer engagement occur in the form of WOM, co-creation, and complaining behaviour.[122]

Detecting the value of social networks and their growing relevance within the marketing discipline, GUMMERUS ET AL. (2012) investigate the concept of customer engagement in a Facebook gaming community.[123] The authors lean their conceptual perception on the definition provided by VAN DOORN ET AL. (2010) which is cited earlier in this paragraph. They extend the definition by arguing that reading too is a behavioural manifestation, though it is passive behaviour.[124] The study showed that there are two kinds of customer engagement behaviours in the Facebook gaming community:

(a) community engagement behaviours
(b) transaction engagement behaviours

Among the community engagement behaviours there are activities that are directed to other members or fulfil the users own needs like reading Game Club messages, "liking" messages of other users or writing comments, so taking part in the conversa-

---

[120] Cf. VAN DOORN ET AL. (2010), p. 255.

[121] Cf. VAN DOORN ET AL. (2010), pp. 255 et seq.

[122] Cf. BIJMOLT ET AL. (2010).

[123] Cf. GUMMERUS ET AL. (2012), p. 857.

[124] GUMMERUS ET AL. (2012) state that "consumers engage in non-interactive behaviors such as reading others' comments, or lurk" GUMMERUS ET AL. (2012), p. 860.

tion. Activities that lead directly to any business are titled transaction engagement behaviours like playing or spending money.[125]

Their findings reveal that the majority of community members only passively consume the content and benefit from the information or entertaining content. Only few actively engage in social networks. Unfortunately, they could not deliver the barriers that prevent people from interacting. Without any users participating and contributing, the company is challenged with providing content. Further, the study shows that within social networks consumers are interested in connecting to the brand rather than to each other.[126]

Some of those results are confirmed in a study conducted by JAHN/KUNZ (2012).[127] They investigate consumer engagement in the context of brand pages in social networks. The authors distinguish between brand page engagement and mere brand page usage which means watching and absorbing information. They claim: "we define fan-page engagement as an interactive and integrative participation in the fan-page community and would differentiate this from the solely usage intensity of a member."[128]

With their study, they were able to prove the impact of brand page engagement on the consumer-brand relationship. Most important drivers for attracting users to brand pages in social networks are functional and hedonic content. They further point out, that interaction is essential and nurtures the attractiveness and vitality of a brand page.[129] As most former studies, they were not able to find out what prevents users from engaging in social networks. The key drivers for engagement which they identified were not validated in the results, as all path coefficients were low.[130]

---

[125] Cf. GUMMERUS ET AL. (2012), p. 863.

[126] Cf. GUMMERUS ET AL. (2012), p. 870.

[127] Cf. JAHN/KUNZ (2012), pp. 344 et seqq.

[128] JAHN/KUNZ (2012), p. 349.

[129] Cf. JAHN/KUNZ (2012), p. 354.

[130] Cf. JAHN/KUNZ (2012), p. 353.

This issue was partly addressed in the article published by WIRTZ ET AL. (2013).[131] They identified moderators that impact the relationship between the drivers of engagement and the actual engagement behaviour. These moderators were divided into product, situational and customer factors. Product factors include involvement and complexity. A highly involved user is more likely to engage, the more complex a product is, the more valuable is the information a user receives. Among the situational factors are the size of the online brand community with a small community facilitating interaction, the valence of information and governance. The latter meaning that information is more credible if the community does not convey the impression of promotional intent. With customer factors the authors describe the members' expertise and membership duration.[132] Unfortunately, these moderators could not be corroborated empirically.

As most studies in recent history treat engagement as a behavioural construct, MALHOTRA/MALHOTRA/SEE (2013) fall into line.[133] They coded over 1,000 wall posts from 98 brand pages on Facebook to investigate which kinds of posts impact engagement. All likes, comments and shares were seen as engagement and used for the analysis.

Simultaneously, Facebook itself started to provide the "engagement rate" as a central metric to its customers. The engagement rate is calculated as[134]:

$$Post\ engagement\ rate = \frac{\#\ of\ Likes + Comments + Shares\ on\ a\ given\ day}{Total\ \#\ of\ Fans\ on\ a\ given\ day}$$

Although the debate on engagement being an attitudinal versus behavioural construct seemed to have vanished from academic dialogue, BRODIE ET AL. (2013) defend their rationale that engagement is a multidimensional concept which offers a comprehensive view on a consumer's experience of interaction and co-creation.[135]

---

131 Cf. WIRTZ ET AL. (2013), pp. 232 et seqq.

132 Cf. WIRTZ ET AL. (2013), pp. 232 et seqq.

133 Cf. MALHOTRA/MALHOTRA/SEE (2013), pp. 17 et seqq.

134 Cf. SOCIALBAKERS (2013a).

135 Cf. BRODIE ET AL. (2011), p. 257.

This perception makes it difficult to identify the drivers of participation though. Especially when defining the concept as an iterative process.

Their working definition is: "*Consumer engagement in a virtual brand community involves specific interactive experiences between consumers and the brand, and/or other members of the community. Consumer engagement is a context-dependent, psychological state characterized by fluctuating intensity levels that occur within dynamic, iterative engagement processes. Consumer engagement is a multidimensional concept comprising cognitive, emotional, and/ or behavioral dimensions, and plays a central role in the process of relational exchange where other relational concepts are engagement antecedents and/or consequences in iterative engagement processes within the brand community.*"[136]

In summary, it can be agreed, that the conceptualisation of engagement is not consistent though the behavioural perception is dominant according to BRODIE ET AL. (2011).[137] Current research is not able to provide arguments for why engagement is low on brand pages.[138] Finally, to look at engagement only, is not the solution; **a psychological pre-behavioural concept needs to be introduced** and moderators that prevent consumers from participating need to be identified.

2.2 Participation

Engagement and participation are often used synonymously. Participation in the context of social media and also in the community research is understood as actively taking part in the discussions or activities.[139] As engagement is also considered to consist of behavioural components, the two concepts overlap. The meaning of participation is clearer though. Researchers leave no doubt that it only contents a behavioural dimension while the discussion on engagement is still ongoing. ALGESHEIMER/DHOLAKIA/HERRMANN (2005) see participation as a consequence of en-

---

[136] Cf. BRODIE ET AL. (2013), p. 107.

[137] Cf. BRODIE ET AL. (2011), p. 254.

[138] Cf. GUMMERUS ET AL. (2012), p. 870.

[139] Cf. WOISETSCHLÄGER/HARTLEB/BLUT (2008), p. 248.

gagement. They differentiate the two concepts by postulating that engagement is the motivation to join the communication and get into contact with others while participation intention then reflects the actual plan to take part.[140] The discrimination is quite weak. Some researchers make no difference between the concepts at all and define engagement through different participation activities.[141] CASALÓ/CARLOS F.; GUINALÍU/GUINALÍU (2010) are more precise in this case. Determinants of participation are solely affective or cognitive.[142] Participation in the online community reflects actual behaviour like contributing, providing valuable information or specialist knowledge[143] or posting and answering to messages.[144] Similar actions apply in the context of social networks where participation mostly consists of liking, sharing, commenting.[145]

2.3 Rationale for a psychographic measure

For the evaluation of brand page performance and explaining consumer behaviour in favour of the brand, both concepts engagement and participation bear several problems. First, the conceptualisation of current constructs is not consistent. Within community research "community engagement" was initially defined through cognitive and affective components. It describes the motivation to participate in community communication and activity. A few years later, VAN DOORN ET AL. (2010) define engagement as a behavioural construct by declaring "customer engagement behaviours go beyond transactions, and may be specifically defined as a customer's behavioural manifestations that have a brand or firm focus, beyond purchase, resulting from motivational drivers."[146] The definition has been picked up by other authors and integrated into their research, also in the context of brand pages in social networks.[147]

---

[140] Cf. ALGESHEIMER/DHOLAKIA/HERRMANN (2005), pp. 21-22, pp. 32-33.

[141] Cf. PARENT/PLANGGER/BAL (2011), pp. 221 et seqq.

[142] Cf. CASALO/CARLOS F.; GUINALIU/GUINALIU (2010), p. 144.

[143] Cf. WIERTZ/DE RUYTER (2007), p. 347.

[144] Cf. CASALO/CARLOS F.; GUINALIU/GUINALIU (2010), p. 166.

[145] Cf. ZAGLIA (2013), p. 220, cf. GUMMERUS ET AL. (2012), p. 876.

[146] VAN DOORN ET AL. (2010), p. 254.

[147] Cf. BIJMOLT ET AL. (2010), cf. GUMMERUS ET AL. (2012).

Likewise, Facebook defines its engagement rate as a behavioural construct.[148] BRODIE ET AL. (2013) view engagement as a "multidimensional concept comprising cognitive, emotional, and/or behavioural dimensions."[149] Though the behavioural perspective seems to have prevailed against the other conceptions, there is no common agreement. Some researchers avoid the confusion altogether and speak about participation instead.

Second, whether it is participation or engagement, with a behavioural metric rating the performance of a brand page, consumers' privacy concerns regarding certain topics are neglected completely. In other words: if a bank sets up a brand page on Facebook and there is little to no interaction, is that due to the quality of the brand page or because users do not want to talk about their bank concerns publicly? They might still be loyal followers of the brand page without actively participating. CARLSON/SUTER/BROWN (2008) argue that research on brand communities has narrowed too much on interactivity. In their eyes "a psychological sense of brand community may exist even in the absence of social interaction."[150] According to them "it is quite possible that many consumers perceive a sense of community, yet never engage in social intercourse with one another."[151]

Hence, **a psychological construct that incorporates pre-behavioural measures is necessary**.[152] The emotional bond to the brand page needs to be measured. Rather than tracking the level of participation by users on brand pages, the focus should lie on how connected they feel to the brand page. SMITH (2013) found that people who claimed to have positive emotions visiting a Facebook brand page are more likely to comment positively about the brand in public.[153] This can be confirmed by REN ET AL. (2012) who identified the "affective connection to [...] an online community" to be crucial.

---

[148] Cf. SOCIALBAKERS (2013a).

[149] BRODIE ET AL. (2013), p. 107.

[150] CARLSON/SUTER/BROWN (2008), p. 284.

[151] CARLSON/SUTER/BROWN (2008), p. 285.

[152] Cf. LANGNER/MÜLLER (2013), p. 22.

[153] Cf. SMITH (2013), p. 365.

In summary, a clear conceptualisation of **a construct that reflects the consumers bond to a brand page in social networks** is missing.[154] It is the aim of this thesis to establish this construct.

Whether or how social media impact brand equity is often called into question. A lot of research was conducted to deliver evidence.[155] To date, this discussion is not of relevance anymore. The impact of social media on brand measures (e.g. brand awareness, consideration or brand image) was proven across different industries and social media has earned a central role in brand communication strategy.[156] Global research companies have established models that quantify the impact of social media communication.[157] Hence, this topic shall not be central to this thesis. Rather, a more in-depth understanding of what drives attraction and bonding to a brand page shall be the outcome.

Before the relevant research gaps will be listed, the concept of brand pages shall be elucidated and its anchorage in marketing theory shall be determined.

3 The position of brand pages in marketing theory

Users discuss brands openly in social networks.[158] Some consumers create groups for people with shared interest in a brand or even set up profiles in the name of a brand and update them regularly.

Businesses and organisations can also set up profiles for their brands, products and services themselves.[159] They have the opportunity to create so called brand (fan)

---

[154] Cf. CARLSON/SUTER/BROWN (2008), p. 284.

[155] Cf. EILERS (2014), pp. 218 et seqq., cf. BRUHN ET AL. (2011), pp. 40 et seqq., cf. JAHN/KUNZ (2014), p. 353 et seqq.

[156] Cf. BHARADWAJ ET AL. (2013), pp. 471 et seqq.

[157] GfK measures "Experience Effects", a cross-media analysis that delivers insight into how different media affect brand perceptions, cf. GFK (2014), MillwardBrown offers a "CrossMedia Research™" approach that is conceptualised to analyse media effects including the effects of sponsorship, events, PR, word of mouth, user-generated content, and retail-based activities, cf. MILLWARDBROWN (2014).

[158] Cf. SMITH/FISCHER/YONGJIAN (2012), pp. 102 et seqq.

pages on Facebook.[160] It keeps its followers informed with status updates. The brand can also upload photos, videos or create applications such as games or raffles.[161] When users click on the "like" button of a brand page, they consequently become "fans" and receive regular posts and updates from the brand in their personal newsfeed.[162] They also have the option to comment, ask questions, participate in discussions or create and share content.

The term "brand *fan* page" is misleading as it indicates an intensive bond between user and brand.[163] A "fan" in common parlance typically describes someone who is an enthusiastic admirer of a favoured sports team for instance.[164] The connection of a brand page follower to the brand does not have to be of high intensity though. The follower sometimes is not even a customer of the brand.[165] JAHN/KUNZ (2012) state that someone who follows a brand on Facebook "can be anything from a devotee to an enthusiast of a particular object."[166] In actual fact, anyone can click "like" of a page that is set up by a brand on facebook. Thus, it makes more sense to use the terminology *brand pages* and *followers* instead of fan pages and fans. In the following, whenever the term brand page is used, a brand page in social networks (e.g. Facebook) is meant.

In academia, brand pages are often allocated to the brand community research.[167] Findings from the community research that base on social identity theory[168] are ap-

---

[159] Cf. NELSON-FIELD/RIEBE/SHARP (2012), p. 262.

[160] Cf. FACEBOOK (2014).

[161] Cf. JAHN/KUNZ (2014), p. 2.

[162] Cf. NELSON-FIELD/RIEBE/SHARP (2012), p. 262.

[163] Cf. BURMANN/KLEINE-KALMER (2013), p. 100.

[164] The Oxford Dictionaries define a fan as "a person who has a strong interest in or admiration for a particular sport, art form, or famous person." OXFORD DICTIONARIES (2014a); cf. SCHADE (2012), pp. 29 et seq.

[165] In the case of premium or luxury products, not all "fans" are customers. Porsche for examples has over 7.1 million "fans" but not all of them are customers. Cf. PORSCHE (2014).

[166] JAHN/KUNZ (2012), p. 346.

[167] Cf. GUMMERUS ET AL. (2012), pp. 857 et seqq.

[168] For further detail please read chapter B 2.3.4.

plied to social network studies. TRUSOV/BODAPATI/BUCKLIN (2010) for instance suggest that social networking sites are a „unique type of online community."[169] DEVRIES/GENSLER/LEEFLANG (2012) claim that managers can enhance the customer-brand relationship by setting up "brand communities in the form of brand fan pages in social networks."[170]

However, recent studies reveal dissimilarities between brand communities and brand pages on Facebook.[171] Therefore, it is necessary to clarify the conceptualisation of brand pages. For this purpose, the subsequent chapters will at first define the concept of a brand community followed by a rational for the conceptual differentiation between brand pages in social networks and brand communities.

3.1 Research on brand communities

Researchers began to investigate the phenomenon of subcultures that evolve around brands in the 1990ies when SCHOUTEN/MCALEXANDER (1995) conducted their studies on the Harley-Davidson owner group. In their ethnography of bikers, they describe Harley-Davidson drivers as "subcultures of consumption."[172] With this term they characterise a group of people that associate because of their consuming habits. In the context of the Harley-Davidson owner group this means that people gather as drivers of the same motorcycle brand where the brand functions as the basis for their lifestyle. Beyond that, they share ethos and ideology of consumption in which the brand inherits the status of a "religious icon."[173] This research delivered fundamental insights for marketing theory.

Parallel, COVA (1997) developed his theory on postmodern tribes.[174] COVA/PACE (2006) understand tribes in the same way as communities and define both as "any

[169] TRUSOV/BODAPATI/BUCKLIN (2010), p. 646.

[170] DEVRIES/GENSLER/LEEFLANG (2012), p. 83.

[171] Cf. ZAGLIA (2013), pp. 220 et seqq.

[172] SCHOUTEN/MCALEXANDER (1995), pp. 43 et seqq.

[173] SCHOUTEN/MCALEXANDER (1995), p. 50.

[174] Cf. COVA (1997).

group of people that possess a common interest in a specific brand and create a parallel social universe (subculture) rife with its own myths, values, rituals, vocabulary and hierarchy."[175] COVA (1997) states that postmodern individuals freed themselves from traditional expectations of society and social bonds.[176] The longing for independence and uniqueness has led to a fragmentation of society and consumption.[177] Customisation of products and services allow for egocentrism and individuality. With the vast development of digital technology and ease of physical mobility, isolation and separatism form late modern lifestyle. At the same time, a "desperate search for the social link"[178] can be observed. Hence, different forms of subcultures evolve, so called "tribes", which are ephemeral and built around shared emotions, beliefs, lifestyles and consumption patterns.[179] The consumers are connected through the shared experience.[180]

MUNIZ/O'GUINN (2001) build on these findings and introduce the term "brand community".[181] Leaving the boundaries of geographical limitation and focusing on a more commercial perception, they define brand community as a "specialized, non-geographically bound community, based on a structured set of social relations among admirers of a brand."[182] These communities can basically build around any brand, but typically around brands that have a strong image, long history and serious competition. According to MUNIZ/O'GUINN (2001) these brands do not need to be unconventional or require a niche positioning. But they are more likely to be consumed out of home where they are displayed in public. In their research on the brand communities around Ford Bronco, Macintosh and Saab they found that members of a

[175] COVA/PACE (2006), p. 1089.
[176] Cf. COVA (1997), pp. 297 et seqq.
[177] Cf. COVA (1997), pp. 297 et seqq.
[178] COVA (1997), p. 300.
[179] Cf. COVA (1997), p. 301.
[180] Cf. COVA/COVA (2002), pp. 602 et seqq.
[181] MUNIZ/O'GUINN (2001).
[182] MUNIZ/O'GUINN (2001), p. 412.

brand community are not necessarily homogenous in their consumption patterns or gather because they share the same lifestyle. The link between them is the brand.[183]

In their community research MUNIZ/O'GUINN (2001) redefined the relation of dependency between consumer and brand and developed the „consumer-brand-consumer triad."[184] Besides the connection between consumer and brand, their concept includes communication paths and relationships amongst consumers (Figure 5). The traditional one dimensional relation between brand and consumer is therefore replaced.

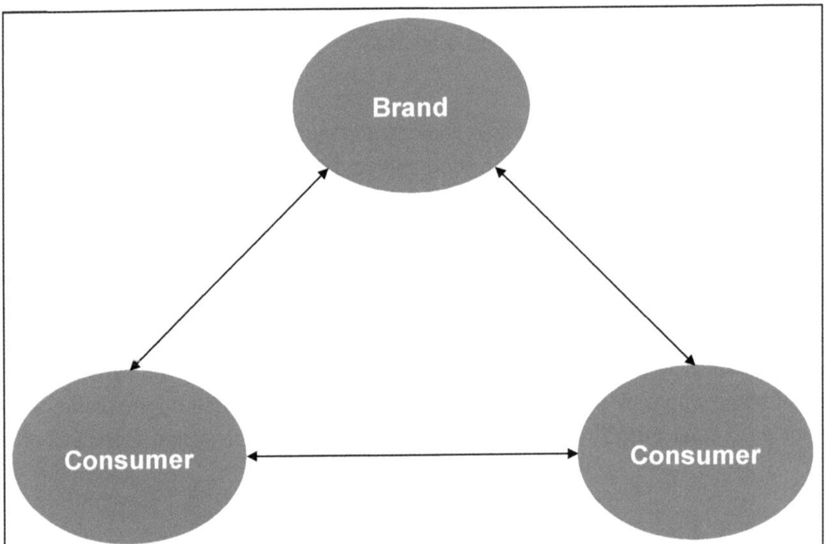

Figure 5: **Consumer-brand-consumer triad**
Source: Based on MUNIZ/O'GUINN (2001) and MCALEXANDER/SCHOUTEN/KOENIG (2002).

According to MUNIZ/O'GUINN (2001) there are three characteristics of a community. Referring to sociologic literature, they state that the most important element is con-

[183] Cf. MUNIZ/O'GUINN (2001), p. 415.
[184] MUNIZ/O'GUINN (2001), p. 427.

sciousness of kind. It implies the feeling of belonging to something that is unique and that differentiates the members from those who are not in the community. The second characteristic represents shared rituals and traditions. Third, community members feel moral responsibility towards the community as a whole but also towards its individual members.[185]

McAlexander/Schouten/Koenig (2002) expand the consumer-brand-consumer triad and add relationships from the consumer's branded environment. That includes relations to the brand, other customers, branded goods and marketing employees of the brand. They suggest a shift of focus, which puts the customer in the centre of the model (Figure 6). In their definition, the value of a brand community is built on customer experience rather than the brand itself.[186]

[185] Cf. Muniz/O'Guinn (2001), p. 413.

[186] Cf. McAlexander/Schouten/Koenig (2002), p.39.

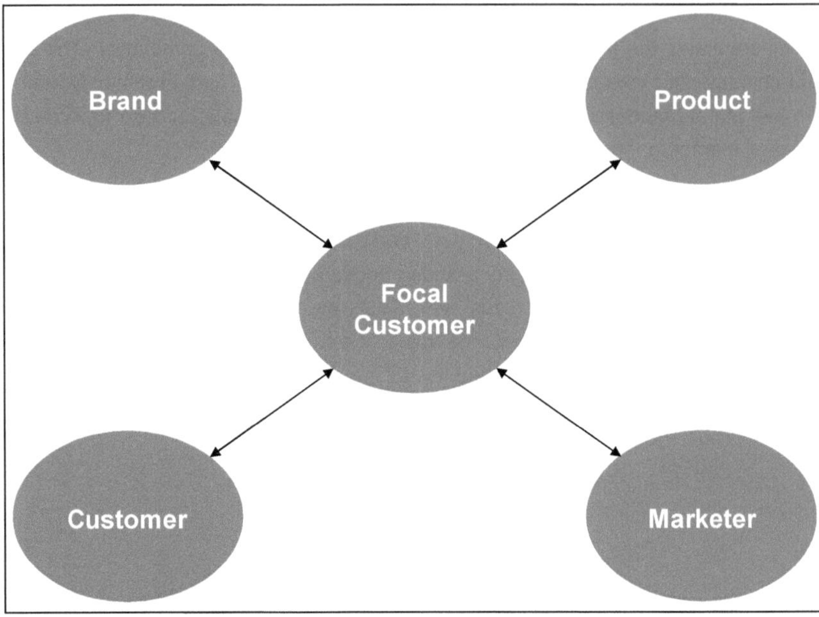

Figure 6: Customer-centric model of brand community
Source: Based on McAlexander/Schouten/Koenig (2002).

Brand communities do not have to be situated locally; they can be anywhere including the internet.[187] Some are based entirely virtually. With the increasing popularity of social media, new forms of brand communities occur within social media.[188] The question arises whether the concept of brand community can be transferred to brand pages in social networks like Facebook. The answer will be provided in the next chapter.

---

[187] Cf. Thompson/Sinha (2008), p. 66.

[188] Cf. Zaglia (2013), p. 217.

3.2 Differentiating brand pages and brand communities

In their study on customer engagement, GUMMERUS ET AL. (2012) investigate user behaviour towards brands in Facebook. They describe brand pages as "Facebook brand communities"[189] and herewith initially transfer the community concept to social networks. Albeit, their findings reveal elementary differences compared to prior studies on brand communities. The impact of social activities on a Facebook gaming page was not as high as expected though research on brand communities declares personal relationships between community members to be of high importance. Furthermore, GUMMERUS ET AL. (2012) found active participation of users to be quite low.[190] In community research on the contrary, members are usually highly active. The authors trace this back to the nature of gaming and the reluctance of members to publish content on Facebook.[191] But, it also raises the question whether it might be necessary to distinguish between brand communities and brand pages in social networks.

To answer this question, ZAGLIA (2013) takes a netnography approach[192] to prove the existence of brand communities embedded into social networks. Facebook was chosen as her subject of research. The author investigates two different entities that occur within a branded environment in Facebook: sub-groups and brand pages. *Subgroups* are established around a certain topic which can be a particular hobby, a geographic region, an alumni club or a brand. *Brand pages* on the contrary have the character of a bulletin board. ZAGLIA (2013) chose to analyse the Canon Camera Malaysia *brand page* with 151,380 followers in comparison to the Canon Digital Photog-

---

[189] GUMMERUS ET AL. (2012), p. 857.

[190] GUMMERUS ET AL. (2012) postulate that "only a small portion of customers actively interact with the content and with other members, while most customers use the brand community mainly as a source of information, reading messages rather than contributing with "likes" or comments." GUMMERUS ET AL. (2012), p. 870.

[191] Cf. GUMMERUS ET AL. (2012), pp. 869 et seq.

[192] The netnography approach was developed by KOZINETS (2002). KOZINETS (2002) defines his methodology "as an online marketing research technique for providing consumer insight. Netnography is ethnography adapted to the study of online communities. As a method, netnography is faster, simpler, and less expensive than traditional ethnography and more naturalistic and unobtrusive than focus groups or interviews. It provides information on the symbolism, meanings, and consumption patterns of online consumer groups." KOZINETS (2002), p. 61.

raphy group with 108,259 members which is a *sub-group* within Facebook.[193] Within her explorative research ZAGLIA (2013) was able to find strong indications for the *sub-group* to function as a community. However, her findings could not be verified for the Canon *brand page*.[194] She concludes that brand pages are "a weaker form of a brand community."[195] But in actual fact, the findings clearly advocate (a) a distinct conceptualisation for brand pages and (b) a differentiation from brand communities. This will be done in the following. The differentiation will be executed along the characteristics of brand communities developed by MUNIZ/O'GUINN (2001). Subsequently, the definition and concept of brand pages will be introduced.

MUNIZ/O'GUINN (2001) defined three characteristics of a community: consciousness of kind, shared rituals and traditions as well as moral responsibility towards the community as a whole and towards its individual members.[196]

For brand pages in social networks these criteria do not fully apply. The next passage will unveil the arguments.

- Consciousness of kind:

  Consciousness of kind implies the feeling of belonging to something that is unique and that differentiates community members from non-members. In social networks (e.g. Facebook) on the contrary, anyone is able to "like" a brand page. There is unlimited access to brand pages. There are no requirements apart from an active profile; people do not have to be customers of the brand they want to follow.

  Users can connect to numerous brand pages in social networks. On average, online users in Germany are connected to nine brands via social networks.[197]

---

193 Cf. ZAGLIA (2013), p. 219.

194 Cf. ZAGLIA (2013), pp. 220 et seqq.

195 ZAGLIA (2013), p. 222.

196 Cf. MUNIZ/O'GUINN (2001), p. 413.

197 People with online affinity that live in Germany are connected to 9 brands or organizations on average via social networks. Cf. TNS (2012).

Hence, the brand that creates a profile in a social network does not own the user exclusively. Brand pages are embedded into a network of relationships between users that are friends or family. These relationships usually also exist in the offline world and have nothing to do with brands but with emotional connections between humans. In a "traditional" brand community, these ties between users only form on the cause of a brand they jointly admire.[198] People, who like the same brand in social networks, do not even need to be connected to each other. Therefore the term "community" in the context of brand pages is misleading.

- Shared rituals and traditions:

Shared rituals and traditions are habits or practices that have established in the community during the course of time. They are set by members and give guidance for behaviour. Through rituals and traditions culture and history of the community are acknowledged.[199]

Users that have a profile in a social network (e.g. Facebook) can connect to a brand by "liking" the brand page. They will then be updated with recent stories and news via their newsfeed.[200] This way, they automatically receive information about the brand on a regular basis. They can browse the brand page and post comments or questions onto the brand's "wall". Interaction is therefore possible if initiated or wanted by the user. There is no obligation for a user to authorise the brand access to his profile. Therefore the connection between user and brand in social networks is in most cases "uni-directional."[201] With "liking" the brand, they are able to passively consume the content that is provided by the brand, but they do not have to contribute actively. Ultimately, there are no common practices that are shared between users. Brand pages are mainly operated and filled with content by the firm. Consequently,

---

[198] Cf. JAHN/KUNZ (2012), pp. 347 et seq.

[199] Cf. MUNIZ/O'GUINN (2001), p. 413.

[200] Cf. NELSON-FIELD/RIEBE/SHARP (2012), p. 262.

[201] TAYLOR/LEWIN/STRUTTON (2011), p. 259.

JAHN/KUNZ (2012) conclude that the motivation to participate in brand communities rituals and traditions differs from brand pages.[202]

- Moral responsibility

  With moral responsibility MUNIZ/O'GUINN (2001) refer to unwritten rules that exist within the community culture and imply a feeling of obligation to act in favour of the community.

  Brand pages in social networks are often used to vent feelings of disappointment. As the criticism is publicly visible, users expect direct feedback from the brand.[203] In many cases other users do not take a position. But sometimes other followers defend the brand and answer directly to the complaining customer. Hence, the feeling of moral responsibility among followers of brand pages cannot be negated completely but is certainly not a constitutive characteristic for brand pages.

In summary, several arguments support the conceptual distinction between brand communities and brand pages. The central point of difference is the sense of belonging which is given in the case of communities but not necessarily on brand pages. Yet, brand pages may accommodate forms of communities.[204] Subgroups of followers can establish links among each other and create a feeling of togetherness. But this is not generalisable. Hence, the differentiation between the two concepts is obligatory and justifies an own focus for brand pages. However, due to the relatedness of the two concepts, the research on communities is insightful for brand pages and will be part of the framework for this thesis.

---

[202] Cf. JAHN/KUNZ (2012), p. 348.

[203] Cf. ZAGLIA (2013), p. 221.

[204] Cf. ZAGLIA (2013), p. 222.

3.3 The concept of brand pages

Brand pages can be defined as sites that are set up by brands within social networks. Any user gains access to a brand page. When s/he clicks the "like" button, s/he automatically follows the brand pages and gets updates in her/his newsfeed.[205]

Users can consume passively or avail themselves of the opportunity to actively interact with the brand.[206] They can also communicate with other users or post comments, pictures or videos, ask questions or use applications.[207]

Some brand pages may be able to create a sense of togetherness for a number of their users.[208] Those are typically highly interactive.[209] Other brand pages are just like bulletin boards with no interaction at all. Still, they might be able to establish bonds with their audience through informative content.

The brand page is integrated into a social network (e.g. Facebook). Therefore, the media is neither owned by the brand nor the users.

4 Gaps in current research evaluating brand pages

The relevance of social media for brand management has been questioned many times. In recent history, several studies were able to dispel the doubts. The impact of social media on brand awareness and brand image has been proven across different industries.[210] Researchers have moved on from this topic and accepted social media as an integral part of brand communication strategy.[211]

---

205 Cf. ZAGLIA (2013), p. 218.

206 Cf. ZAGLIA (2013), p. 218.

207 Cf. GUMMERUS ET AL. (2012), p. 869.

208 Cf. ZAGLIA (2013), p. 222.

209 Cf. ZAGLIA (2013), p. 222.

210 Cf. EILERS (2014), pp. 218 et seqq., cf. BRUHN ET AL. (2011), pp. 40 et seqq., cf. JAHN/KUNZ (2014), p. 353 et seqq.

211 Cf. BHARADWAJ ET AL. (2013), pp. 471 et seqq.

At the present, the social media research cluster strives to establish a concept that reflects the performance of brands in social networks.[212] Progress has been made on the exploration of the research field.[213] Still, there are some deficiencies that need to be explored further. This thesis shall unveil and close some of these gaps in the current research.

First, measuring engagement seems to be high in fashion in social media research. Yet, this concept bears several shortcomings. The main issue is the behavioural conceptualisation that does not accrue for moderating effects. Instead, a pre-behavioural metric is obligatory. To date, there is no common agreement on a suitable concept that reflects the consumers bond to a brand page in social networks. **A clear definition and conceptualisation on a construct, that measures the user's psychological bond to a brand page is necessary**.

Second, the items that are employed for measurement often do not reflect the conceptualisation of the construct. Intangible variables that are supposed to be qualitative are measured through quantitative indicators such as number of likes, number of comments or number of followers as in the case of the Facebook interaction rate.[214] Moreover, concepts are named engagement but operationalised by items that measure identification.[215] **Evidently, a distinct operationalisation of the construct is needed.**

Third, transferring all findings from the brand community research to research on brand pages in social networks is problematic due to arguments listed in chapter A 3.2. Because communities are closed groups that build on shared interest in a brand and forms ties between users, interaction is facilitated and becomes intense. Hence, customer engagement is vital to community management. On the contrary, brand pages are basically digital walls set up and filled with content by brand management. Key benefits from a consumer perspective are obtaining entertaining and informative

---

[212] Cf. JAHN/KUNZ (2014), p. 2.

[213] Cf. BRODIE ET AL. (2013), p. 105.

[214] Cf. SOCIALBAKERS (2013a).

[215] Cf. PENTINA ET AL. (2013), p. 72

content.[216] Entertainment and information can be consumed passively and do not require active engagement. Hence, focussing on user engagement in the context of social networks excludes those users that do not interact actively but absorb content passively and still have a strong bond towards the brand page. **Accordingly, it is necessary to take a step back and at first investigate the emotional bond to the brand page, i.e. how attached[217] users become to a brand page.**

Fourth, for companies it is essential to know which factors impact brand page attachment. Only then are they able to manage the brand page and get users to regularly read and update information about the brand which again leads to higher attachment and consumers investing time. **Hence, brand managers should know what influences users to become bonded to the brand page.**

Fifth, little is known about the consequences of users' attachment to brand pages. A meta-introspective investigation delivered insights into how addictive Facebook can become and how some people constantly check their profile to see if there is any update in their network.[218] A positive connection between user and social network leads to behavioural intentions towards it like recommending it to friends and the intention for continuous usage.[219] So, an investigation on what "attached" consumers are willing to invest (e.g. time, participation, co-creation, personal information) is required as HOFFMAN/FODOR (2010) recommend. **Further research on behavioural reactions highly bonded users show in social networks is of relevance.**

Sixth, positioning engagement or participation as a construct to evaluate the quality of brand pages in social networks neglects the fact that participating in communications in social networks not only depends on the attractiveness of the brand page but also on the user's propensity to interact.[220] Another shortcoming is the disregard of

---

[216] Cf. BURMANN/KLEINE-KALMER (2013), p. 102.

[217] The words attached, bonded and connected are used interchangeably. Cf. THOMSON/MACINNIS/PARK (2005), p. 80.

[218] Cf. PATTERSON (2012), p. 530.

[219] Cf. PENTINA ET AL. (2013), p. 75.

[220] Cf. WIERTZ/DE RUYTER (2007), cf. WOISETSCHLÄGER/HARTLEB/BLUT (2008).

privacy concerns. A representative online survey[221] of 1.000 interviewees revealed: consumers allege companies to collect data only for their own benefit. They do not want companies to be in possession of their personal data let alone the passing on of data to third party contractors.[222] Facebook is known for their disastrous privacy protection and their violation of personal privacy.[223] Users who are aware of this issue hesitate to interact with brands in social networks out of fear of disclosure.[224] This fact has not been deliberated within the engagement research. **Thus, an analysis of moderators that prevent bonded users from participating with brands in social networks needs to be accomplished**.

Generally, all research questions above need to be viewed given the impact brand pages have on consumer attitudes and behaviours towards brands. Verifying the impact of brand pages is not central to this study due to several reasons. First, the correlation between social media and brand image, brand loyalty as well as purchase intention has been confirmed in former studies already.[225] Second, the extent of a research project analysing the impact of brand pages on brand perception justifies a separate project and cannot be subsumed under this study. And third, the necessity of a construct discussion is of higher relevance to the social media research progress than another validation of social media impact.[226]

5 Research objective, research questions and outline of the study

In the context of the challenges outlined above, a professional management of brand pages in social networks is imperative. Concomitant is the evaluation of the brand

---

[221] The study has been conducted in Germany by the Chair of innovative Brand Management instigated by the Wissenschaftlichen Gesellschaft für Marketing und Unternehmensführung e.V. The online survey was carried out in March 2013. A sample of 1.000 people between the age of 14-69 years representative for the German population was used.

[222] Cf. BURMANN/KLEINE-KALMER/HEMMANN (2013), p. 28.

[223] Cf. GUARINI (2013).

[224] Cf. TAYLOR/LEWIN/STRUTTON (2011), p. 263.

[225] Cf. ARNHOLD (2010), pp. 331 et seqq., cf. BRUHN ET AL. (2011), pp. 40 et seqq., cf. EILERS (2014), pp. 218 et seqq., cf. JAHN/KUNZ (2014), pp. 353 et seqq.

[226] Cf. JAHN/KUNZ (2014), pp. 354 et seqq.

page's impact. Current approaches still fall short in delivering constructs that can be implemented into the perpetual controlling of brand pages. Hence, the main objective of this thesis is to establish a construct that measures the user's bond to brand pages in social networks as well as its consequence and antecedents.

Consequently, the following research questions will be pursued:

1) What is attachment and why is it the best construct to measure the bond between user and brand page?

2) How can brand page attachment be conceptualised and measured in the context of social networks?

3) Which antecedents, consequences and moderators have to be considered?

To fulfil the research objectives, the outline of the study is as follows.

In the next chapter B, the theoretical basis will be laid out and a research model with corresponding hypotheses will be developed. The first part of chapter B covers the approach of identity-based brand management. The approach is the foundation for branding in social networks. The concept of brand pages in social networks will be integrated into the framework of identity-based brand management. The main objective of this thesis is to measure the user's bond to a brand page. For this purpose, the construct attachment will be introduced and discriminated from rival concepts. Antecedents and consequences will be deduced from relevant literature and integrated into the research model. Further, moderators that impact the relation between brand page attachment and consumer behaviour will be identified.

Chapter C introduces the relevant statistical methodology and operationalisation of constructs. It also comprises the empirical study that was conducted to validate the hypotheses arrayed in chapter B. Facebook users that follow brand pages of brands belonging to the categories FMCG, automobile or restaurant chains were surveyed with regard to their attachment to the brand pages.

The thesis closes with a summary of results in chapter D and implications for management and academia. The structure of the thesis is illustrated in Figure 7.

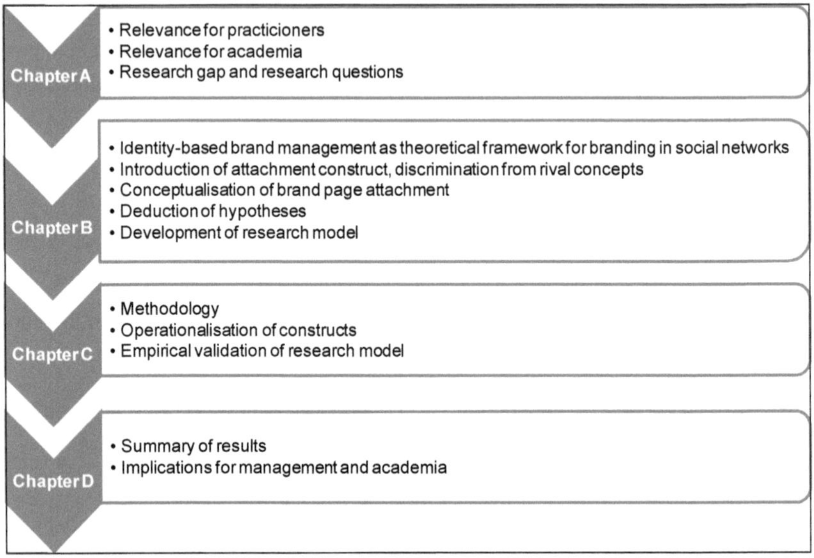

Figure 7: **Structure of thesis**

Source: Own illustration.

B Theoretical foundations

1 Identity-based brand management model as theoretical basis

1.1 Development of the identity-based brand management model

The corner stone for branding was set with the start of mass production at the beginning of the twentieth century. Producers labelled their supplies for recognition purposes. Those labels were employed as a guarantee for steady product quality and recognisable product (packaging) design. During the course of the early twentieth century branding became more and more sophisticated. With the beginning of the 1960s markets for consumer goods were saturated and products converged, so branding became the only way of differentiation.[227] The role of marketing in those days was to impact the consumer's subjective perception of a brand: the brand image.[228] In the beginning of the 1990s globalisation led to an interchange of knowledge and technology. Consequently, products became convertible and hardly discernible. Pricing became even more competitive and brands eroded. During this time academics saw the necessity for rethinking the theory of brand management. The market perspective that put the consumer's view on the brand in the centre of research was extended by an internal view that focuses on competencies of the firm. The identity-based brand management approach was developed parallel by KAPFERER (1992), AAKER (1996) and MEFFERT/BURMANN (1996).[229]

The identity-based brand management model broadens the former one-dimensional concept of image-oriented brand management by taking the internal competences and resources of a company into account. The model merges two opponent perspectives by integrating the external and internal view on a brand into one holistic approach: The inside-out perspective of internal stakeholders and the outside-in per-

---

[227] Cf. BURMANN/HALASZOVICH/HEMMANN (2012), pp. 20 et seqq.

[228] Cf. KELLER (1993).

[229] Cf. BURMANN/HALASZOVICH/HEMMANN (2012), pp. 20 et seqq.

spective of external stakeholders.[230] The inside-out perspective is determined through internal stakeholders like employees, executives, intermediaries and therefore builds the brand identity. The brand identity expresses the values and attributes that the brand stands for. It is actively formed through the firm itself and ultimately determines the perception of external groups through postulating the brand promise. The outside-in perspective, the brand image, is the perspective of external stakeholders, e.g. consumers. A brand in the context of identity-based brand management is understood as "a bundle of consumer benefits with specific attributes that - from the view of relevant target groups - differentiate this bundle from other bundles that fulfil the same basic needs".[231] Consumers experience the brand at various brand touch points[232] and therefore constitute a perception of the brand in their minds. Trough mutual exchange between internal and external groups at various brand touch points both concepts – brand identity and brand image – sharpen over time.[233] The approach is illustrated in Figure 8.

[230] Cf. MEFFERT/BURMANN/KIRCHGEORG (2012), p. 359.

[231] The original definition is phrased in the German language: „ein Nutzenbündel mit spezifischen Merkmalen, die dafür sorgen, dass sich dieses Nutzenbündel gegenüber anderen Nutzenbündeln, welche dieselben Basisbedürfnisse erfüllen, aus Sicht der relevanten Zielgruppen nachhaltig differenziert." BURMANN/HALASZOVICH/HEMMANN (2012), p. 28, BURMANN/BLINDA/NITSCHKE (2003), p. 3.

[232] SCHULTZ ET AL. (2009) describe the approach of customer touchpoints as follows: "This term allows marketers to focus on all the ways their organization touches the customer or prospect, whether through outbound marketing communication or any other of a myriad points of interaction. This idea of touchpoints is truly the differentiating factor between customer-brand relationship and traditional marketing for it starts with the customer, not the delivery system." SCHULTZ ET AL. (2009), pp. 202-203.

[233] Cf. BURMANN/HALASZOVICH/HEMMANN (2012), p. 29.

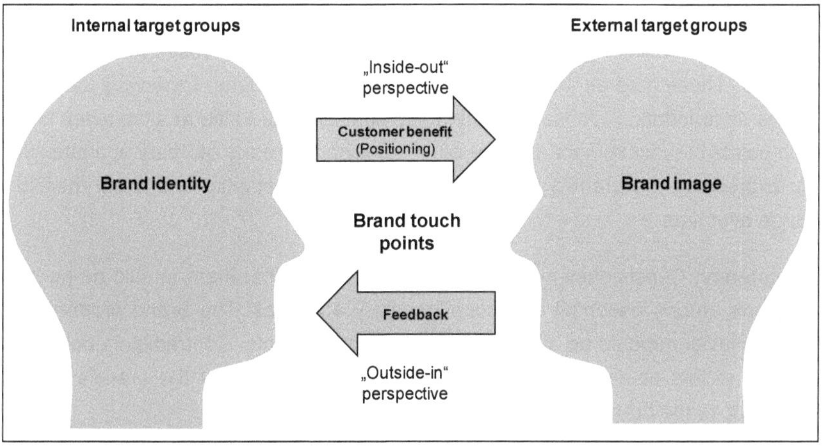

Figure 8: **Identity-based brand management basic model**
Source: Own illustration based on BURMANN/HALASZOVICH/HEMMANN (2012), p. 29.

1.2 Brand identity

The identity of a brand comprises those spatio-temporal features of a brand that form the character of a brand on a long-term basis from the view of internal target groups.[234] The identity is continually matched to the perception of external groups and assimilates if there are discrepancies. There are four fundamental characteristics that constitute a brand's identity:[235]

Reciprocity: An identity can only be formed through relationships between a brand and its consumers and other external groups. The interactions between brands and customers are decisive for the composition of a brand identity. Especially the long-term relationships are relevant for the stability of the brand identity. Hence the consumer relation can be seen as an integrative part of the identity.

---

[234] Cf. BURMANN/HALASZOVICH/HEMMANN (2012), p. 39.

[235] Cf. BURMANN/HALASZOVICH/HEMMANN (2012), p. 36.

Continuity: Essential characteristics of a brand have to be maintained over time. An identity is formed through a set of attributes that define the essence of a brand's character. These core attributes should be preserved over time. Otherwise the identity loses its foundation. Those core attributes should come to life at all relevant brand touch points that consumers experience. In addition, there are auxiliary attributes that help expressing the brand's identity but are not as substantial and might therefore change over time.

Consistency: Consistency in a brand's identity means that there should be no contradictions among essential and supplementary attributes. The brand promise and brand behaviour should be aligned at all brand touch points. Contradictory behaviour of ambassadors or employees leads to a misunderstanding of the brand's identity and damages the brand image.

Individuality: A brand should differentiate itself from competitor brands by one or more relevant attributes. Otherwise consumers see the brand as exchangeable.

The essence of the brand identity foots on several components. The identity-based brand management approach developed by MEFFERT/BURMANN (1996) offers six constitutive components (see Figure 9). A clear description of the identity components builds the foundation for implementing brand identity as an internal management concept. The basis for a brand's identity is the **heritage**. It determines the roots of a company not only historically but also regionally and regarding company or industry origin.[236] Regional roots can impact the quality perception of a brand. The good reputation of a region or country for a certain competence can be transferred to the brand. Examples for brands referring to regional origin are IKEA, Jever, VW[237] who use the German subtitle "Das Auto" in communication abroad.[238] Closely linked to the brand's heritage is the **brand vision**. The exploration of company roots directly leads to the question of where the company is going in future. The orientation of the brand vision is long-term and can be seen as an umbrella under which the beliefs

---

[236] Cf. BECKER (2012), p. 60.

[237] Cf. BURMANN/HALASZOVICH/HEMMANN (2012), p. 45.

[238] For more detailed information on brand heritage in the context of the identity-based brand management approach, please see BECKER (2012).

and aims are subsumed. It gives employees orientation and direction. The statement of a company vision does not have to be specified to the last detail, but it needs to be realistic and achievable.[239]

Competencies of a company help to obtain competitive advantage in a market.[240] Only through its competencies is a company able to deliver unique products or service that cannot or not easily be imitated by competitors.[241] Competencies of a brand or company are distinguished from branding competencies.[242] The latter are seen as an important ability for managing a brand and preparing it for future challenges.[243] Competencies are developed over time and result from organisational abilities and resources. Hence, investment in human resources that inherit and redefine competencies is seen as crucial.[244] A strong commitment of employees and the intention to stay in the company is therefore important.[245] The behaviour of employees is an expression of their beliefs. Ideally the behaviour mirrors the **brand values**. Brand values bring an emotional component to the brand identity. They reflect the company's responsibility for employees, products, environment and stakeholders. The brand values are typically summarised in concise statements. They can only have a positive impact on consumer perception if they are brought to life by employees.[246] The style of brand behaviour and communication is an expression of the **brand's per-**

---

[239] Cf. BURMANN/HALASZOVICH/HEMMANN (2012), p. 49.

[240] In the first part of the last century researchers argued that competitive advantage results from market and industry structure. This market-based view has been criticised for neglecting internal capabilities by researchers in the 1950s which was the basis for the development of the resource-based and later the competence-based view that foots on the theory of dynamic capabilities. Cf. BLINDA (2007), pp. 6 et seqq., cf. BURMANN/HALASZOVICH/HEMMANN (2012), pp. 6-16, cf. DAY (2011), cf. FREILING/GERSCH/GOEKE (2008).

[241] Cf. BLINDA (2007), p. 6.

[242] For a detailed analysis of brand management competencies in the context of identity-based brand management, please see BLINDA (2007).

[243] Cf. BLINDA (2007), p. 174.

[244] Cf. BURMANN/HALASZOVICH/HEMMANN (2012), pp. 50 et seqq.

[245] For a detailed review on the construct of brand commitment and internal branding in general, please see PIEHLER (2011).

[246] Cf. SCHALLEHN (2012), pp. 69-71.

sonality.[247] A brand personality according to AAKER (1997) is a "set of human characteristics associated with a brand."[248] GILMORE (1919) acknowledges in his "theory of animism" that people bring objects to life by assigning human personality traits to them.[249] The brand personality is essential for a brand's identity. Depending on the self-concept of the target group, congruence between the brand's and the consumer's personality can lead to high identification benefits which again impact the image of a brand positively.[250]

These five components of brand identity are the foundation for the **brand assortment**, the sixth component. They determine the type of products and services a company offers.[251]

The brand identity composed of the six dimensions explained above has to be credible. Only a brand that is authentic finds acceptance and is trusted by consumers.[252]

---

[247] The brand personality research was coined by AAKER (1997) who developed a scale that consisted of five dimensions to measure brand personality. SCHADE (2012) provides a detailed review on brand personality literature and researches the construct in the context of identity-based brand management for professional sport teams.

[248] AAKER (1997), p. 347.

[249] Cf. GILMORE (1919).

[250] In his dissertation, SCHADE (2012) was able to empirically prove that the higher the self-congruence the higher the identification with the brand which again impacts the brand image positively. Cf. SCHADE (2012), pp. 169-171.

[251] Cf. BURMANN/HALASZOVICH/HEMMANN (2012), pp. 56 et seq.

[252] Brand authenticity in the context of identity-based brand management has been researched in depth by SCHALLEHN (2012). The study he conducted confirmed the impact of perceived brand authenticity on brand trust empirically. Cf. SCHALLEHN (2012), p. 168.

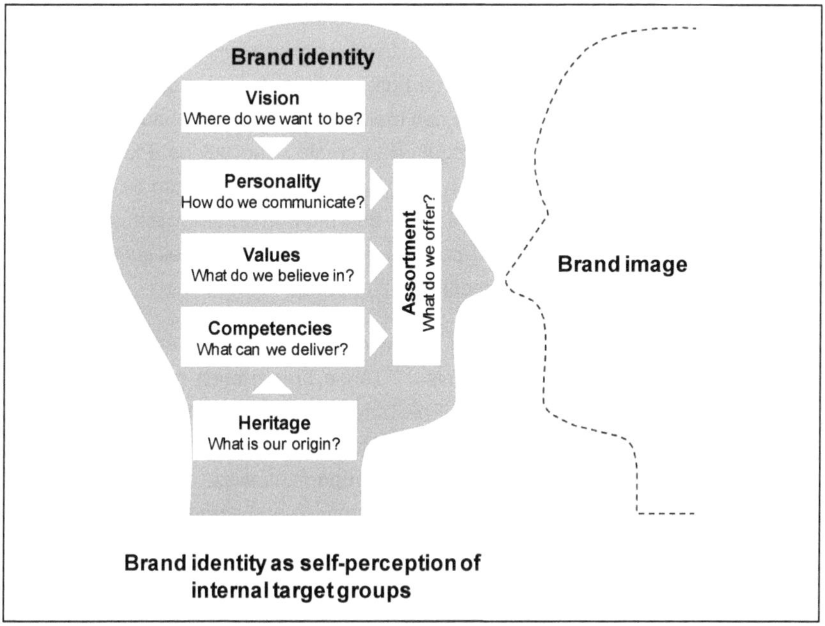

Figure 9: Components of the brand identity

Source: Own illustration based on BURMANN/HALASZOVICH/HEMMANN (2012), p. 44, ARNHOLD (2010), p. 39.

1.3 Brand image

The brand image is a multidimensional construct that consists of attitudes towards a brand and has a significant influence on the consumer's purchase intention.[253] It subsumes various subjective impressions of a product or a brand. Those impressions can occur in the form linguistic, metaphoric, episodic or visual stimuli.[254]

---

[253] Cf. TROMMSDORFF/TEICHERT (2011), p. 130.

[254] Cf. TROMMSDORFF/TEICHERT (2011), pp. 133 et seq.

The brand image is formed through consumers' expectations and experiences of a brand.[255] It is not only cognitive but also contains emotional, experiential and evaluative dimensions.[256] An image can only be built on the premise of brand awareness. Only if a person knows the brand, s/he can make up her/his mind about it.[257] Further, certain knowledge about a brand is required to create associations. Plus, the brand has to fulfil consumer needs adequately.[258] The consumer benefit can be either functional or symbolic. The latter becomes more and more important because in industries with high saturation, functional benefits of brands are not delivering sufficient reasons for differentiation from competitors.

The brand image is impacted through an individual's experience and perception of the brand at various brand touch points.[259] Those brand touch points include any contact between brand and consumer. This may include media impressions, contact at point of sale, customer service, brand outlets and many more.[260] At those touch points, the brand's ambassadors (employees, representatives, agencies) bring the components of the brand identity to life. Brand promise and brand performance need to be aligned, so the consumer can form a clear brand image in her/his mind.[261]

1.4 The relevance of interaction for identity-based brand management

A consumer experiences a brand at different touch points.[262] Brand touch points[263] can occur in the form of product usage, commercials, customer service or direct brand-consumer interaction. Whereas in the traditional concept of marketing, brand

---

[255] Cf. BURMANN/HALASZOVICH/HEMMANN (2012), p. 59.

[256] Cf. TROMMSDORFF/TEICHERT (2011), p. 134.

[257] Cf. BURMANN/HALASZOVICH/HEMMANN (2012), p. 59.

[258] Cf. BURMANN/HALASZOVICH/HEMMANN (2012), p. 59.

[259] Cf. BURMANN/HALASZOVICH/HEMMANN (2012), p. 103.

[260] Cf. BURMANN/HALASZOVICH/HEMMANN (2012), p. 104.

[261] Cf. BURMANN/ULBRICHT (2013), p. 15.

[262] Cf. BURMANN/HALASZOVICH/HEMMANN (2012), p. 103, cf. MEFFERT/BURMANN/KIRCHGEORG (2012), p. 361.

[263] Brand touch points include all contact points between the relevant target group and the brand. Cf. BURMANN/HALASZOVICH/HEMMANN (2012), p. 103.

touch points are created by the brand owner, in the context of social media brand touch points can also be created by consumers.[264] Social media touch points offer opportunity for interaction. Interaction comprises the exchange of content between various parties involved in the communication. Central element to interaction is reciprocity.[265] Only under the condition of reciprocity[266] does communication become interaction.[267] Hence, the exchange happens under the circumstance of mutual action. EILERS (2014) distinguishes between three forms of interaction:[268]

- "human-to-computer"[269] interaction

  With human-to-computer interaction EILERS (2014) describes a user interacting with a computer system or an internet application. The system or software has the ability to respond to the action of the user. This could be a website that is reacting towards the content the user activates or provides.

- "human-to-human"[270] interaction

  This category contains all kinds of interactions that happen between two or more individuals. Sociologists point towards the geographic component in the human-to-human interaction. Herewith, they highlight that individuals involved are usually gathered in one place at the same time.

- "computer-mediated"[271] interaction

---

264 Cf. ARNHOLD (2010), p. 48.

265 Cf. TROPP (2011), pp. 47 et seq, cf. EILERS (2014), p. 60.

266 "Reciprocity refers to the mutuality or bi-directionality" of a relationship. THOMSON/JOHNSON (2006), p. 715.

267 Cf. EILERS (2014), p. 63.

268 In her thesis, EILERS (2014) investigates the impact of social media on brand image and purchase behaviour. She compares different tools of social media communication for the industries automobile and food. For further details please see EILERS (2014).

269 EILERS (2014), p. 61.

270 EILERS (2014), p. 61.

271 EILERS (2014), pp. 61 et seq.

> Computer-mediated interaction has similarities with human-to-human interaction only that the communication is arbitrated through a medium. The parties involved in the communication are geographically not bound to be at the same place. They can be in different places and connect via internet. Neither is it required for the time to overlap. One individual can write a comment or post online and the other individual is able to answer or react later on.

For the context of social networks the computer-mediated interaction is predominant. Unlike media like television, radio or print, for social networks the criteria of reciprocity is fulfilled.[272] Consumers are able to interact with the brand mediated through computer software e.g. social networks. But different types of interaction need to be considered.[273] EILERS (2014) differentiates between interactive social media stimuli and passively consumed social media stimuli.[274] Among the interactive social media stimuli she subsumes personal communication between brand and user. That includes writing **personal messages**, **post comments**, **like posts** that the brand published on its wall or **share content** that the brand provided (see Figure 10). These activities can be defined as interaction because reciprocity is given. They happen as a reaction towards a stimulus provided by the brand.[275]

---

[272] Cf. EILERS (2014), p. 63, cf. TROPP (2011), p. 48.

[273] Cf. EILERS (2014), pp. 218 et seqq.

[274] Cf. EILERS (2014), p. 100.

[275] Cf. EILERS (2014), p. 65.

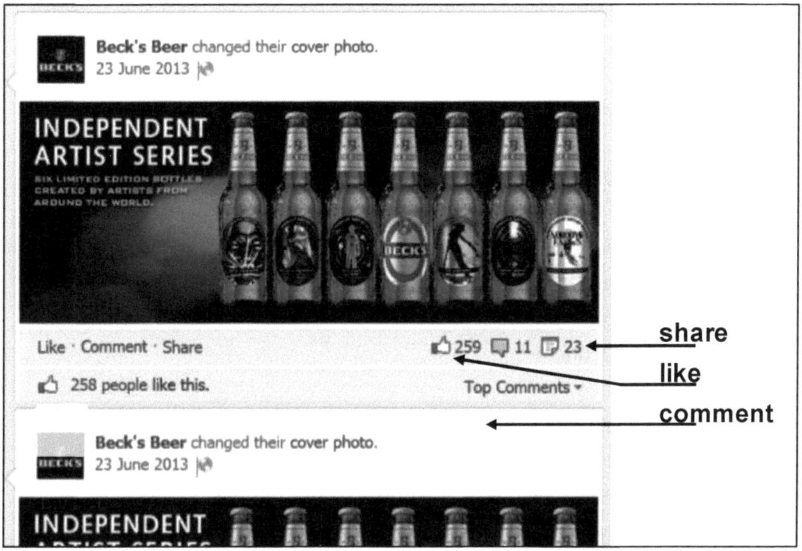

Figure 10: **Brand post and user comments on Facebook wall**
Source: Own illustration, Facebook brand page of Beck's Beer

Further, **passive consumption** of brand related user generated content[276] and brand generated content[277] has to be considered. The gratification a user gains from following a brand page, does not require active participation. In fact, only 1.3% of users that follow a brand page are interacting with the brand according to a study[278] conducted by the Ehrenberg-Bass Institute.[279] Interaction in this case was measured by

---

[276] Brand related user generated content comprises published material that refers to a brand and has been created by users. The content does not have any commercial purpose and is available online. For a detailed review, definition and examples, please see ARNHOLD (2010), pp. 31 et seqq., EILERS (2014), pp. 51 et seqq., MEFFERT/BURMANN/KIRCHGEORG (2012), pp. 667 et seqq.

[277] Brand generated content comprises published material that is provided by the brand owner. It is available online and issued on account of commercial purposes. For a detailed review, please see EILERS (2014), p. 56, MEFFERT/BURMANN/KIRCHGEORG (2012), p. 669.

[278] The study analysed the user engagement of 200 brand pages on Facebook during a time span of six weeks. To measure engagement, they used the publicly available metric "people talking about this" cf. HEDEMANN (2012), cf. FACEBOOK (2012), cf. DARWELL (2012).

[279] Cf. HEDEMANN (2012), cf. EILERS (2014), p. 72.

the metric "people talking about this"[280] provided by Facebook. This metric includes the following user activities:

- post on the page wall
- like a post
- comment on a post
- share a post
- answer a question
- RSVP[281] to a page's event
- mention the page in a post
- tag the page in a photo
- check-in at a place
- share a check-in deal
- like a check-in deal
- write a recommendation
- like a page (new followers within a seven days period)
- claim an offer.[282]

Another study validated these findings by finding out that 77% of brand page followers are rather just reading posts from the brand instead of actively participating in the communication on the brand page.[283] Hence, analysts that are evaluating engagement or interaction rates for social media performance measurement only examine a small portion of their target group. The majority of brand page followers is neglected. For this reason, there is a clear need for a new metric that includes the passive users into the research. EILERS (2014) also detected the relevance of the passively consumed content.[284] In her thesis, she lays focus on the differences between the attitudes towards different kinds of postings and the impact of frequency and analysed

[280] FACEBOOK (2012).

[281] RSVP is a common abbreviation of répondez s'il vous plaît.

[282] Cf. DARWELL (2012).

[283] A 15 minute online questionnaire was filled out by 1,491 US consumers, older than 18 years in January 2011. Cf. CHADWICK MARTIN BAILEY (2011), cf. EILERS (2014), p. 72.

[284] Cf. EILERS (2014), p. 73.

their impact on brand uses and brand image. But, an overall evaluation metric for brand pages was not included in her model.

The aim of this present work is to address this reoccurring issue and establish a construct that measures the bond a user feels toward the brand page. Further, the impact of this bond on consumer behaviour should be analysed. For brand management this scale should deliver an instrument for assessing brand pages in terms of their power to bind a consumer, gain her/his attention and evoke supportive behaviour. Because interaction and engagement rates are not delivering the necessary insights towards the emotional bond[285], this work advocates measuring the consumer's attachment toward a brand page.

2 Attachment as central construct for assessing brand pages

Several constructs have been employed to measure emotional bonds between consumers and brands.[286] Important research areas are brand attachment[287], brand relationships[288] containing constructs like customer-brand relationship[289], brand satisfaction[290], brand loyalty[291] or brand love[292]. This theory and constructs will be differentiated from brand attachment in chapter B 2.3. Before the differentiation, it needs to be clarified, what attachment stands for.

---

[285] Cf. CARLSON/SUTER/BROWN (2008), p. 284.

[286] Cf. FOURNIER (1998), pp. 343 et seqq.

[287] Cf. THOMSON/MACINNIS/PARK (2005), cf. PARK ET AL. (2010), cf. PARK/MACINNIS/PRIESTER (2006a), cf. PARK/EISINGERICH/PARK (2013), cf. LACOEUILHE (2000).

[288] Cf. FOURNIER (1998), cf. FOURNIER/DOBSCHA/MICK (1998), cf. WENSKE (2008), EICHEN (2010).

[289] Cf. WENSKE (2008).

[290] More insights into the differentiation between brand satisfaction and brand love are provided by FOURNIER/MICK (1999) or CARROLL/AHUVIA (2006).

[291] For more details on the concept of brand loyalty, please see TUCKER (1964), JACOBY/KYNER (1973), DAY (1976), JACOBY/CHESTNUT (1978), BLOEMER/KASPER (1995), FOURNIER/YAO (1997), CHAUDHURI/HOLBROOK (2001).

[292] For further detail on brand love research, please see CARROLL/AHUVIA (2006), ALBERT/MERUNKA/VALETTE-FLORENCE (2008), BATRA/AHUVIA/BAGOZZI (2012), LANGNER/KÜHN/BRUNS (2013).

The rationale for employing the attachment construct to measure the bond a consumer feels toward a brand page will be provided in the following subchapters. For this purpose, first, the construct attachment will be illuminated. The state of the art research on brand attachment and brand *community* attachment will be explained in detail. Based on these chapters, the concept of brand *page* attachment will be developed accordingly. This is accompanied by a rationale for why attachment is superior to competing constructs.

2.1 The attachment construct

The attachment construct has been long established in academia.[293] Psychological science led the way into attachment theory. BOWLBY (1979) researched bonds between parents and children. In this context, he sees attachment as an emotional connection between two people.[294] Those early bonded social ties usually endure a lifetime.[295] The level of attachment characterises the strength of the bond.[296] Some individuals form weak and some form strong bonds to attachment objects in order to gain protection from external threats.[297] Each individual is equipped with a range of attachment levels.[298] Individuals that feel strong attachment toward a person or an object are likely to strive for closeness.[299] In turn, being separated from the attachment target would cause negative stress for the person.[300] Building on these findings that are based on mother-child observations, the attachment construct has been further explored in the context of places, people, gifts, objects and brands.[301]

---

[293] Cf. HAZAN/SHAVER (1994), p. 1, cf. MOONEY (2010), pp. 8 et seqq.

[294] Cf. BOWLBY (1979).

[295] Cf. MOONEY (2010), p. 7.

[296] Cf. HAZAN/SHAVER (1994), p. 3.

[297] Cf. PARK/MACINNIS/PRIESTER (2006b), p. 193.

[298] Cf. PARK/MACINNIS/PRIESTER (2006b), p. 193.

[299] Cf. PARK/MACINNIS/PRIESTER (2006b), p. 193.

[300] Cf. BOWLBY (1979), cf. BOWLBY (1980).

[301] Cf. THOMSON/MACINNIS/PARK (2005), pp. 77 et seq.

2.2 Reviewing the concept of attachment

2.2.1 State of the art research on *brand* attachment

As described above the attachment research stems from psychology and originally explored emotional connections between people.[302] Still, despite the transfer into other research areas[303], the original meaning of attachment was kept.[304] Attachment represents the bond between a human and a subject or an object.[305] Those objects may range from places[306] to brands[307], gifts[308], possessions[309], celebrities[310] or communities[311].

To ultimately derive a definition for brand *page* attachment, the understanding of attachment in former work needs to be scrutinised. To take a broad approach, the construct of *brand* attachment will be considered. A search in EBSCOhost®[312] for the term *brand attachment* delivered 97 results, the amount of issued articles annually is shown in Figure 11.

---

302 Cf. BOWLBY (1979), cf. BOWLBY (1980).

303 Cf. PARK/MACINNIS/PRIESTER (2006b), p. 194.

304 Cf. PARK ET AL. (2010), p. 1.

305 Cf. THOMSON/MACINNIS/PARK (2005), p. 78, cf. KLEINE/KLEINE/ALLEN (1995), p. 327.

306 Cf. HILL/STAMEY (1990), pp. 303 et seqq.

307 Cf. THOMSON/MACINNIS/PARK (2005), pp. 77 et seqq., cf. PARK ET AL. (2010), pp.1 et seqq., cf. SCHOUTEN/MCALEXANDER (1995).

308 Cf. MICK/DEMOSS (1990), pp. 322 et seqq.

309 Cf. BABAD (1987), pp. 231 et seqq., cf. WALLENDORF (1988), pp. 531 et seqq., cf. RICHINS (1994), pp. 522 et seqq.

310 Cf. THOMSON (2006), pp. 104 et seqq.

311 Cf. REN ET AL. (2012), pp. 841 et seqq.

312 EBSCOhost® is a US-American database service. The company offers databases for full-text and secondary research as well as e-books and e-journals. The search service is widely spread among academic institutions and used in researching academic literature worldwide. The search was executed in November 2013. Only academic journals and peer-reviewed publications were taken into account. Cf. EBSCO INDUSTRIES (2013).

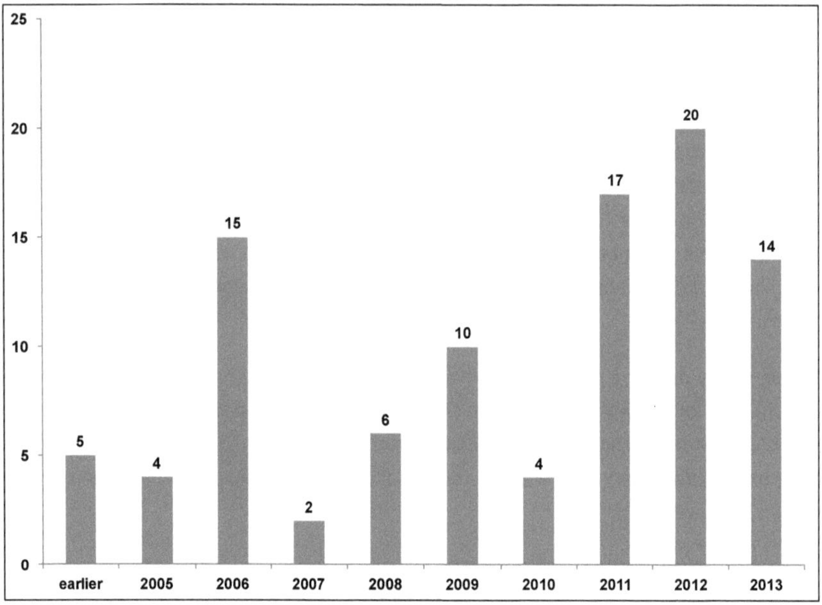

Figure 11: **Number of peer-reviewed publications in academic journals issued on brand attachment by year, November 2013**

Source: Own illustration

The aim of this chapter is not to review all publications in detail[313], but to point out to those that have been cited most and had a big impact. The article written by THOMSON/MACINNIS/PARK (2005) and published in the Journal of Consumer Psychology had a high impact as it inspired a lot of following publications[314].[315] It is commonly seen as fundamental piece of work that needs to be looked at when executing research on emotional attachment to brands.[316] Various academics quote this source

[313] For a detailed review and summary on the research on the construct of attachment, please read the work of THOMSON/MACINNIS/PARK (2005), PARK ET AL. (2010), MENDE/BOLTON/BITNER (2013).

[314] Please see Table 2 and Table 3.

[315] Cf. THOMSON/MACINNIS/PARK (2005).

[316] Cf. BRAKUS/SCHMITT/ZARANTONELLO (2009), p. 53.

when assembling literature for brand attachment.[317] A search in Google scholar[318] revealed that the paper was cited 525 times. The essay investigated **emotional attachment to brands** under the assumption that the construct is solely set up by affective dimensions.

THOMSON/MACINNIS/PARK (2005) developed a scale to measure emotional attachment to brands.[319] The foundation of their perception of attachment is the research by BOWLBY (1979) on infants and their relations to parents.[320] Citing BOWLBY (1979), THOMSON/MACINNIS/PARK (2005) define attachment as "an emotion-laden target-specific bond between a person and a specific object. Attachments vary in strength, and stronger attachments are associated with stronger feelings of connection, affection, love, and passion [...]."[321] Thus, the concept is highly emotional and defined by different affective dimensions.[322] Through this emotional bond, consumer behaviour can be predicted.[323] Strong emotional attachment to an item leads to the desire of proximity[324] to object one is attached.[325] The person wishes to stay close and gain shelter provided by the object in times of emotional stress. Further, separation distress may happen when the connection to the object is threatened to split up.[326] In addition, attachment predicts commitment. The authors define commitment "as the degree to which an individual views the relationship from a long-term perspective and has a willingness to stay with the relationship even when things are difficult (VAN

317 Cf. BRAKUS/SCHMITT/ZARANTONELLO (2009), BATRA/AHUVIA/BAGOZZI (2012), MALÄR ET AL. (2011), ZHOU ET AL. (2012), LAMBERT-PANDRAUD/LAURENT (2010), ALBERT/MERUNKA/VALETTE-FLORENCE (2013), TSAI (2011).

318 Cf. GOOGLE SCHOLAR (2014).

319 Cf. THOMSON/MACINNIS/PARK (2005).

320 Cf. BOWLBY (1979).

321 THOMSON/MACINNIS/PARK (2005), pp. 77-78.

322 Cf. BOWLBY (1997), p. 209.

323 Cf. KLEINE/KLEINE/ALLEN (1995), p. 341, cf. PARK ET AL. (2010), p. 14.

324 Proximity and closeness are used synonymously as to their similar interpretation with closeness being defined as "only a short distance away or apart in space or time" and proximity as "nearness in space, time, or relationship" cf. OXFORD DICTIONARIES (2014b), OXFORD DICTIONARIES (2014c).

325 Cf. WALLENDORF (1988), pp. 542 et seqq.

326 Cf. THOMSON/MACINNIS/PARK (2005), p. 78.

LANGE ET AL. (1997))."[327] So according to them[328], commitment describes a state of mind that results from attachment to the object.[329]

THOMSON/MACINNIS/PARK (2005) differentiate their concept of emotional attachment from related constructs like **brand attitudes, satisfaction, and involvement**.[330] For the differentiation of *brand attitudes*[331] the authors argue that consumers can have evaluative reactions (attitudes) towards objects without any direct contact with it. Attachment on the contrary can only develop over time. They matter, develop a meaning for the individual and inflame emotions regarding the attachment object.[332] Attachments link the object to the self and to individual memories[333] whereas attitudes not necessarily do. A positive attitude can still lead to switching. High attachment according to the authors predicts loyalty.[334] *Satisfaction*[335] for them is an evaluative judgment and hence different from the emotionally laden attachment construct. The construct of satisfaction is commonly used in relation to product or service performance rather than emotional connections to brands.[336] FOURNIER/MICK (1999) state that "satisfaction generally is conceptualized as an attitude-like judgment following a purchase act or based on a series of consumer-product interactions."[337] Grading the

[327] THOMSON/MACINNIS/PARK (2005), p. 78.

[328] The constructs commitment and attachment bear similarities and are therefore often employed in the same way. However, THOMSON/MACINNIS/PARK (2005) among others advocate the differentiation of the two constructs. For the research community studying attachment, "commitment is a psychological pledge regarding future behavior. Attachment is a characteristic of a relationship between a consumer and a brand." PARK/MACINNIS/PRIESTER (2006b), p. 198.

[329] The distinct differentiation between the two concepts attachment and commitment will follow in chapter B 2.3.5.

[330] Cf. THOMSON/MACINNIS/PARK (2005), pp. 78 et seq.

[331] PARK ET AL. (2010) define "attitude valence as the degree of positivity or negativity with which an attitude object (in the current context, a brand) is evaluated." PARK ET AL. (2010), p. 1. More insights into the research on brand attitudes, please read: PARK/YOUNG (1983), pp. 320 et seqq., cf. GARDNER (1985), pp. 192 et seqq., cf. AAKER/JACOBSON (2001), pp. 485 et seqq.

[332] Cf. THOMSON/MACINNIS/PARK (2005), p. 78.

[333] Cf. KLEINE/KLEINE/ALLEN (1995), p. 340.

[334] Cf. THOMSON/MACINNIS/PARK (2005), p. 86.

[335] More detail and a literature review on satisfaction are provided by FOURNIER/MICK (1999).

[336] Cf. FOURNIER/MICK (1999), p. 5.

[337] FOURNIER/MICK (1999), p. 5.

level of satisfaction is an "active, dynamic process"[338]. This process can be influenced through external sources like family members whose opinion has an impact on the level of satisfaction of the purchase maker. It is also dependent on former expectations and the overall contentment with an individual's life situation.[339]

Involvement[340] is a state of mental readiness that typically influences the allocation of cognitive resources to a consumption object, decision, or action. Hence, involvement is composed of cognitive dimensions; the definition and conceptualisation of attachment in the view of THOMSON/MACINNIS/PARK (2005) contains only emotional components.[341] This differentiation was not only declared conceptually but proven empirically. In an exploratory factor analysis[342] the items loaded onto five factors which were: involvement, satisfaction and loyalty[343], brand attitude, dissatisfaction and emotional attachment.[344] In summary, the authors establish a distinct construct which measures the emotional bond between consumers and their brands. For this reason they compose the construct of the three affective dimensions: affection, connection and passion.[345] Further details on the discrimination of the attachment construct against competing constructs are provided in chapter B 2.3.

The perception and conceptualisation of emotional brand attachment coined by THOMSON/MACINNIS/PARK (2005) was cited and conveyed in many ensuing studies. The definition as an emotional bond[346] was predominant in succeeding work by other

---

[338] FOURNIER/MICK (1999), p. 15.

[339] Cf. FOURNIER/MICK (1999), pp. 15 et seqq.

[340] Detailed insights into the involvement construct are delivered by LAURENT/KAPFERER (1985), pp. 41 et seqq., see also KNOX (2003), pp. 271 et seqq.

[341] Cf. THOMSON/MACINNIS/PARK (2005), pp. 77 et seqq.

[342] For this study 179 respondents were recruited with an average age of 27 years. Cf. THOMSON/MACINNIS/PARK (2005), p. 83.

[343] The items of those two construct loaded onto one factor which is in line with former research and proved the relatedness of those two constructs. Cf. THOMSON/MACINNIS/PARK (2005), p. 85.

[344] Cf. THOMSON/MACINNIS/PARK (2005), p. 86.

[345] Cf. THOMSON/MACINNIS/PARK (2005), p. 80.

[346] Cf. THOMSON/MACINNIS/PARK (2005), p. 78.

researchers as shown in Table 2 below. Until two of the authors[347] came to the conclusion that measuring attachment solely from an emotional point of view, neglects the cognitive components which have been disregarded so far but are nonetheless existent. PARK ET AL. (2010) conducted a follow up study which was published in the Journal of Marketing and cited 170 times according to Google scholar[348].[349] The study endorsed the existence of cognitive components in the attachment construct.

PARK ET AL. (2010) articulate in their paper that was published in the Journal of Marketing in 2010 that the conceptual properties of the attachment construct are still ambiguous.[350] Instead of speaking about emotional brand attachment, they remove the adjective "emotional" and utilise the term brand attachment. For them, brand attachment is (as cited in Table 2) "**the strength of the bond connecting the brand with the self**. Consistent with attachment theory (MIKULINCER/SHAVER (2007)), this bond is exemplified by a rich and accessible memory network[351] (or mental representation) that involves thoughts and feelings about the brand and the brand's relationship to the self. Two critical factors reflect the conceptual properties of brand attachment: brand–self connection and brand prominence."[352] With this definition the authors integrate the cognitive component into the attachment construct.

They entitle the first dimension **brand-self connection**, which includes the cognitive comprehension of the brand's importance or meaning in relation to the self concept.[353] The connection between a person and a brand inherits emotions about the brand[354], e.g. happiness, fear of separation or pride, yet the process of appreciation

---

[347] The research on emotional brand attachment published in 2005 was conducted by Matthew Thomson, Deborah J. MacInnis and C. Whan Park. One of the succeeding studies on brand attachment was carried out by C. Whan Park, Deborah J. MacInnis, Joseph Priester, Andreas B. Eisingerich and Dawn Iacobucci in 2010.

[348] Cf. GOOGLE SCHOLAR (2014).

[349] Cf. PARK ET AL. (2010).

[350] Cf. PARK ET AL. (2010), p. 2.

[351] Cf. BIELEFELD (2012), pp. 123 et s.eqq for details on neural networks.

[352] PARK ET AL. (2010), p. 2.

[353] Cf. PARK ET AL. (2010), p. 2.

[354] Cf. THOMSON/JOHNSON (2006), p. 712.

and understanding the relevance of the brand is cognitive[355]. Hence, this dimension of attachment represents both cognitive and affective components. They distinguish between two kinds of brand-self connections: one foots on the *identity* and the other has an *instrumentality basis*.[356] The connections that are built on the *identity* arise because the brand stands for what the consumer believes in. This condition is grounded in the research on identity-based brand management.[357] A brand evokes highest behavioural relevance for an individual if the brand's identity matches the self-concept[358] of the individual.[359] The brand displays the consumer's personality[360] and helps her/him to express her-/himself.[361] For example if an individual wears clothes from a brand that produces outdoor clothing, s/he wants to express her/his sportiness as well as her/his natural and adventurous lifestyle. An *instrumentality basis* is given when the connection to the brand helps the consumer to pursue personal targets or interests.[362] Coming back to the example of outdoor clothing, the waterproof rain jacket and extra durable hiking shoes supports the individual while climbing a mountain and fulfil her/his personal dream.

The brand-self connection dimension is verified by other researchers[363] in the context of attachment to possessions.[364] SCHULTZ/KLEINE (1989) state that attachment "represents the degree of linkage perceived by an individual between him/her self and a particular object."[365] In their eyes, attachments to possessions are linked to previous

---

[355] Cf. PARK ET AL. (2010), p. 3.

[356] Cf. PARK ET AL. (2010), p. 2.

[357] Cf. BURMANN/HALASZOVICH/HEMMANN (2012), pp. 19 et seqq.

[358] Please see chapter 2.4.2 for the self-congruency theory.

[359] Cf. SCHADE (2012), p. 77, cf. BURMANN/HALASZOVICH/HEMMANN (2012), p. 55.

[360] For a thorough literature review on brand personality research, please read SCHADE (2012), pp. 60 et seqq.

[361] Cf. PARK/MACINNIS/PRIESTER (2006b), p. 195.

[362] Cf. PARK ET AL. (2010), p. 2.

[363] Cf. SCHULTZ/KLEINE (1989) pp. 359 et seqq., KLEINE/KLEINE/ALLEN (1995), pp. 340 et seqq.

[364] According to KLEINE/BAKER (2004) attachment to brands and attachment to possessions are related research areas. While most findings can be transferred, they point out that brands are intangible while possessions are tangible objects. This may have an impact on interpreting research results and theory development. Cf. KLEINE/BAKER (2004), pp. 2 et seq.

[365] SCHULTZ/KLEINE (1989), p. 360.

and current self-definitional experiences.[366] KLEINE/KLEINE/ALLEN (1995) study attachment to possessions and their linkage to the consumer's identity. Their findings reveal that individuals have different facets of attachment to possessions to reflect different parts of their identity.[367] The facets occur in the form of attachments to possessions that connect the consumer to its own past and memory, attachments that link to the consumer's identity in present, attachments to possessions that are gifts from other people.[368]

The existence of the dimension self-brand connection becomes evident through consumers displaying brands on clothes, watches, cars and their desire to join brand communities and liaise with others attached brand admirers.[369] Statements that express the linkage of the brand to the self are used for measurement.[370] Examples are: "part of me", "reflecting me", "an extension of myself", "aesthetically appealing to me" or "emotionally relating to me".[371]

The original scale employed by PARK ET AL. (2010) to measure the dimension brand-self connection of the construct brand attachment[372] contains the following items:

366 Cf. SCHULTZ/KLEINE (1989), p. 366.

367 Cf. KLEINE/KLEINE/ALLEN (1995), p. 340.

368 Cf. KLEINE/KLEINE/ALLEN (1995), p. 340.

369 Cf. PARK/MACINNIS/PRIESTER (2006b), p. 195.

370 Cf. BALL/TASAKI (1992), p. 162.

371 PARK/MACINNIS/PRIESTER (2006b), p. 195.

372 Cf. PARK ET AL. (2010), p. 6.

Dimension	Items
Brand-self connection	*To what extent is (brand name) part of you and who you are?*
	To what extent do you feel personally connected to (brand name)?
	To what extent do you feel emotionally bonded to (brand name)?
	To what extent is (brand name) part of you?
	To what extent does (brand name) say something to other people about who you are?

Figure 12: Items for brand-self connection of the brand attachment scale by PARK ET AL. (2010)
Source: PARK ET AL. (2010), p. 6.

Note that only the italicised items were used for brand-self connection in the final attachment scale.[373] Due to reasons of simplification, PARK ET AL. (2010) employed a reduced scale.[374]

The second dimension is labelled **brand prominence**. Brand prominence indicates how present the brand is in a consumer's mind.[375] That means when a person thinks about a category or industry, automatically thoughts about one specific brand come up. According to the latest neuroscientific research, the storage of brand information in a consumer's mind is deeper when the coding of symbolic brand attributes is highly detailed.[376] Individuals that deeply processed brand information and symbolic meaning are able to recall brand information.[377] Prominence reflects the strength of thoughts and emotions about a brand. The stronger they are the more the brand is top of mind.[378] Thus, high brand prominence represents one facet of high attach-

[373] Cf. PARK ET AL. (2010), p. 6.

[374] Cf. PARK ET AL. (2010), pp. 5 et seq.

[375] Cf. ALBA/CHATTOPADHYAY (1986), p. 363.

[376] Cf. BIELEFELD (2012), pp. 188 et seqq. For detailed information on consumer neuroscience, please read BIELEFELD (2012).

[377] Cf. BIELEFELD (2012), pp. 199 et seqq.

[378] In marketing research, top of mind brand awareness plays an important role as determines first choice and purchase intention or consideration. Cf. NEDUNGADI/HUTCHINSON (1985), pp. 498 et seqq., cf. THELEN/WOODSIDE (1997), pp. 125 et seqq.

ment.[379] PARK ET AL. (2010) describe this as the "salience"[380] of the consumer's bond to a brand. [381] This salience is characterised by how easy and how often thoughts about a brand pop up.[382] ROMANIUK/SHARP (2004) argue that salience or prominence cannot be conceptualised and measured by equalising it to "top of mind" or brand awareness.[383] The concept of brand salience is broader and reflects "the quantity and quality of the network of memory structures buyers' hold about the brands"[384] also referred to as "share of mind"[385]. If the brand prominence is high, the more thoughts come into the buyer's mind and the association of brand attributes is stronger. This leads to an overall higher likelihood to be chosen in buying situations.[386] HONG/WANG/DE LOS SANTOS (2008) compare salience to arousal which they define as "the level of activation associated with an emotional response".[387]

ROMANIUK/SHARP (2003) were able to prove a direct inverse relationship between brand salience and customer defection.[388] They advocate regarding brand salience levels to measure the effectiveness of branding activities[389] that aim at customer retention.[390] A change in brand salience of one percentage point leads to a decrease of 0.25 of a percentage point in defection rates.[391] These results were verified over sev-

---

[379] Cf. COLLINS (1996), p. 813.

[380] PARK ET AL. (2010), p. 2.

[381] Prominence is also referred to as salience. ALBA/CHATTOPADHYAY (1986) describe salience as "the prominence or "level of activation" of a brand in memory." ALBA/CHATTOPADHYAY (1986), p. 363.

[382] Cf. PARK ET AL. (2010), p. 2.

[383] Cf. ROMANIUK/SHARP (2004), p. 327.

[384] ROMANIUK/SHARP (2004), p. 327.

[385] Cf. ROMANIUK/SHARP (2004), p. 334.

[386] Cf. BUILDING BRAND SALIENCE FOR COMMODITY-BASED WINE REGIONS (2009), p. 82.

[387] HONG/WANG/DE LOS SANTOS (2008), p. 106.

[388] Cf. ROMANIUK/SHARP (2003), pp. 25 et seqq.

[389] Other researchers confirm this, e.g MILLER/BERRY (1998) in the context of advertising effectiveness, cf. MILLER/BERRY (1998), pp. 77 et seqq. or VAN DER LANS/PIETERS/WEDEL (2008) in the context of shelf visibility in store, cf. VAN DER LANS/PIETERS/WEDEL (2008), pp. 922 et seqq, or JOHNSTONE/DODD (2000) in the context of product placement in a motion picture, cf. JOHNSTONE/DODD (2000), pp. 141 et seqq.

[390] Cf. ROMANIUK/SHARP (2003), p. 40.

[391] Cf. ROMANIUK/SHARP (2003), p. 40.

eral different set ups including different pricing, service, origin and expertise of the brand.[392]

The original scale employed by PARK ET AL. (2010) to measure the dimension brand prominence of the construct brand attachment[393] contains the following items:

Dimension	Items
Brand prominence	*To what extent are your thoughts and feelings toward (brand name) often automatic, coming to mind seemingly on their own?*
	To what extent do your thoughts and feelings toward (brand name) come to your mind naturally and instantly?
	To what extent do your thoughts and feelings toward (brand name) come to mind so naturally and instantly that you don't have much control over them?
	To what extent does the word (brand name) automatically evoke many good thoughts about the past, present, and future?
	To what extent do you have many thoughts about (brand name)?

Figure 13: Items for brand prominence of the brand attachment scale by PARK ET AL. (2010)
Source: PARK ET AL. (2010), p. 6.

Here too, only the italicised items were used for brand prominence in the final attachment scale.[394] Due to reasons of simplification, PARK ET AL. (2010) employed a reduced scale.[395]

To sum up, both dimensions are crucial for the measurement of brand attachment. While brand-self connection is the central element of the construct as it is inherent in its definition, brand prominence helps specifying how strong the connection really is.[396] The dimension prominence indicates the accessibility of thoughts and feelings about a brand.[397] It is therefore inherent to the attachment construct. If the brand is not accessible in the consumer's mind, the self-brand connection may be strong, but

392 Cf. ROMANIUK/SHARP (2003), p. 40.
393 Cf. PARK ET AL. (2010), p. 6.
394 Cf. PARK ET AL. (2010), p. 6.
395 Cf. PARK ET AL. (2010), pp. 5 et seq.
396 Cf. PARK ET AL. (2010), p. 2.
397 Cf. PARK ET AL. (2010), p. 2.

attachment overall should be weak.[398] Only the combination of both dimensions completes the construct of attachment. Further, the researchers postulate that prominence is a reliable predictor for behaviour and that there is greater long-term commitment when the brand is prominent.[399]

The rationale behind the integration of cognitive elements to the attachment measurement foots on three arguments:

First, THOMSON/MACINNIS/PARK (2005) define emotional attachment by three factors affection, connection and passion that consists of in total ten emotional items "affectionate", "loved", "friendly", "peaceful", "passionate", "delighted", "captivated", "connected", "bonded", "attached".[400] PARK ET AL. (2010) argue that those items are random and could always be supplemented by other emotional items like "joy, excitement, pride, contentment, relief, nostalgia"[401] to name a few. The authors agree that attachment is inherently emotional, but the goal of their research is not to identify the specific type of emotions. They question if it is even possible to build a comprehensive scale that captures all types of emotions signifying attachment.[402]

Second, the use of passion as indicator in the view of PARK ET AL. (2010) is not suitable, as passion very much depends on the duration of the brand-consumer relationship.[403] In an enduring relationship passion may fade with time.[404] On the contrary, attachment should grow. In this case, the factor passion would give a wrong indication of the degree of attachment.[405]

---

[398] Cf. PARK ET AL. (2010), pp. 2 et seqq.

[399] Cf. PARK ET AL. (2010), p. 2.

[400] THOMSON/MACINNIS/PARK (2005), p. 80.

[401] PARK ET AL. (2010), p. 3.

[402] Cf. PARK ET AL. (2010), p. 3.

[403] Cf. PARK ET AL. (2010), p. 3.

[404] Cf. AHUVIA/BATRA/BAGOZZI (2009).

[405] Cf. PARK ET AL. (2010), p. 3.

Third, PARK ET AL. (2010) believe that attachment goes beyond emotions.[406] The construct also reflects a cognitive evaluation of the connection to the brand and memories from the past that are evoked.[407] Therefore, they suggest not to use emotion items as indicators for attachment but to integrate the emotional element of the construct within the dimensions brand-self connection and brand prominence.[408]

The work by THOMSON/MACINNIS/PARK (2005) and PARK ET AL. (2010) has been cited many times and inspired other researchers for further exploration of the attachment concept. During the course of time, attachment has been transferred to other objects than brands, e.g. brand communities.

2.2.2 State of the art research on *brand community* attachment

To tie on to the prior section that illustrated the work on the attachment construct by PARK ET AL. (2010)[409], the publications on community attachment will be reviewed next. This section delivers arguments for why the construct of attachment is applicable in the context of brand communities and therefore also transferable to brand pages because of the relatedness of the two concepts. In the context of communities there are four[410] relevant studies that investigate attachment.

Among the researchers who saw the relevance of a psychological construct – namely *psychological sense of brand community*[411] – were CARLSON/SUTER/BROWN (2008). The authors define their construct "as the degree to which an individual perceives relational bonds with other brand users."[412] CARLSON/SUTER/BROWN (2008) prove

[406] Cf. PARK ET AL. (2010), p. 3.

[407] Cf. PARK ET AL. (2010), p. 3, cf. MIKULINCER/SHAVER (2007).

[408] Cf. PARK ET AL. (2010), p. 3.

[409] Cf. PARK ET AL. (2010).

[410] The studies have been identified based on a research on EBSCOhost®, a US-American database service. The search was executed in November 2013. Only academic journals and peer-reviewed publications were taken into account. Cf. EBSCO INDUSTRIES (2013).

[411] Cf. CARLSON/SUTER/BROWN (2008), p. 284.

[412] CARLSON/SUTER/BROWN (2008), p. 286.

empirically that interaction is not essential for the creation of a community sense.[413] Interaction may increase the feeling of attachment though.[414] In their eyes, it is the psychological sense of a brand community that fosters any positive consumer behaviour toward the brand.

In the study executed by PARK/CHO (2012) community attachment is conceptualised with regard to the community characteristic established by MUNIZ/O'GUINN (2001). The authors split the psychological attachment to the community into three components: we-ness, moral responsibility, shared culture.[415] Those components together define the psychological attachment and were categorised as antecedents of community commitment. The perception of attachment versus commitment is vague in their article. Overall, a clear conceptualisation of constructs in the context of perceived connectedness toward online communities is missing.

LEE ET AL. (2011) examine an online brand community for a notebook computer brand in South Korea. Their results, too, show a strong impact from emotional attachment to the community on behaviours in favour of the brand.[416] Their perception of emotional attachment is that it "can be developed through shared emotional ties with an independent entity of consumer group"[417].

REN ET AL. (2012) differentiate this further. They declare that attachment in a community can be fostered through a) identification with the group and b) interpersonal bonds. They conceptually distinguish between those two types of communities. Users of the first type identify with the idea behind the community but do not focus on relations among users. The second type of communities is built around interpersonal relationships. Their investigation shows that group identification mechanism has a stronger effect on community attachment than interpersonal bonds. While their study

---

[413] The researchers argue that the creation of a community feeling is purely psychological and does not depend on interaction. Even without any participation this feeling or sense can be established. Cf. CARLSON/SUTER/BROWN (2008), pp. 285 et seq.

[414] Cf. CARLSON/SUTER/BROWN (2008), p. 286.

[415] Cf. PARK/CHO (2012), p. 402.

[416] Cf. LEE ET AL. (2011), p. 225.

[417] LEE ET AL. (2011), p. 217.

contributes significantly to community research theory, it also has limitations. Namely, the study is based on only one community. Further, they do not conceptualise the construct attachment thoroughly. They note that it is used interchangeably with the constructs commitment and identification[418]. These differ significantly and therefore should be conceptually differentiated. This will be done in chapter B 2.3.

In summary, the studies on brand community attachment deliver valuable insights. They reveal that a psychological bond between members and brand communities exists. This central learning can be transferred to brand pages. Accordingly, users that like brand pages in social networks can also become attached and feel a psychological bond.

2.3 Distinction from related constructs

Within the research of analysing bonds between consumers and objects (e.g. brand communities or brand pages in the case of this thesis), there are several constructs that have been used to depict the feeling of connectedness. Besides attachment, several constructs have been utilised to measure bonds between people and objects. As research on brand pages in social networks is still relatively young, it is essential for succeeding research to have a distinct concept and to discriminate rival concepts from each other. This is still missing in the present marketing theory. Most papers only point towards the relatedness of constructs.[419] Consequently, this chapter will compile the literature that has been produced on the relevant constructs and demarcate them from the attachment construct.

2.3.1 Brand attitude strength

PARK ET AL. (2010) validated the differentiation from **brand attitude strength** empirically. The results show that attachment as a second order construct consisting of the

[418] Cf. REN ET AL. (2012), p. 842.

[419] Cf. REN ET AL. (2012), p. 842.

two dimensions brand-self connection and brand prominence is a better predictor[420] for separation distress which has been identified as an indicator for attachment.[421]

Conceptually, they spotted four dissimilarities between the two constructs brand attachment and brand attitude strength.[422] The first aspect they describe reflects the type of affection the constructs measure. While *attachment* reflects the "hot" aspect of a connection, i.e. emotions, *attitude* mirrors the "cold" affect, i.e. evaluations about the brand.[423] In the opinion of the authors, the former is a more valid antecedent for behaviour and delivers results that are more precise. Second, both constructs somehow measure strength. Attachment measures the intensity of the bond between a person and a brand. The degree of intensity is indicated through brand prominence. With attitude on the other hand the strength of the judgement about a brand is measured. Strength in this case means the confidence with which a person rates a brand as being good or bad. While attitudes can also have underlying emotions, they are evaluated and rated cognitively. The third aspect illuminates the degree of valence. Attitudes range from positive to negative; they are typically measured on bipolar scales. A strong positive attitude may have the same strength of impact on behavioural consequences as a strong negative attitude.[424] Attachment on the other hand reaches from weak to strong attachment. So the behavioural consequence only results from one pole of the scale. The last point the authors make is the impact of time. Attachments get stronger with more time spent with the brand. Attitudes on the

---

[420] Cf. PARK ET AL. (2010), p. 8.

[421] Cf. BOWLBY (1980), THOMSON/MACINNIS/PARK (2005).

[422] Cf. PARK ET AL. (2010), pp. 3 et seq.

[423] Cf. PARK ET AL. (2010), p. 3, cf. MIKULINCER/SHAVER (2007).

[424] This proposition shall be clarified through an example: A person is very content coming back from her/his holidays and has a strong positive attitude toward a hotel where s/he had spent some time. Hence, this person is likely to share word-of-mouth and recommend the place to friends or family. Given the person is familiar with social media, s/he might even enter a platform and provide word-of-mouth publicly. Another person was disappointed with the service in a hotel and therefore has a very bad attitude toward the hotel. The impact on behavior is the same, if not stronger. The person is likely to share word-of-mouth with family and friends and maybe write a review online. Only in this case the word-of-mouth is negative.

contrary can be built immediately and are not necessarily an indicator for building long-term relations with the brand.[425]

The attitude construct is a long established concept in marketing theory. In 1935 ALLPORT (1935) already highlights the importance and high relevance of the construct.[426] Amongst consumer behaviour researchers it is considered as one of the most explored concepts within the discipline.[427] Many articles have been published relating to the subject of attitudes. A search in google scholar delivers 2,9 million results on the subject of "attitudes".

Despite the comprehensiveness of research, academics are still debating whether affective or cognitive processes are dominating.[428] PARK/MACINNIS (2006) describe attitudes as "generalized predispositions to behave toward an object".[429] KROEBER-RIEL/WEINBERG/GRÖPPEL-KLEIN (2009) define attitudes as "motivation and cognitive evaluation" of an object or situation.[430] Still, there is no common agreement on a definition within marketing research.

The attitude construct belongs to those concepts that have been researched in depth and thoroughly. But it is also considered as being applicable to almost every marketing issue[431], which makes it less distinct and less distinguishable from other concepts.

One research area where the concept has been employed is the discipline of measuring advertising effectiveness where the *attitude toward the ad* concept plays an

---

[425] Cf. PARK ET AL. (2010), pp. 3 et seq.

[426] Cf. ALLPORT (1935), pp. 798 et seqq.

[427] Cf. KROEBER-RIEL/WEINBERG/GRÖPPEL-KLEIN (2009), pp. 210 et seqq.

[428] Cf. KROEBER-RIEL/WEINBERG/GRÖPPEL-KLEIN (2009), p. 211.

[429] PARK/MACINNIS (2006), p. 16.

[430] KROEBER-RIEL/WEINBERG/GRÖPPEL-KLEIN (2009), p. 212.

[431] Cf. KROEBER-RIEL/WEINBERG/GRÖPPEL-KLEIN (2009), p. 210.

important role.[432] In the context of social media this construct has again been transferred and is used to measure attitudes towards social media stimuli.[433]

While conceptually the *attachment* construct is considered to be the better predictor for consumer behaviour due to the arguments listed above, currently, many studies use the *attitude toward the ad* construct for measuring social media likeability.[434] To provide evidence for the benefits of the *attachment* construct, the superiority of *attachment* will be proven empirically during the course of this thesis.[435]

2.3.2 Consumer-brand relationship

This leads to another conceptual differentiation which is compulsory at this point: the difference between **brand relationship** and brand attachment. For this purpose, the construct of relationships needs to be illuminated in sufficient detail. The OXFORD DICTIONARIES (2014d) defines a relationship as "the way in which two or more people or things are connected, or the state of being connected: 1. the state of being connected by blood or marriage, 2. the way in which two or more people or groups regard and behave towards each other, 3. an emotional and sexual association between two people."[436] This definition emphasises the reciprocity[437] of relationships, especially the second point. Transferring this to brand management, most studies on brand relationships foot their theoretical framework on the triangular theory of interpersonal love established by STERNBERG (1986).[438] According to the author, the "triangle of love"[439] consists of the components intimacy, passion and deci-

---

[432] Cf. NÖCKER (2014), p. 63.

[433] Cf. CHU (2011), pp. 32 et seqq., cf. TAYLOR/LEWIN/STRUTTON (2011), pp. 258 et seqq., cf. EILERS (2014), p. 77.

[434] Cf. EILERS (2014), p. 77.

[435] See C 4.4 for an empirical comparison of both contructs.

[436] OXFORD DICTIONARIES (2014d).

[437] According to THOMSON/JOHNSON (2006) "reciprocity refers to the mutuality or bi-directionality" of relationship quality. THOMSON/JOHNSON (2006), p. 715.

[438] Cf. STERNBERG (1986), cf. STERNBERG (1997), cf. FETSCHERIN/CONWAY-DATO-ON (2010), p.4.

[439] STERNBERG (1986), p. 119.

sion/commitment.[440] The first component intimacy consists of several feelings[441] including "mutual understanding with the loved one, receipt of emotional support from the loved one, intimate communication with the loved one."[442] Those items clearly indicate a bi-directional relationship. Conceptualisations of consumer-brand relationships assume a bi-directional relationship between consumer and brands.

FOURNIER (1998) investigated the construct of consumer-brand relationships and established a measurement scale in marketing academia.[443] Her scale has been employed to related research and enhanced by other academics. She argues that brands can indeed function as partners as brands are being humanised by consumers.[444] She bases her argument on the theory of animism introduced by GILMORE; G.W. (1919). The theory of animism postulates that humans feel a need to anthropomorphise things and allocate personality attributes to objects, e.g. brands.[445] Hence, consumers can establish relationships to brands. In her view, marketing activities executed by the brand qualify the brand as a contributing member of the dyadic relationship.[446]

One modification of FOURNIER (1998) scale has been applied by WENSKE (2008) who integrated the **customer-brand relationship** into identity-based brand management.[447] The customer-brand relationship as modelled by WENSKE (2008) shows several shortcomings. Primarily, she conceptualises the customer-brand relationship

[440] Cf. STERNBERG (1986), p. 119.

[441] The feeling of intimacy is expressed through "(a) desire to promote the welfare of the loved one, (b) experienced happiness with the loved one, (c) high regard for the loved one, (d) being able to count on the loved one in times of need, (e) mutual understanding with the loved one, (f) sharing of one's self and one's possessions with the loved one, (g) receipt of emotional support from the loved one, (h) giving of emotional support to the loved one, (i) intimate communication with the loved one, and (j) valuing the loved one in one's life." STERNBERG (1986), pp. 120 et seq.

[442] STERNBERG (1986), p. 121.

[443] Cf. FOURNIER (1998), cf. FOURNIER/MICK (1999), cf. FOURNIER/YAO (1997), cf. FETSCHERIN/CONWAY-DATO-ON (2010).

[444] Cf. FOURNIER (1998), p. 344.

[445] Cf. FOURNIER (1998), p. 344, cf. AAKER (1997), pp. 347 et seqq.

[446] Cf. FOURNIER (1998), p. 345.

[447] Cf. WENSKE (2008), cf. BURMANN/HALASZOVICH/HEMMANN (2012), pp. 74 et seqq.

as bi-directional, but measures and operationalises the construct as an attitude toward a relationship. Further, the term customer-brand relationship is misleading as it only considers customers as target group for a brand. As a result, the concept neglects consumers that are not customers but might still have a strong emotional bond to the brand. This applies in the case of high price premium brands like sports cars, boats, watches, fashion. Consumers might not be able to afford such a brand (yet) but still are admirers and therefore highly attached.

In the work of FOURNIER (1998) and WENSKE (2008) among others, the relations between humans and brands are assumed to be similar to interpersonal relationships. This comparison is problematic. As WHANG ET AL. (2004) postulate "love is an outcome of bi-directional interaction between two partners, yet its highly dynamic interactivity makes it challenging for researchers to study. But, when the target of love is replaced with an object (e.g., a product or brand), love becomes **uni-directional** and thus less dynamic."[448] Hence, transferring the concept of interpersonal relationships to consumer-brand relationships cannot be supported. A brand is not able to provide the reciprocity that an interpersonal relationship requires.[449] Even when the consumer interacts with a human being that represents the brand like customer service or sales people, reciprocity stays an illusion.[450] It is a figment of a consumer's imagination. There is no "mutual understanding" or "intimate communication."[451] Instead, FETSCHERIN/CONWAY-DATO-ON (2010) describe consumers' relations to brands as "parasocial"[452]. A parasocial relationship is characterised by one-sidedness. This can be explained by the unequal distribution of knowledge. One individual might have wide-ranging information about the other but the latter cannot match it.[453] This phenomenon has been researched much in the context of celebrities.[454] THOMSON (2006) researches human brands (i.e. celebrities) and makes a case for the differences be-

---

448 WHANG ET AL. (2004), p. 320.

449 Cf. FETSCHERIN/CONWAY-DATO-ON (2010), p. 4.

450 Cf. FETSCHERIN/CONWAY-DATO-ON (2010), p. 4.

451 STERNBERG (1986), p. 121.

452 FETSCHERIN/CONWAY-DATO-ON (2010), p. 4.

453 Cf. FETSCHERIN/CONWAY-DATO-ON (2010), p. 4.

454 Cf. FETSCHERIN/CONWAY-DATO-ON (2010), p. 4.

tween interpersonal bonds and consumer attachment to brands. In his view these conceptual differences are underrepresented in research and the concept of interpersonal relationships cannot be transferred to brands.[455]

To sum up, the term relationship in a uni-directional context is misleading and therefore the recommendation is to employ the construct of attachment. Attachment measures the uni-directional cognitions and emotions an individual has about her/his bond to a brand. What should be measured is the **bond[456] to the brand** rather than a relationship. Bi-directional relationships with brands do not exist, only in a consumer's mind which again makes them uni-directional.

In the context of brand pages, the construct is as inappropriate as it is for measuring bonds to brands. There is no relationship with a brand page. But in contrast, there is proof that consumers are able to develop attachment to online communities.[457] Therefore it can be deduced that the same applies to brand pages.

2.3.3 Brand love

Brand love is currently a frequently researched construct in academia.[458] FETSCHERIN/HEINRICH (2014a) recently conducted a citation meta-analysis to structure the research that has been carried around consumer-brand relationships. Brand love in their view "focuses on extreme emotions (positive and negative) consumers can have for brands."[459] They declare brand love as "passionate emotional attach-

---

[455] Cf. THOMSON (2006), p. 105.

[456] Bond in this context means the emotional connection a person establishes to an object (a brand in this case). Neuroscientific research reveals that emotions related to brands are saved in a person's memory and recalled when a person has contact to the object. The recall is stronger when emotions rather than just cognitive elements are associated to the object. Cf. BIELEFELD (2012), pp. 194 et seqq.

[457] Cf. REN ET AL. (2012), p. 856.

[458] Cf. FETSCHERIN/HEINRICH (2014a), p. 1.

[459] FETSCHERIN/HEINRICH (2014a), p. 7.

ment"[460] to a brand. It is stronger for brands that offer a symbolic benefit and address the consumers need for hedonism.[461]

The construct **brand love** measures the emotion towards a brand under the circumstance of a parasocial relationship.[462] "Brand love is defined as the degree of passionate emotional attachment a satisfied consumer has for a particular trade name."[463] Some researchers consider the construct of brand love as multidimensional. BATRA/AHUVIA/BAGOZZI (2012) see brand love as a higher order construct subsuming seven distinct elements including behavioural dimensions: "(1) passion-driven behaviors reflecting strong desires to use it, to invest resources into it, and a history of having done so; (2) self–brand integration, including a brand's ability to express consumers' actual and desired identities, its ability to connect to life's deeper meanings and provide intrinsic rewards, and frequent thoughts about it; (3) positive emotional connection that is broader than just positive feelings, including a sense of positive attachment and having an intuitive feeling of "rightness"; (4) anticipated separation distress if the brand were to go away; (5) long-term relationship, which includes predicting extensive future use and a long-term commitment to it; (6) positive attitude valence; and (7) attitudes held with high certainty and confidence."[464] Their research gains insight into how brand liking can be changed into brand love.[465] Some of these dimensions are taken from the attachment construct.

FETSCHERIN/HEINRICH (2014b) explain brand love by setting it into the context of consumer-brand relationship constructs.[466] They explain how consumers' bonds towards brands can be divided into functional and emotional connections.[467] Functional connections exist when functional consumer needs are fulfilled. The consumer likes the

[460] FETSCHERIN/HEINRICH (2014a), p. 7.

[461] Cf. FETSCHERIN/HEINRICH (2014a), p. 7, cf. ALBERT/MERUNKA (2013), pp. 258 et seqq.

[462] Cf. FETSCHERIN/CONWAY-DATO-ON (2010), p. 6.

[463] CARROLL/AHUVIA (2006), p. 81.

[464] BATRA/AHUVIA/BAGOZZI (2012), p. 13.

[465] Cf. BATRA/AHUVIA/BAGOZZI (2012), p. 13.

[466] Cf. FETSCHERIN/HEINRICH (2014b), pp. 366 et seqq.

[467] Cf. FETSCHERIN/HEINRICH (2014b), p. 367.

brand, but has a tendency to switch between brands. Emotional connections exist when the brand meets emotional needs. Brand love can be built when both, functional and emotional connections are strong and the consumer is fully invested (see Figure 14).[468]

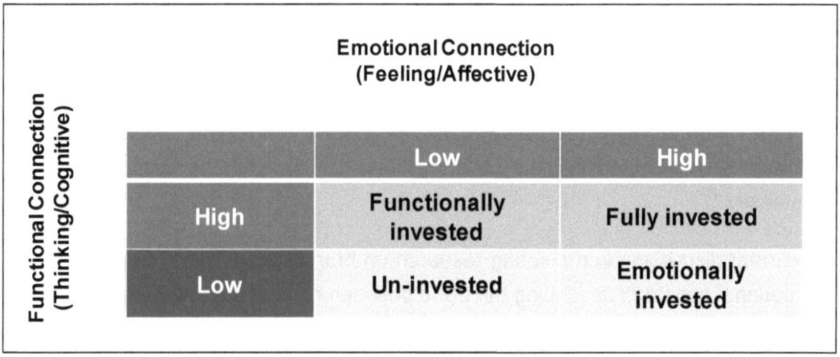

Figure 14: **Brand connection matrix**
Source: FETSCHERIN/HEINRICH (2014b), p. 368.

Most studies on brand love only reflect the currents status of the consumer-brand relationship. LANGNER ET AL. (2014) argue that brand love develops over time. The authors conduct a study by interviewing participants that investigates the development of feelings towards beloved brands.[469] Five different ways of forming brand love were categorized: “slow development,” “liking becomes love,” “love all the way,” “bumpy road,” and “turnabout.”[470] They identify personal memories (i.e. from childhood) and highly emotional experiences from the past as highly relevant for the development of brand love.[471] Hence, there is only little control for brand managers to influence these events that lead to brand love.[472]

---

[468] Cf. FETSCHERIN/HEINRICH (2014b), pp. 367 et seqq.

[469] Cf. LANGNER ET AL. (2014), pp. 1 et seqq.

[470] Cf. LANGNER ET AL. (2014), p. 1.

[471] Cf. LANGNER ET AL. (2014), pp. 10 et seqq.

[472] Cf. LANGNER ET AL. (2014), pp. 1 et seqq.

According to RAUSCHNABEL/AHUVIA (2014) brand love is mainly determined by anthropomorphism.[473] Extraverts and neurotics are most likely to love their brands as they see them as potential partners.[474] They recommend anthropomorphism to brand managers as brand love has a positive impact on consumer behaviour, i.e. the willingness to pay a price premium.[475] The authors introduce the example of the successful Lindt chocolate brand HELLO which "talks" to consumers on the packaging in first person: Hello, my name is Nougat Crunch.[476] Another example of anthropomorphism is the usage of human traits in product design, i.e. car fronts that imitate human faces. Further, they see social media as a great tool for anthropomorphism as the brand "speaks" directly to the consumer and can therefore be associated to humans easily.[477]

The current discussion in marketing research on brand love justifies the relevance of an emotional construct describing the bond between consumers and their brands and also brand pages.

However, for the purpose of measuring bonds to *brand pages* the construct of "love" is not applicable. This is due to several reasons. First, love already implies a strong feeling, leaving little room for a wider continuum. Second, it ultimately reflects a stronger verbalisation for high attachment. Third, the integration of conative components makes it worthless to predict behavioural intentions.

2.3.4 Identification

The research on social media is to a large extent based on brand community research and Facebook brand pages are labelled Facebook brand communities.[478] Though there are many similarities that justify this association, the differences ex-

---

[473] Cf. RAUSCHNABEL/AHUVIA (2014), p. 387.

[474] Cf. RAUSCHNABEL/AHUVIA (2014), p. 373.

[475] Cf. ALBERT/MERUNKA (2013), pp. 263 et seqq.

[476] Cf. RAUSCHNABEL/AHUVIA (2014), p. 389.

[477] Cf. RAUSCHNABEL/AHUVIA (2014), p. 389.

[478] Cf. GUMMERUS ET AL. (2012).

plain why the construct of attachment should be preferred over identification in a context of measuring consumers' bonds to brand pages in social networks.[479] To illustrate why attachment fits better, it first needs to be clarified what identification means.

Identification is a broadly discussed construct in the marketing literature. In the context of brand communities, researchers refer back to the social identity theory which was coined by Henri Tajfel and John C. Turner in 1986. It describes an individual's self-perception in relation to others and the social categories they belong to. Social categories are built up in people's minds to ease the comprehension of the society's structure. It allows an individual to locate where s/he belongs and offers orientation. The individual's identification is therefore relative to the social group. The individual defines her-/himself in comparison to people from other social categories. So, the social identity "consists [...] of those aspects of an individual's self-image that derive from the social categories to which he perceives himself as belonging."[480] The concept foots on three general assumptions[481]:

- Individuals desire a positive self-worth, so they aim for a positive concept of the self.
- Social categories are recognised as being good or bad. So the individual's social identity is perceived to be positive or negative according to the social groups it belongs to.
- The perception of the social group an individual considers her-/himself belonging is made up by the comparison to other groups. This implies a clear definition of in- and out-groups. If the in-group is evaluated to be better than (an)other out-group(s), this leads to high prestige and vice versa.

---

[479] For a detailed explanation on the differences between brand community and brand pages in social networks, see chapter A 3.2.

[480] TAJFEL/TURNER (1986), p. 16.

[481] Cf. TAJFEL/TURNER (1986), p. 16.

The idea of self-categorisation is also discussed by BERGAMI/BAGOZZI (2000) who investigate the identification construct from the organisational perspective.[482] In their study, they survey n=409 employees of an Italian food service company which reflects the inner perspective of a company.

Organisational identification is seen "as a form of social identification whereby a person comes to view him- or herself as a member of a particular social entity, the organisation."[483] This reflects the definition worked out by TAJFEL/TURNER (1986).

According to the authors, self-categorisation is a cognitive process since an individual is well aware of its belonging to a social group. They state, identification has to be treated separately from emotional or behavioural responses that evolve from it. Hence, the construct of identification should only reflect cognitive components. They discover affective commitment as a consequence of identification but suggest differentiating the emotional notions from the cognitive state of identification.[484]

BHATTACHARYA/SEN (2003a) put this into a branded environment and investigate the construct of consumer-company identification.[485] The authors integrate the research on social and organisational identification into their work. They postulate that relationships between consumers and brands are built on the premise of identification. If a consumer can identify with a company it helps her/him to define her-/himself. Precondition is the company's identity which needs to be congruent to the individual's identity. These circumstances can serve as a fertile basis for identification.[486] The authors agree with the cognitive composition of the construct.

DHOLAKIA/BAGOZZI/KLEIN PEARO (2004) research the phenomenon of social identity in the community context.[487] In this case social identity functions as antecedent of "we-

---

[482] Cf. BERGAMI/BAGOZZI (2000).

[483] BERGAMI/BAGOZZI (2000), p. 557.

[484] Cf. BERGAMI/BAGOZZI (2000), pp. 557 et seq.

[485] Cf. BHATTACHARYA/SEN (2003a).

[486] Cf. BHATTACHARYA/SEN (2003a), p. 86.

[487] Cf. DHOLAKIA/BAGOZZI/KLEIN PEARO (2004), p. 241.

intentions"[488] which they describe as the motivation for collaboration, i.e. to act together as one group.[489]

Identification with the community is influenced by the consumer's bond to the brand.[490] A positive perception of the brand will lead to a higher identification with the brand community. This is found out in a study executed by ALGESHEIMER/DHOLAKIA/HERRMANN (2005) who surveyed European car club members. They advocate that identification consists of cognitive and affective dimensions. The cognitive part reflects the self-categorisation described above, the affective dimension is formed through emotional involvement with the group: "the person construes himself or herself to be a member - that is, as "belonging" to the brand community. In contrast to other identities, which may render a person unique and separate, this is a shared or collective identity."[491] Their model proposes that high identification with the community leads to community engagement. This assumption is self-evident as joining a brand community implies the willingness to engage. The scale that ALGESHEIMER/DHOLAKIA/HERRMANN (2005) developed is often applied in research on community identification.[492]

The subject of "collective identity"[493] is also reflected in the paper written by JOHNSON/MASSIAH/ALLAN (2013) who study consumer-to-consumer helping in brand communities. Their perception of identification related to the group which mirrors the view of other researchers.[494] A strong sense of community and connectedness to other members lead to the belief that the community's fortune is linked to the individual's.[495] The consequence is a strong feeling of responsibility and finally a high willingness to participate and help other members.

---

[488] DHOLAKIA/BAGOZZI/KLEIN PEARO (2004), p. 242.

[489] Cf. DHOLAKIA/BAGOZZI/KLEIN PEARO (2004), p. 242.

[490] Cf. ALGESHEIMER/DHOLAKIA/HERRMANN (2005), p. 20.

[491] ALGESHEIMER/DHOLAKIA/HERRMANN (2005), p. 20.

[492] Cf. YEH/CHOI (2011), cf. PAI/TSAI (2011), cf. MATZLER ET AL. (2011).

[493] ALGESHEIMER/DHOLAKIA/HERRMANN (2005), p. 20.

[494] Cf. TAJFEL/TURNER (1986), cf. ASHFORTH/MAEL (1989), cf. BHATTACHARYA/SEN (2003a).

[495] Cf. JOHNSON/MASSIAH/ALLAN (2013), p. 123, cf. ASHFORTH/MAEL (1989).

Transferring the theoretical implications from the studies summarised above into the research on social networks is problematic. The identification construct is very much based on social entities like groups or communities. Becoming a member in most cases implies a certain activity like setting up a profile or paying membership fees which have higher barriers than just click the "like" button on a brand page in a social network. Further it requires a feeling and an awareness of membership, a feeling of belonging to a certain social group.[496] For communities this sense of "we-ness"[497] can be proven. Users who follow a brand page in social networks would not automatically think of themselves as "members" of the brand page. They are called "fans" in colloquial language but they are not "fans" in the way the term is used in sports language. The often cited "sense of emotional involvement with the group"[498] is not given in the environment of brand pages. There is no "shared or collective identity."[499] ZAGLIA (2013) compares Facebook brand pages to Facebook groups[500] in order to investigate whether brand communities exist embedded into social networks. She found evidence for social identity and perceived membership within the sub-group, but could not find the same degree of social relatedness for the brand page[501], even though her research attends a topic with highly involved consumers.

Consequently, the identification construct is not appropriate in the context of measuring the consumer's bond to a brand page.

2.3.5 Commitment

The distinction between commitment and attachment is the most difficult as many authors use both terms synonymously.[502] But a closer look at the conceptualisation

---

[496] Cf. MUNIZ/O'GUINN (2001), p. 418.

[497] MUNIZ/O'GUINN (2001), p. 418.

[498] DHOLAKIA/BAGOZZI/KLEIN PEARO (2004), p. 245.

[499] ALGESHEIMER/DHOLAKIA/HERRMANN (2005), p. 20.

[500] In her study she chose the brand Canon and investigated the Canon Camera Malaysia brand page with 151,380 followers in comparison to the Canon Digital Photography group with 108,259 members which is a sub-group within Facebook. Cf. ZAGLIA (2013), p. 219.

[501] Cf. ZAGLIA (2013), p. 221.

[502] Cf. O'REILLY/CHATMAN (1986), p. 492, cf. MEYER/ALLEN (1991), p. 63.

reveals disparity. To differentiate between commitment and attachment, the first step is to look at the expressions from a linguistic point of view. The Oxford Dictionary describes attachment as "affection, fondness, or sympathy for someone or something."[503] Commitment on the contrary is defined as "the state or quality of being dedicated to a cause, activity, etc."[504] It is further depicted as "a pledge or undertaking, an engagement or obligation that restricts freedom of action."[505] Because of this notion, the construct of commitment and its conceptualisation as attitudinal versus behavioural has been discussed controversially by academics.

Commitment is a construct that originates from organisational theory. The research on organisational commitment can be traced back to the 1950ies. There are more than 2,000 articles published in peer-reviewed journals on the subject of organisational commitment.[506] The construct describes the relationship of employees with the organisation s/he works for.[507] Companies depend on the loyalty and brand citizenship behaviour[508] of their employees; therefore commitment is a central success factor. In the context of internal branding brand commitment is seen as the central determinant for brand citizenship behaviour.[509]

The meaning of the commitment construct has been long discussed in academic circles. MEYER/ALLEN (1997) summarise the research streams into two areas: one that investigates the nature i.e. different forms of commitment and the other classifies units or objects to which someone becomes committed.[510] The discussion in both

---

[503] OXFORD DICTIONARIES (2013a).

[504] OXFORD DICTIONARIES (2013b).

[505] OXFORD DICTIONARIES (2013b).

[506] Cf. PIEHLER (2011), p. 193.

[507] Cf. MEYER/ALLEN (1997), p. 2.

[508] PIEHLER (2011) was able to provide evidence for the impact from brand commitment on brand citizenship behaviour. Brand citizenship behaviour in this context is defined as a "global concept which reflects the employee's behaviour which is consistent with the brand identity and the brand promise and overall strengthens the brand." Cf. PIEHLER (2011), p. 543 and p. 303.

[509] Cf. PIEHLER (2011), p. 354.

[510] Cf. MEYER/ALLEN (1997), pp. 8 et seq.

areas is determined through the debate of commitment being an *attitudinal* versus *behavioural* concept.[511] This discussion splits academics into two camps.[512]

One faction views commitment as an *attitudinal* (or psychological) construct. According to MEYER/ALLEN (1997), the attitudinal view was originally established to facilitate the measurement of commitment in relation to its behavioural consequences.[513] A construct that contains behavioural components cannot be integrated into a structural equation model that calculates the impact on behaviour. Hence, it is due to practicability and statistical validity that the attitudinal concept was introduced.

MOWDAY/STEERS/PORTER (1979) argue in favour of the attitudinal conceptualisation for organisational commitment but state that "commitment represents something beyond mere passive loyalty to an organization. It involves an active relationship with the organization such that individuals are willing to give something of themselves in order to contribute to the organization's well being."[514] For them, commitment embodies three key elements: an internalisation of the aims and value of the company, enthusiasm to put in effort and a willingness to stay within the company or organisation.[515] Two of three elements contain behavioural persistence.

MEYER/ALLEN (1991) define commitment as "a psychological state that (a) characterizes the employee's relationship with the organization, and (b) has implications for the decision to continue or discontinue membership in the organization."[516] The widely accepted three-component model of organisational commitment developed by MEYER/ALLEN (1991) conveys that commitment consists of the three components *affective, continuance*, and *normative* commitment.[517] Affective commitment stands for identification and involvement with the company. Continuance commitment means

---

[511] Cf. MEYER/ALLEN (1997), p. 9.

[512] Cf. MOWDAY/STEERS/PORTER (1979), p. 226.

[513] Cf. MEYER/ALLEN (1997), p. 8.

[514] MOWDAY/STEERS/PORTER (1979), p.226.

[515] Cf. MOWDAY/STEERS/PORTER (1979), p. 226.

[516] MEYER/ALLEN (1991), p. 67.

[517] Cf. MEYER/ALLEN (1991), p. 67.

the purpose to stay within the organisation and avoid the expenditure for leaving. Normative commitment expresses the feeling of pressure to stay within the organisation.[518] Although the authors take the standpoint of psychological construal, the two dimensions of continuance and normative commitment represent behavioural persistence.

This approach was criticised by O'REILLY/CHATMAN (1986) and PIEHLER (2011) who raise the issue of mixing up commitment and its consequences in the conceptualisation of the construct commitment by MEYER/ALLEN (1991).[519] PIEHLER (2011) addresses this issue by defining brand commitment as the "extent of psychological attachment of employees to the brand."[520] So his definition of brand commitment is for the most part synonymous to brand attachment. But his conceptualisation differs from the conceptualisation of brand attachment by PARK ET AL. (2010). His conceptualisation is based on O'REILLY/CHATMAN (1986) who identify three dimensions of commitment: compliance, identification and internalisation.[521] He excludes the compliance dimension due to several reasons but mainly because its empirical relevance could not be proven[522]. This leaves the two dimensions identification and internalisation, the latter is understood as the person-organisation-fit and particularly relevant in the context of organisations.[523]

These dimensions are to some extend reflected in the construct attachment through the component *self-brand connection* conceptualised by PARK ET AL. (2010).[524] But additionally relevant in the context of buyer-brand relations is the factor *brand prominence* which enhances the attachment construct. It signifies how present the brand is in a consumer's mind and is highly relevant for resulting behaviour. This can be illustrated as follows: if a consumer feels the same degree of brand-self connection to

---

518 Cf. MEYER/ALLEN (1991), p. 67.

519 Cf. PIEHLER (2011), pp. 209 et seqq.

520 PIEHLER (2011), p. 200.

521 Cf. O'REILLY/CHATMAN (1986), p. 493.

522 For a detailed assessment of the compliance dimension, please read PIEHLER (2011), pp. 211 et seqq.

523 Cf. PIEHLER (2011), p. 220.

524 Cf. PARK ET AL. (2010), p. 2.

two brands, the attachment is higher for the brand that is more prominent.[525] This might not be important for organisations as an employee typically has the company top of mind whenever s/he goes to work. Thus, there is no new decision process or cognitive choices for a company each day people go to work. This clearly differentiates attachment from the attitudinal perception of commitment.

To summarise, although the definition of brand commitment by PIEHLER (2011) and the definition of brand attachment by PARK ET AL. (2010) are mostly synonymous, the conceptualisation and subsequent measurement of the construct differs as a results of origination from different research streams. Yet, in the context of brand pages, the brand attachment construct is more applicable.

The other faction of academics supports a *behavioural* construal of commitment. This coincides with the linguistic definition the Oxford Dictionary provides (see above). There is no "freedom of action"[526] which means that the intention for certain behaviour is already implicit in the commitment construct; "the state or quality of being dedicated"[527] implies that the dedicated individual has already made an active and cognitive decision of acting in favour of the company. There are several advocates for the behavioural composition.

BLOEMER/KASPER (1995) understand brand commitment as a pledge towards the choice of brand. The authors reflect this pledge in the composition of items used for commitment: "If my preferred brand of blank audio cassettes were not available at the store, I will go to another store"[528] is only one of the six indicators. The items are all phrased on the premise of loyal purchase behaviour.[529]

VAN LANGE ET AL. (1997) state that "commitment represents the degree to which an individual experiences long-term orientation toward a relationship, including intent to persist through both good and lean times, feelings of psychological attachment, and

---

[525] Cf. PARK ET AL. (2010), p. 2.

[526] OXFORD DICTIONARIES (2013b).

[527] OXFORD DICTIONARIES (2013b).

[528] BLOEMER/KASPER (1995), p. 327.

[529] Cf. BLOEMER/KASPER (1995), pp. 326 et seq.

implicit recognition that one needs a relationship."[530] MORGAN/HUNT (1994) investigate the construct of relationship commitment which they define "as an exchange partner believing that an ongoing relationship with another is so important as to warrant maximum efforts at maintaining it; that is, the committed party believes the relationship is worth working on to ensure that it endures indefinitely."[531]

THOMSON/MACINNIS/PARK (2005) describe brand commitment as "the degree to which an individual views the relationship from a long-term perspective and has a willingness to stay with the relationship."[532] This willingness to stay again emphasises the cognitive decision and clearly implies a behavioural intention.

Later, the construct has been transferred community research.[533] It relates to the connection an individual has to the community. The majority of researchers vindicate the intentional component in the construct. PARK/CHO (2012) state that "commitment is related to the positive feelings toward a community and the desire to maintain a long-term membership."[534] This is also expressed by the choice of items WIERTZ/DE RUYTER (2007) utilise to measure community commitment.[535] They contain an intentional indication to continue the relationship with the community. CASALÓ/CARLOS F.; GUINALÍU/GUINALÍU (2010) agree on this as they say commitment "indicates a long-term orientation in the relationship"[536] KIM ET AL. (2008) operationalise their scale for community commitment integrating the continuance dimension: "I expect that I will continuously participate in community activities."[537] These conceptions of commit-

---

[530] VAN LANGE ET AL. (1997), p. 1374.

[531] MORGAN/HUNT (1994), p. 23.

[532] THOMSON/MACINNIS/PARK (2005), p. 78.

[533] Cf. JANG ET AL. (2008), cf. KIM ET AL. (2008).

[534] PARK/CHO (2012), p. 403. They refer back to the work of MOORMAN/ZALTMANN/DESHPANDE (1992) and PORTER (2004).

[535] Cf. WIERTZ/DE RUYTER (2007), p. 376. The items utilised by the authors are: "The relationship I have with the X community is something to which I am very committed. The relationship I have with the X community deserves my effort to maintain. The relationship I have with the X community is one I intend to maintain indefinitely."

[536] CASALO/CARLOS F.; GUINALIU/GUINALIU (2010), p.140.

[537] KIM ET AL. (2008), p. 418.

ment cannot be transferred to measure the bond to a brand page and its behavioural outcomes as the behavioural consequence are part of the commitment construct.

The dispute between behavioural or attitudinal conceptions is ongoing since more than 30 years. Though the psychological perception is dominant in organisational literature, the behavioural is dominant in community research. Overall, there is no consensus.[538] From a linguistic viewpoint, the implicit behavioural intention is evident. Further, in social media and community research which is the theoretical basis for this work, most concepts integrate a behavioural component into the architecture of commitment. Moreover, the factor *prominence* is missing. Hence, the construct commitment cannot be utilised to measure the bond between user and brand page. It goes one step further as it already inherits an intentional component. Thus, analysing the effect that commitment has on participation would be false. There needs to be a construct that has no behavioural or intentional components: brand page attachment.

2.4 Introducing the concept of brand page attachment

2.4.1 Defining brand page attachment

The previous chapters illuminated the attachment construct, its basis, historical development and areas it has been applied to. From the preceding studies that are recapitulated above, the perception of attachment can be carried over to brand page attachment. It mirrors the bond or connection that someone feels toward the brand page. This is again reflected in the broad overview of definitions provided in Table 2 that summarises the perceptions of attachment in different research projects.

---

[538] There are still publications that advocate a behavioural approach. For instance GERMANN ET AL. (2013) who define brand commitment as follows: "Consumers can become attached to brands, form close relationships with them [...], and have a general desire to maintain this close relationship [...]" in their article in Marketing Letters. Cf. GERMANN ET AL. (2013), p. 3.

Construct	Definition	Author(s)
attachment	"attachment is an emotion-laden target-specific bond between a person and a specific object"[539]	BOWLBY (1979), BOWLBY (1980)
emotional attachment to brands	"According to BOWLBY (1979), an attachment is an emotion-laden target-specific bond between a person and a specific object. Attachments vary in strength, and stronger attachments are associated with stronger feelings of connection, affection, love, and passion [...]."[540]	THOMSON/MACINNIS/PARK (2005)
psychological sense of brand community	"We define psychological sense of brand community as the degree to which an individual perceives relational bonds with other brand users."[541]	CARLSON/SUTER/BROWN (2008)
brand attachment	"We define brand attachment as the strength of the bond connecting the brand with the self. Consistent with attachment theory (MIKULINCER/SHAVER (2007)), this bond is exemplified by a rich and accessible memory network (or mental representation) that involves thoughts and feelings about the brand and the brand's relationship to the self. Two critical factors reflect the conceptual properties of brand attachment: brand–self connection and brand prominence."[542]	PARK ET AL. (2010)
emotional brand attachment	"Thus, emotional brand attachment reflects the bond that connects a consumer with a specific	MALÄR ET AL. (2011)

539 BOWLBY (1979).

540 THOMSON/MACINNIS/PARK (2005), pp. 77-78.

541 CARLSON/SUTER/BROWN (2008), p. 286.

542 PARK ET AL. (2010), p. 2.

	brand and involves feelings toward the brand. These feelings include affection, passion, and connection (THOMSON/MACINNIS/PARK (2005)), which represent "hot" affect from the brand's linkage to the self (MIKULINCER/SHAVER (2007))."[543]	
emotional attachment to the community	"Accordingly, emotional attachment can be developed through shared emotional ties with an independent entity of consumer group (brand, individual, place, or a specific subject and so on) in the form of an attachment based on relationship (PARK/MACINNIS (2006))."[544]	LEE ET AL. (2011)
attachment to the large community	"[...] members' affective connection to and caring for an online community in which they become involved."[545]	REN ET AL. (2012)
psychological attachment to the community	"This psychological attachment can be divided into three aspects: consciousness of a kind, moral responsibility, and "shared rituals and traditions"."[546]	PARK/CHO (2012)
emotional bonding	"In addition to these positive emotions, other researchers have also noted that consumers are likely to feel a strong desire to maintain proximity with their loved objects, even feeling "separation distress" when they anticipate or experience being distanced from them (HAZAN/ZEIFMAN (1999), PARK ET AL. (2010), THOMSON/MACINNIS/PARK (2005))."[547]	BATRA/AHUVIA/BAGOZZI (2012)

543 MALÄR ET AL. (2011), p. 36.
544 LEE ET AL. (2011), p. 217.
545 REN ET AL. (2012), p. 842.
546 PARK/CHO (2012), p. 402.
547 BATRA/AHUVIA/BAGOZZI (2012), p. 4.

brand attachment	"BOWLBY (1979) seminal research defines attachment as an emotion-laden, target-specific bond between a person and a specific object, typically a caregiver."[548]	ZHOU ET AL. (2012)
brand attachment	"Deep-seated passion for the brand and persistent longing to take it into possession, coupled with willingness to make necessary sacrifices in order to acquire the brand."[549]	TSAI (2011)

Table 2: Definitions of attachment
Source: Own illustration.

Overall, the definitions collectively reflect the bond to the object.[550] Yet, for the definition of brand page attachment, it is important to incorporate both, affective and cognitive elements into the connotation of the construct, as argued by PARK ET AL. (2010). Their perception and the learnings from prior studies shall be transferred to the measurement of bonding to brand pages. Thus, based on the findings, the construct brand page attachment can be defined based on PARK ET AL. (2010) as:

***Brand page attachment** reflects the strength of the connection a person feels toward a brand page.*[551]

2.4.2 Conceptualising brand page attachment

In previous chapters, the concepts of brand attachment and community attachment have been discussed. In a thorough literature review, the attachment theory and concepts of attachment have been analysed. The widely accepted publications of THOMSON/MACINNIS/PARK (2005) and PARK ET AL. (2010) proved helpful in defining brand page attachment. This chapter shall validate to which extent the conceptualisa-

---

[548] ZHOU ET AL. (2012), p. 891.

[549] TSAI (2011), p. 526.

[550] Cf. BOWLBY (1979).

[551] Cf. PARK ET AL. (2010), p. 2.

tions of the attachment construct are useful for measuring brand *page* attachment. For this purpose, a broad range of conceptualisations for attachment will be reviewed. The purpose is, to find the best conceptualisation for brand page attachment. These are summarised in Table 3 at the end of this chapter. A selection of publications with *dissimilar* approaches is illustrated in the next paragraphs.

The concepts used for brand *community* attachment cannot be utilised for brand *page* attachment as they build on the premise of relationships among members.[552] Relationships between followers are not given in the context of brand pages; therefore the constructs are not applicable.[553] Instead, the conceptualisations for *brand* attachment will be discussed in detail.

An often cited and empirically validated[554] conceptualisation of emotional attachment to brands is provided by THOMSON/MACINNIS/PARK (2005). They partition the construct into three emotional dimensions: affection, passion, connection.[555] Leaning on the rationale in chapter B 2.2.1, measuring solely emotional components of attachment neglects cognitive components of attachment.

LACOEUILHE (2000) advocates a uni-dimensional measurement of brand attachment.[556] His perception of brand attachment is based on the presumption that attachment is an emotional construct and should be measured through items that express affection to the brand. This is reflected in the definition: "attachment to the brand is a psychological variable that reveals a lasting and inalterable *affective* relationship (separation is painful) to the brand and expresses a relation of psychological closeness to it."[557] This approach, too, disregards cognitive elements of attachment.

---

552 Cf. CARLSON/SUTER/BROWN (2008), cf. LEE ET AL. (2011), cf. PARK/CHO (2012).

553 For a detailed discussion on conceptual differences between brand communities and brand pages in social networks, please read chapter A 3.2.

554 Studies that refer and employ the scale developed by THOMSON/MACINNIS/PARK (2005) are listed in Table 3.

555 Cf. THOMSON/MACINNIS/PARK (2005), p. 80.

556 Cf. LOUIS/LOMBART (2010), p. 119; p. 121, cf. LACOEUILHE (2000).

557 LOUIS/LOMBART (2010), p. 118 who cite and translate LACOEUILHE (2000). The original definition is: "l'attachement à la marque est une variable psychologique qui traduit une relation affective du-

(Continued on next page)

ESCH ET AL. (2006) measure brand attachment using a scale that consists of two items whereby one reflects the connection to the brand and the other one refers to the separation anxiety aspect.[558] Their scale was developed for practitioners.[559] The use of only two items was employed due to reasons of simplicity.[560] They admit this as limitation of their research and recommend a more thorough approach to measure brand attachment as introduced by THOMSON/MACINNIS/PARK (2005).[561] As there is no information for the validity of the scale, this conceptualisation cannot be recommended for transfer to brand pages.

SWAMINATHAN/STILLEY/AHLUWALIA (2009) measure brand attachment using only the dimension "connection"[562] developed by THOMSON/MACINNIS/PARK (2005).[563] In the opinion of SWAMINATHAN/STILLEY/AHLUWALIA (2009), the other two dimensions "affection"[564] and "passion"[565] are too closely linked to the personality of the brand. Brands which are "sincere"[566] would accordingly be rated higher on the items that display affection. Brands that are perceived as cool or "exciting"[567] would be evaluated higher on the passion items. Hence, both dimensions affection and passion are dependent on the brand personality. For this reason the authors reduce the scale to the dimension *connection*.

A summary of the conceptualisations is provided in Table 3.

---

rable et inaltérable (la séparation est douloureuse) envers la marque et qui exprime une relation de proximité psychologique avec celle-ci." LACOEUILHE (2000), p. 66.

558 Cf. ESCH ET AL. (2006), p. 101.

559 Cf. ESCH ET AL. (2006), p. 103.

560 Cf. ESCH ET AL. (2006), p. 103.

561 Cf. ESCH ET AL. (2006), p. 103, cf. THOMSON/MACINNIS/PARK (2005).

562 Cf. THOMSON/MACINNIS/PARK (2005), p. 80.

563 Cf. SWAMINATHAN/STILLEY/AHLUWALIA (2009), p. 989, cf. THOMSON/MACINNIS/PARK (2005), p. 80.

564 Cf. THOMSON/MACINNIS/PARK (2005), p. 80.

565 Cf. THOMSON/MACINNIS/PARK (2005), p. 80.

566 Cf. SWAMINATHAN/STILLEY/AHLUWALIA (2009), p. 989.

567 Cf. SWAMINATHAN/STILLEY/AHLUWALIA (2009), p. 989.

Author(s)	Construct	Dimensions
THOMSON/MACINNIS/PARK (2005)	emotional attachment to brands	affection connection passion[568]
LACOEUILHE (2000), LOUIS/LOMBART (2010)	l'attachement à la marque, attachment to the brand	one-dimensional construct[569]
ESCH ET AL. (2006)	brand attachment[570]	
SWAMINATHAN/STILLEY/AHLUWALIA (2009)	brand attachment	connection[571] based on THOMSON/MACINNIS/PARK (2005)
PARK ET AL. (2010)	brand attachment	brand–self connection brand prominence[572]
MALÄR ET AL. (2011)	emotional brand attachment	affection connection passion[573] based on THOMSON/MACINNIS/PARK

568 Cf. THOMSON/MACINNIS/PARK (2005), p. 80.

569 Cf. LACOEUILHE (2000), p. 69, cf. LOUIS/LOMBART (2010), p. 119, p. 121.

570 Cf. ESCH ET AL. (2006), p. 101.

571 Cf. SWAMINATHAN/STILLEY/AHLUWALIA (2009), p. 989.

572 Cf. PARK ET AL. (2010), p. 2.

573 Cf. MALÄR ET AL. (2011), p. 41.

		(2005)
ZHOU ET AL. (2012)	brand attachment	affection connection passion[574] based on THOMSON/MACINNIS/PARK (2005)
SCHMALZ/ORTH (2012)	brand attachment	affection connection passion[575] based on THOMSON/MACINNIS/PARK (2005)
MERCHANT/ROSE (2013)	brand attachment	brand-self connection brand prominence[576] based on PARK ET AL. (2010)
CHIOU/HSU/HSIEH (2013)	brand attachment	brand-self connection brand prominence[577] extended scale based on PARK ET AL. (2010)

574 Cf. ZHOU ET AL. (2012), p. 893.

575 Cf. SCHMALZ/ORTH (2012), p. 875.

576 Cf. MERCHANT/ROSE (2013), p. 2623.

577 Cf. CHIOU/HSU/HSIEH (2013), p. 917.

MUEHLING/SPROTT/SULTAN (2014)	brand attachment	brand-self connection[578] based on PARK ET AL. (2010)
LAM/SHANKAR (2014)	brand attachment	own scale development[579], refer to similarities with PARK ET AL. (2010)

Table 3: Conceptualisations of attachment
Source: Own illustration.

The concept that is most distributed beside the work on emotional attachment introduced by THOMSON/MACINNIS/PARK (2005), is the concept of brand attachment developed by PARK ET AL. (2010). To date this is the most state of the art measure of brand attachment. Therefore it will also function as basis for conceptualising brand *page* attachment. It is based on the assumption that brand attachment assembles two dimensions: *brand-self connection* and *brand prominence*.[580]

The first and central dimension of the construct is *brand-self connection* which represents a bond between a brand and the individual's self. The brand-self connection can be built on (a) the brand becoming part of the person's identity.[581] It means that the brand helps expressing the consumer's identity.[582] It becomes a part of the consumer's self.[583] In this case, the consumer experiences a cognitive and emotional "oneness"[584] with the brand. The brand-self connection can also consist of (b) the brand's instrumental value. In this case, the brand helps to fulfil personal goals, is-

578 Cf. MUEHLING/SPROTT/SULTAN (2014), p. 77.
579 Cf. LAM/SHANKAR (2014), p. 32.
580 Cf. PARK ET AL. (2010), p. 2.
581 Cf. KLEINE/KLEINE/ALLEN (1995), p. 327.
582 Cf. SCHULTZ/KLEINE (1989), p. 361.
583 Cf. BALL/TASAKI (1992), p. 155.
584 Cf. PARK ET AL. (2010), p. 2.

sues, and projects. A smart phone for example can fulfil entertainment-, aesthetic- but also work-related or personal goals.[585]

The dimension brand-self connection relates back to the congruence theory. Congruence theory postulates that brand personality traits offer symbolic benefits for consumers when personality attributes are congruent with the self-concept of a person.[586]

People assign human personality traits to certain brands. A brand's personality can therefore be expressed through particular attributes. Congruence theory postulates that the symbolic benefit for consumers is high when the brand's personality is congruent with the self-concept of a person.[587] High congruence between a person's self-concept and the brand's personality generates affection, attitudes and behaviour in favour of the brand.[588] SIRGY (1982) differentiates between the actual self-concept and the ideal self-concept.[589] The *actual* self-concept mirrors who the person believes s/he really is. It is a reflection of the true self without any projections or figments. The *ideal* self-concept stands for who the person would like to be.[590] A person assigns attributes to her/his ideal personality that s/he does not have but desires to. This may result through comparisons with other people, role models or reference groups. When someone perceives a high fit between the brand's personality and her/his own personality, it is more likely that the person buys the brand. A person strives for high congruity between its *actual* self and the brand's personality out of motives for self-consistency.[591] A person strives for congruity between its *ideal* self and the brand's personality to attain "goals that maintain and/or increase positive self-regard"[592], i.e. to enhance her/his self-esteem.[593]

---

[585] Cf. PARK ET AL. (2010), p. 3.

[586] Cf. AAKER (1999), p. 45.

[587] Cf. AAKER (1999), p. 45.

[588] Cf. MALÄR ET AL. (2011), p. 35, cf. SCHADE (2012), p. 77.

[589] Cf. SIRGY (1982), p. 288.

[590] Cf. SIRGY (1982), p. 288.

[591] Cf. SIRGY (1985), p. 197.

[592] Cf. SIRGY (1985), p. 197.

MALÄR ET AL. (2011) investigate whether brands with an aspirational positioning that enhance the *ideal* self-concept are able to create stronger attachment than brands that fit with consumer's *actual* self.[594] Their results which are published in the Journal of Marketing show that under the circumstance of actual self-congruence, attachment to brands is stronger than for brands with ideal self-congruence.[595] In other words, brands that present themselves in a natural and modest way, find more acceptance from consumers who want to retrieve their true self when buying the brand. This wish for veracity can be illustrated by a recent example: cosmetic brands have always tried to create a sense of elusiveness, using models that portray people with ultimate beauty. This connotes that when consumers apply those products, they too will obtain fantastic appearances. Unilever chose a different approach. They selected "normal" size women with average looks to advertise their Dove beauty products. Because consumers felt closer to these women and identified with their real-life appearances, the campaign was a huge success in creating emotional connections to consumers.[596]

What does this imply for brand pages in social networks? If the attachment to the brand gets higher when congruity is given as proven in the study by MALÄR ET AL. (2011), it is also likely that brand activities have a higher appeal. Hence, the attachment to a brand page in a social network (e.g. Facebook) is stronger when someone perceives high congruity between her-/himself and the brand. If the person believes the brand represents who s/he actually is or who s/he wants to be, s/he is more likely to evaluate the brand page's content positively and become emotionally attached to it.

Thus, the dimension of self-brand connection by PARK ET AL. (2010) can be transferred to context of brand pages and will be termed **brand page connectedness** in the following. Integrating the dimension of brand page connectedness into the brand *page* attachment construct bears the problem of whether to operationalise *actual* or

---

[593] Cf. SIRGY (1985), p. 197.

[594] Cf. MALÄR ET AL. (2011), p. 35.

[595] Cf. MALÄR ET AL. (2011), p. 43.

[596] Cf. MALÄR ET AL. (2011), p. 35.

ideal self perception. PARK ET AL. (2010) never addressed this issue. However, MALÄR ET AL. (2011) were able to prove that *actual* self-congruence is a significant determinant of brand attachment whereas *ideal* self-congruence is not significant.[597] Hence, the integration of ideal self-congruence into the attachment construct would theoretically deliver wrong results as it only works for brand pages that reflect the *actual* self-concept not the *ideal* self-concept. This corresponds to consumers striving for authenticity[598] and their wish to express their actual or true self.[599]

Thus, the dimension of **brand page connectedness** has to be conceptualised as a connection from the user's *actual* self to the brand page. This would reflect the emotional conceptualisation of the *connection* dimension established by THOMSON/MACINNIS/PARK (2005) or SWAMINATHAN/STILLEY/AHLUWALIA (2009).[600] For brand pages, this dimension can be defined as:

> ***Brand page connectedness** reflects the emotional linkage between a brand page and the person's self and expresses to what extent s/he feels drawn towards or mesmerised by it.*

The conceptualisation is reflected in the operationalisation of the dimension. The items are illustrated and explained in detail in chapter C 3.2.

The second factor *brand prominence*[601] measures the strength of the attachment. This dimension represents how present the brand is in a consumer's mind.[602] It further indicates the quality and quantity of memory structures about the brand.[603] When a brand has a great share of a consumer's mind, it influences preference and pur-

---

[597] Cf. MALÄR ET AL. (2011), pp. 35 et seqq.

[598] Cf. SCHALLEHN (2012), cf. SCHALLEHN/BURMANN/RILEY (2014), pp. 192 et seqq. Authenticity is defined "as the degree to which personal identity is causally linked to individual behavior" SCHALLEHN/BURMANN/RILEY (2014), p. 193.

[599] Cf. MALÄR ET AL. (2011), p. 44.

[600] Cf. SWAMINATHAN/STILLEY/AHLUWALIA (2009), p. 989.

[601] Cf. PARK ET AL. (2010), p. 2.

[602] Cf. ALBA/CHATTOPADHYAY (1986), p. 363.

[603] Cf. ROMANIUK/SHARP (2004), p. 327.

chase decisions.[604] This dimension is highly relevant for brand pages following the same rationale as for brands. Only those pages that come into a user's mind when thinking about social networks have obviously left traces. Hence, for the measurement of the strength of brand page attachment, the dimension *prominence* should definitely be transferred. It can be defined as:

> ***Brand page prominence*** *represents the quality of recollection about a brand page.*[605] *It reflects how easy and often a brand page comes into a person's mind whenever s/he thinks about social networks.*

The conceptualisation is also reflected in the operationalisation of the dimension. Here too, the items are illustrated and explained in detail in chapter C 3.2.

In summary, the construct **brand page attachment** consists of two dimensions **brand page connectedness** and **brand page prominence** which leans on the construct structure of brand attachment developed by PARK ET AL. (2010).[606]

2.5 Summary

The review on relevant literature on the attachment construct delivers the following key findings:

- The construct attachment reflects the emotional bond from a person to an object. This bond has been measured in the context of various objects, including brands and brand communities. It is also transferrable to brand pages.
- It is important to incorporate both, affective and cognitive elements into the connotation of the construct.
- The conceptualisation by PARK ET AL. (2010) is widely accepted and has been empirically validated in many studies. Due to its transferability, it also functions as basis for the development of a brand *page* attachment construct in this the-

---

[604] Cf. PARK ET AL. (2010), pp. 2 et seq.

[605] Cf. ROMANIUK/SHARP (2004), p. 327.

[606] Cf. PARK ET AL. (2010), pp. 2 et seqq.

sis. It consists of two dimensions. The first dimension connects the brand page with the *actual* self of a user.[607] It is the perceived *connectedness* that is measured. The second dimension measures the share of mind of a brand page. Hence, **brand page attachment** consists of **brand page connectedness** and **brand page prominence**.

- The distinction from related constructs delivers many reasons why attachment is the superior concept in measuring the bond to a brand page.

3 Antecedents of brand page attachment

There are several antecedents that impact how bonded a person feels towards a brand page. For managers, it is important to be acquainted with those antecedents. If the relevant drivers can be identified and controlled, brand page attachment can be intensified which leads to behavioural responses in favour of the brand.

The following subchapters will summarise the literature review on the identified antecedents. The basis for deducing antecedents is the uses and gratifications (U&G) approach, which researchers have drawn on to explore motivations for the usage of different media.[608] The U&G approach asserts that people are goal-directed in their media usage and select certain media to fulfil their needs.[609] Though originally developed to explain mass media consumption, the U&G theory has been applied to various digital media.[610] From an extant literature review on publications on uses and gratifications of internet, website, and social media usage the following factors could be deduced.

[607] Cf. MALÄR ET AL. (2011), pp. 36 et seqq.

[608] Cf. RUGGIERO (2000), p. 14.

[609] Cf. KO/CHO/ROBERTS (2005), p. 59.

[610] Cf. STAFFORD/STAFFORD/SCHKADE (2004), cf. DHOLAKIA/BAGOZZI/KLEIN PEARO (2004), cf. KO/CHO/ROBERTS (2005), cf. TAYLOR/LEWIN/STRUTTON (2011).

3.1 Information and service

There are several studies that are useful for inferring antecedents of brand page attachment. Drawing back to the U&G approach, the information motive was confirmed in numerous studies investigating digital media gratifications.[611]

DHOLAKIA/BAGOZZI/KLEIN PEARO (2004) explore network- and small-group-based virtual communities. Their antecedent *purposive value* consists of two components. One is informational value, which means that users of communities get gratification from receiving and giving information. Moreover, they derive value from the thoughts and opinions of other members. The other is instrumental value. Under this component the authors subsume the motivation to reach certain goals through participating in communities. This can be an idea that one gets from another member or share with other members, a problem that is solved or support that one receives or gives in a decision process.[612]

In their study on advertisements in social networks, TAYLOR/LEWIN/STRUTTON (2011) found informativeness to be one of the key drivers for the assessment of advertisements.[613] Users like to be informed, find out details about products and brands and be up to date with new launches or releases.[614]

MUNTINGA/MOORMAN/SMIT (2011) conducted unstructured interviews via instant messaging.[615] They found out that there are three levels of activeness in social media: consuming, contributing, and creating.[616] Information proved to be a crucial motivational factor for consumption. The factor can be further split into sub-motivations as surveillance, knowledge, pre-purchase information and inspiration. Under surveil-

---

[611] Cf. DHOLAKIA/BAGOZZI/KLEIN PEARO (2004), p. 255, cf. KO/CHO/ROBERTS (2005), p. 65, cf. PARK/KEE/VALENZUELA (2009), p. 732, cf. TAYLOR/LEWIN/STRUTTON (2011), p. 267, cf. MUNTINGA/MOORMAN/SMIT (2011), pp. 26 et seqq.

[612] Cf. DHOLAKIA/BAGOZZI/KLEIN PEARO (2004), p. 244.

[613] Cf. TAYLOR/LEWIN/STRUTTON (2011), pp. 261 et seq.

[614] Cf. TAYLOR/LEWIN/STRUTTON (2011), pp. 261 et seq., cf. KO/CHO/ROBERTS (2005), p. 60.

[615] Cf. MUNTINGA/MOORMAN/SMIT (2011), pp. 22 et seq.

[616] Cf. MUNTINGA/MOORMAN/SMIT (2011), p. 16.

lance the authors subsume activities like observing what is going on in the social environment. Knowledge can be generated through information provided by the brand or other consumers that provide expertise or special insights. Pre-purchase information is helpful especially in the context of high price categories. Reviews or experiences by other consumers are valuable information before one decides to purchase. Inspiration is induced by content provided by the brand or other users that offer new ideas for usage or alternative designs.[617]

The motivations summarised above can all be transferred to brand pages in social networks. Through the users' personal news feed, followers of brand pages can track recent posts and news that are provided by the brand. For users that seek information and are interested in brand related content, the brand page is a useful tool to keep up to date. Taking advice and reading about other users' opinions can also help reducing the perceived risk when buying a product. Moreover, there is an option of asking product-related questions that are answered in real time by employees of the company. Hence, people that derive value from informational content or value the service that is provided by the brand are likely to become attached to the page. Therefore the following hypotheses can be generated:

H 1a	The benefit of information and service positively impacts brand page attachment.

3.2 Entertainment

In order to get away from everyday life, people enjoy spending time online to have fun or relax.[618] TAYLOR/LEWIN/STRUTTON (2011) describe entertainment as "escapism, enjoyment, and emotional release."[619] The consumption of social media can be amusing; it offers a possibility to get away from stress or negative thoughts and helps

[617] Cf. MUNTINGA/MOORMAN/SMIT (2011), pp. 27 et seq.

[618] Cf. DHOLAKIA/BAGOZZI/KLEIN PEARO (2004), p. 244, cf. KO/CHO/ROBERTS (2005), p. 60, cf. PARK/KEE/VALENZUELA (2009), p. 732, cf. TAYLOR/LEWIN/STRUTTON (2011), p. 262.

[619] Cf. TAYLOR/LEWIN/STRUTTON (2011), p. 262.

to dispel boredom.[620] Content that is distributed virally is often funny or engaging. For most brands, entertaining posts work best in social networks. This can be illustrated through an example: during the Super Bowl in 2013 there was a power outage for several minutes. Some brands made use of it in a clever way: the brand Oreo released an advertisement for its Oreo Cookie and distributed it via social media. With the headline: "Power out? No problem."[621] they posted the image displayed in Figure 15.

Figure 15: Twitter post by Oreo Cookie: Power out? No problem.
Source: Cf. OREO COOKIE (2013).

MUNTINGA/MOORMAN/SMIT (2011) divided consumers' online brand-related activities in social media into three continuous types of usage: consuming, contributing, and cre-

[620] Cf. MUNTINGA/MOORMAN/SMIT (2011), p. 28.
[621] OREO COOKIE (2013).

ating as described above. Entertainment was found to be crucial for all three types.[622] Hence,

H 1b	The benefit of entertainment positively impacts brand page attachment.

3.3 Social value

Social networks bear a lot of opportunities to socialise with friends and family. DHOLAKIA/BAGOZZI/KLEIN PEARO (2004) describe how people see value in keeping in touch or receive support and reassurance through joining network- and small-group-based virtual communities. They are able to interact with their favourite brand and with other admirers of the brand.[623] Some even join communities because they are lonely in their real lives.[624] Through communities they are able to interact, take part in discussions, have social contacts, even if only virtually.[625] Dialogues with like-minded people in social networks or communities may lead to long lasting friendships. The shared interest or passion brings people closer together.[626]

This motive can be transferred to social networks. The users can meet other people that are also passionate about the brand. The communication with other people that like the brand is facilitated via the brand page. Some brands also set up groups in social networks for discussion among users. This leads to the hypotheses:

H 1c	The benefit of social value positively impacts brand page attachment.

[622] Cf. MUNTINGA/MOORMAN/SMIT (2011), pp. 26 et seqq.

[623] Cf. KO/CHO/ROBERTS (2005), p. 60, cf. DHOLAKIA/BAGOZZI/KLEIN PEARO (2004), pp. 243 et seqq.

[624] Cf. DHOLAKIA/BAGOZZI/KLEIN PEARO (2004), p. 244.

[625] Cf. DHOLAKIA/BAGOZZI/KLEIN PEARO (2004), p. 244.

[626] Cf. KO/CHO/ROBERTS (2005), p. 60.

3.4 Economic incentives

Users may also exploit social media for remuneration. For example, for the 50th anniversary, NUTELLA UK & IRELAND (2014) asked their Facebook users to share their favourite Nutella stories. They are up with a chance to win prices for their anecdotes as illustrated in Figure 16.[627]

Figure 16: **Facebook post by Nutella**
Source: Cf. NUTELLA UK & IRELAND (2014).

Some brands also offer discounts or vouchers for their followers via social networks. In their study, MUNTINGA/MOORMAN/SMIT (2011) identified remuneration in form of a holiday trips, freebees or discounts as a motive for consuming brand-related content.[628] Therefore it can be assumed:

H 1d	The benefit of economic incentives positively impacts brand page attachment.

In summary, the hypotheses and relations among constructs that were verbalised in the previous chapters are visualised in Figure 17.

[627] Cf. NUTELLA UK & IRELAND (2014).

[628] Cf. MUNTINGA/MOORMAN/SMIT (2011), p. 29.

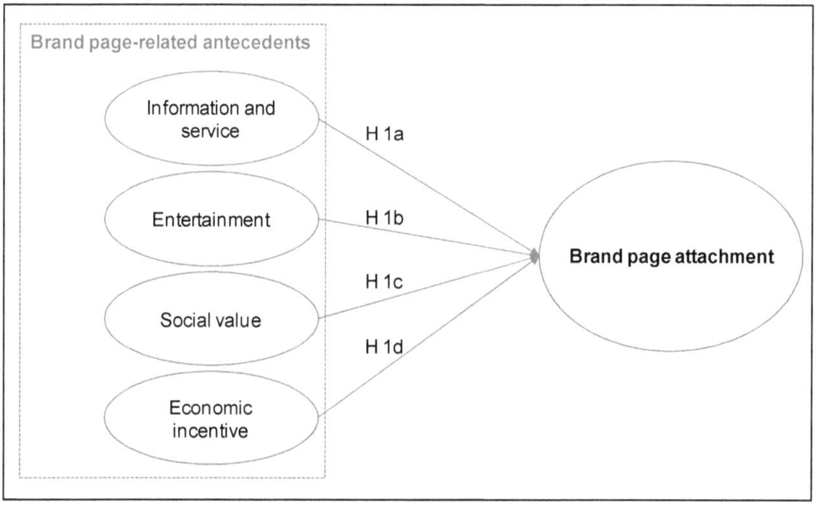

Figure 17: **Antecedents of brand page attachment**
Source: Own illustration.

4 Behavioural consequences of brand page attachment

From attachment research, it can be concluded that strong brand attachment results in consumer behaviour in favour of the brand.[629] As PARK ET AL. (2010) prove, the attachment construct is the strongest predictor for behaviour.[630] They state, these behaviours "require investments of time, money, energy, and reputation"[631] from the attached individual. Ultimately, the attachment construct is able to predict consumer sacrifices. The willingness to sacrifice eventually coincides with long-term loyalty.[632] The same logic can be applied to brand page attachment. The higher the attachment to a brand page, the better it predicts consumer behaviour in favour of the brand page and consequently of the brand. If this assumption can be verified in the empiric

[629] Cf. PARK ET AL. (2010), p. 14.
[630] Cf. PARK ET AL. (2010), p. 14.
[631] PARK ET AL. (2010), p. 14.
[632] Cf. PARK ET AL. (2010), p. 14.

study, it would again highlight the relevance of emotions and justify the measurement of the construct attachment over other constructs with less emotional orientation.

HOFFMAN/FODOR (2010) argue that measuring the effectiveness of social media should be done regarding the consumer investments rather than the company's investments.[633] According to them, those measures could be number of visits, time spent on the platform, or active participation behaviour.[634] Those indicators measured on a continually basis inform managers about the performance of their social media platform. Though the authors appreciate the necessity of hard facts, they advocate the measurement of qualitative variables, too.[635]

On the whole, consumer investments are the logic bracket under which behavioural outcomes of brand page attachment are subsumed. The following subchapters will deliver insights into various types of investments. They are illustrated in summary in Figure 19 at the end of the subchapters.

4.1 Brand page participation

Though most activities on brand pages in social networks happen to be passive, some users like to actively participate. The activities are commonly referred to as *engagement behaviours* and involve activities as liking, commenting, sharing.[636] Engagement behaviours or brand page participation as it is termed here (both expressions can be used synonymously) have been reviewed in detail in chapter B **Fehler! erweisquelle konnte nicht gefunden werden.**. This chapter will not provide more details but enlighten the relation between brand page attachment and participation.

ZAGLIA (2013) delivers some valuable insights into the motives for participation on Facebook brand pages.[637] Users actively ask for help or the opinion of others when

[633] Cf. HOFFMAN/FODOR (2010), p. 42.

[634] Cf. HOFFMAN/FODOR (2010), p. 42.

[635] Cf. HOFFMAN/FODOR (2010), p. 43.

[636] Cf. MALHOTRA/MALHOTRA/SEE (2013), p. 18.

[637] Cf. ZAGLIA (2013), p. 221.

they conceive the brand page as precious source of information.[638] If they obtain data tailored to their needs, they become attached to the brand page. Automatically, they have then also higher propensity to ask questions or deliver answers to other users. This is especially the case, when the product or service requires high financial investments and extensive knowledge.[639] Further, brand pages enhance the knowledge or skills of their followers by providing competitions or challenges where users can compete. The better the brand page is perceived by the user and s/he feels attached, the more likely s/he participates in brand page initiated activities.[640] And last, the brand page offers a platform to share enthusiasm or passion about a brand. Strongly attached users share their dreams, fantasies or wishes related to the brand.[641]

H 2a	Brand page attachment positively impacts the willingness to participate on the brand page.

4.2 Word-of-mouth

Word-of-mouth (WOM) has been identified as a crucial driver for sales as it impacts consumers buying decisions significantly.[642] WOM means the distribution of information about brands and products among consumers.[643] This implies recommending the brand and may also mean defending it against critique from others.[644]

The research on WOM can be traced back to the 1960ies.[645] Traditional WOM transmits within offline conversations between people. DICHTER (1966) distinguishes

638 Cf. ZAGLIA (2013), p. 220, cf. DHOLAKIA/BAGOZZI/KLEIN PEARO (2004), p. 244.

639 Cf. ZAGLIA (2013), p. 220.

640 Cf. ZAGLIA (2013), p. 220.

641 Cf. ZAGLIA (2013), p. 221.

642 Cf. HENNIG-THURAU ET AL. (2004), p. 39.

643 Cf. MILLAN/DIAZ (2014), pp. 260 et seq.

644 Cf. BHATTACHARYA/SEN (2003b) , p. 83, cf. MILLAN/DIAZ (2014), p. 261.

645 Cf. DICHTER (1966).

between two types of WOM, pre-decision and post-decision.[646] The customer who spreads the word after his purchase (post-decision) is highly valuable for the company, as recommendations by friends, family members or acquaintances are more credible than advertisements by the company.[647] With the advent of digital media, WOM was shifted to another level as conversations became publicly visible online. The term eWOM was introduced. HENNIG-THURAU ET AL. (2004) define eWOM as "any positive or negative statement made by potential, actual, or former customers about a product or company, which is made available to a multitude of people and institutions via the Internet".[648] Popular examples for eWOM platforms are consumer-opinion websites like ciao.com[649], holidaycheck.com[650] or epinions.com[651].

In the context of social networks, consumers produce brand related word-of-mouth and distribute it within their network. The more buzz a brand is able to create, the more awareness it gets in social media.[652] Moreover, users recommend brand pages they like and become attached to. Participation in eWOM happens when a user has a positive feeling about the object that s/he refers to.[653] Researchers found that people who participate in WOM are involved or connected with the product, message or cat-

646 Cf. DICHTER (1966), p. 148.

647 Cf. DICHTER (1966), p. 147.

648 HENNIG-THURAU ET AL. (2004), p. 39.

649 "Ciao is a multi-million-strong online community that critically reviews and rates millions of products and services for the benefit of other consumers. Available free of charge to consumers in local-language versions in major western European markets, Ciao combines unbiased consumer reviews and up-to-date price information from hundreds online merchants [...]."CIAO! (2014).

650 "HolidayCheck is a leading travel website where users can easily find and book their perfect holiday and share their holiday experience. The HolidayCheck idea dates back to 1999 when two guys Markus Schott and Sascha Vasic, frustrated with the lack of authentic information when choosing a hotel, decided to create a website which would give others the opportunity to read real opinions and reviews instead of just catalogue descriptions." HOLIDAYCHECK (2014).

651 "Epinions helps people make informed buying decisions. It is a premier consumer reviews platform on the Web and a reliable source for valuable consumer insight, unbiased advice, in-depth product evaluations and personalized recommendations." EPINIONS (2014).

652 Cf. KELLER/FAY (2013), p. 463.

653 Cf. DICHTER (1966), p. 148.

egory.[654] Hence, it can also be assumed that connection to a brand page results in positive WOM.

H 2b	Brand page attachment positively impacts word-of-mouth or the willingness to recommend the brand page.

4.3 Co-creation of value and meaning

As markets change and significance of eWOM rises, users are becoming co-producers of marketing messages[655]. The extent to which a company is able to control brand related user generated content is limited.[656] However, findings in research lead to the conclusion that allowing users to co-create leads to stronger engagement with the brand.[657] SCHAU/MUNIZ/ARNOULD (2009) suggest that firms should encourage their customers to exploit their creativity in social media as that leads to an increase in consumption opportunities and creates value for the brand and other customers.[658] As a result of the expansion of social media, users are enabled to take part in the process of brand development.[659] They are provided with platforms where they can connect to each other and share creativity. Users are co-creating their own experience in social media.[660] PRAHALAD/RAMASWAMY (2004) explain the concept of co-creation as illustrated in Figure 18.[661]

[654] Cf. HENNIG-THURAU ET AL. (2004), p. 41.

[655] Cf. KOZINETS ET AL. (2010), p. 72.

[656] Cf. KAPLAN/HAENLEIN (2010), pp. 59 et seq., cf. ARNHOLD (2010), pp. 31 et seqq.

[657] Cf. BRODIE ET AL. (2011), p. 252.

[658] Cf. SCHAU/MUNIZ/ARNOULD (2009), p. 41.

[659] Cf. KAPLAN/HAENLEIN (2010), p. 62.

[660] Cf. PRAHALAD/RAMASWAMY (2004), pp. 7 et seqq.

[661] Cf. PRAHALAD/RAMASWAMY (2004), p. 8.

What co-creation is
• Co-creation is about joint creation of value by the company and the customer. It is not the firm trying to please the customer. • Allowing the customer to co-construct the service experience to suit her context • Joint problem definition and problem solving • Creating an experience environment in which consumers can have active dialogue and co-construct personalized experiences; product may be the same but customers can construct different experiences • Experience variety • Experience of one • Experiencing the business as consumers do in real time • Continuous dialogue • Co-constructing personalized experiences • Innovating experience environments for new co-creation experiences

Figure 18: **The concept of co-creation**
Source: PRAHALAD/RAMASWAMY (2004), p. 8.

Participating in co-creation activities entails a desire or interest in investing the time and effort. This is only given, if the consumer is attached to the brand page and desires to enhance her/his experience on the brand page. Therefore, it can be concluded:

H 2c	Brand page attachment positively impacts co-creation of value and meaning.

4.4 Willingness to share personal data

Strong attachments lead to different kinds of investments as outlined at the beginning of this chapter. Another type of investment is the willingness of a person to give personal information to the company.[662] This information is highly valuable for brands. With the availability of accurate data, the company is able to tailor products and services to the individual needs of a buyer.[663] The individual data can be analysed in terms of preferences and behaviours and delivers an exclusive brand experience in

[662] Cf. PENTINA ET AL. (2013), p. 65.

[663] Cf. BURMANN/KLEINE-KALMER/HEMMANN (2014), p. 57.

real time.[664] However, due to privacy concerns, a lot of people reject companies to collect and analyse their data from online shopping or search behaviour.[665] Only with building trust is the brand able to acquire this information.[666] Thus, a connection that is able to enhance trust needs to be established. If the brand is able to attach a consumer to its brand page and strengthens the consumer's belief in the authenticity of the brand, the user is more likely to share personal data with the brand. This hypothesis is supported by the research of SMIT/BRONNER/TOLBOOM (2007)[667], who found that a positive attitude towards contact with the brand results in a higher likelihood to share personal information with the company.[668]

H 2d	Brand page attachment positively impacts the willingness to share personal data with the brand.

4.5 Intention to maintain connection

And finally, all behavioural responses above also imply that the user is willing to maintain the connection and will not dislike the brand page nor disable notifications or stop using applications that are offered on the brand page.

H 2e	Brand page attachment positively impacts the intention to maintain the connection to the brand page.

[664] For background information on the subject of generating brand experiences through the use of big data, please see BURMANN/KLEINE-KALMER/HEMMANN (2014) or BURMANN/KLEINE-KALMER/HEMMANN (2013).

[665] Cf. BURMANN/KLEINE-KALMER/HEMMANN (2014), p. 64.

[666] Cf. BURMANN/KLEINE-KALMER/HEMMANN (2014), p. 64.

[667] The researchers interviewed 938 respondents from an online panel provided by TNS NIPO. The brands that were researched were the car brands Ford and Volvo; the computer brands Compaq and IBM; the beer brands Grolsch and Heineken; and the shampoo brands Andrélon and Dove. Cf. SMIT/BRONNER/TOLBOOM (2007), p. 629.

[668] Cf. SMIT/BRONNER/TOLBOOM (2007), p. 632.

All behavioural consequences are summarized in Figure 19.

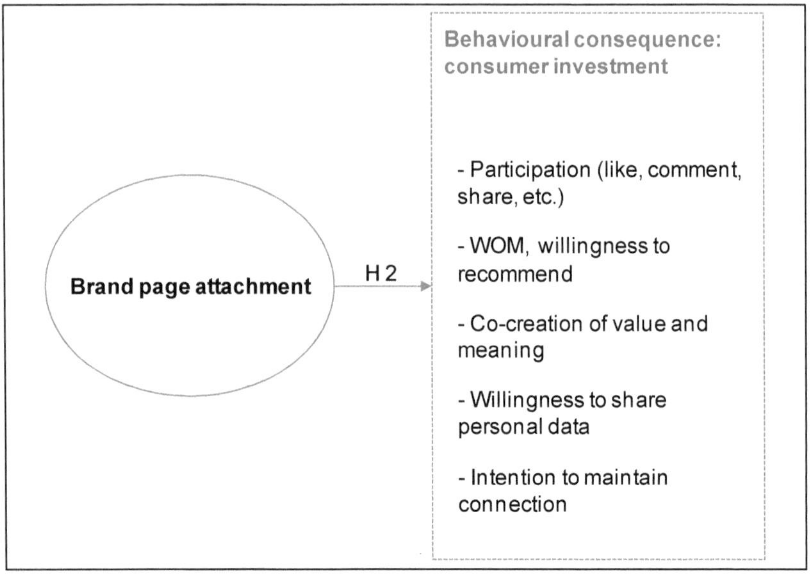

Figure 19: Consequences of brand page attachment
Source: Own illustration.

5 Moderating effects between brand page attachment and its behavioural consequences

Only a small proportion of Facebook users that like brand pages actively interact with brands in Facebook.[669] Though the interaction or engagement rates vary between pages, in general they are all low level.[670] Some researchers trace this back to the type of content and advocate for more engaging topics in social media.[671] But this explanation is unsatisfying because even the top brand pages have relatively low

---

[669] Cf. HEDEMANN (2012).

[670] Cf. SOCIALBAKERS (2013b), cf. EYL (2013).

[671] Cf. PARENT/PLANGGER/BAL (2011), pp. 227 et seq., cf. PHILLIPS (2013).

rates.[672] The next chapters will deliver insights on why followers are not participating. The effects moderate the relation between attachment and behaviour.

5.1 Propensity to interact

Besides industry and page size, participation also depends on the personality of the user.[673] WIERTZ/DE RUYTER (2007) argue that users are different in their inclination to contribute.[674] This is not an online phenomenon. People vary in the way they communicate; extroverts are more likely to engage in conversations or initiate dialogue. Introverts would generally be more passive in their communication behaviour.

To understand personality differences and their consequences for participation behaviour in brand-related online media, MATHWICK (2002) employed clustering methodology to a sample of online shoppers and identified four different groups[675]: transactional community members, socialisers, personal connectors, and lurkers.[676] Lurkers have low interest in participation whether it is discussions or feedback. They are characterised through passive behaviour, monitor what is happening in the community and observe other people's postings. Transactional community members are the exact opposite; they actively engage with other people and give feedback about products and services. Socialisers and personal connectors are more interested in keeping relations to friends, family or in the case of socialisers other fellow customers rather than contributing to transaction related topics. Socialisers are more active than personal connectors and have higher impact due to the amount of connections.[677]

---

[672] Cf. EYL (2013).

[673] Cf. MUNTINGA/MOORMAN/SMIT (2011), p. 15.

[674] Cf. WIERTZ/DE RUYTER (2007), p. 348.

[675] 826 online shoppers that participated in transactional communities were surveyed. They were recruited through news-group announcements, banner ads, and announcements through a mailing list and in the popular media. The survey was administered by Georgia Institute of Technology's Graphic, Visualization & Usability Center (GVU).

[676] Cf. MATHWICK (2002), p. 40.

[677] Cf. MATHWICK (2002), p. 49.

The findings could be confirmed for social media behaviour. In their explorative study on brand-related social media use, MUNTINGA/MOORMAN/SMIT (2011) found that there are three levels of activeness in social media: consuming, contributing, and creating.[678] Further, WIERTZ/DE RUYTER (2007) conducted interviews with members of an online technical support community that is administered by a computer hard- and software supplier.[679] They prove empirically that "customers feel a relational bond with the community that encourages them to assist fellow customers and to share their knowledge."[680] This causal relation is even stronger when customers have a high online interaction propensity.[681] Consequently for brand pages, the same effect can be hypothesised.

H 3a	Users' propensity to interact is moderating the causal relation between brand page attachment and its behavioural consequences: (i) brand page participation (ii) WOM (iii) co-creation of value and meaning.

5.2 Privacy concerns

Trust in the compliant handling of confidential personal data is very low in Germany. A study on the topic of big data[682] that was executed by the Chair of innovative Brand Management at the University of Bremen revealed that 51% of respondents believe

---

678 Cf. MUNTINGA/MOORMAN/SMIT (2011), p. 16.

679 Cf. WIERTZ/DE RUYTER (2007), p. 360.

680 WIERTZ/DE RUYTER (2007), p. 369.

681 Cf. WIERTZ/DE RUYTER (2007), p. 369.

682 An online survey was executed in Germany, n= 1.040, representative for the German population. Cf. BURMANN/KLEINE-KALMER/HEMMANN (2014), pp. 62 et seq. The authors define big data as: Big data are unstructured consumer data, extracted from social media, websites, online purchase and GPS information. The challenge is to link these unstructured data to existent company owned structured customer data and to analyse and use these data providing value to the consumer. Cf. BURMANN/KLEINE-KALMER/HEMMANN (2014), p. 59.

that companies buy people's personal data from third-party suppliers. A further 28% are of the opinion that companies collect people's personal data through tracking and analysis of online activities without informing them. Only 21% acknowledge that they provide personal data through filling out online forms or participating in online raffles.

The respondents were further asked what they think how companies handle their personal data. As Figure 20 shows, 63% answered "I believe that some companies pass on my data without my approval." Only 8% trust in the responsible handling of sensitive data.

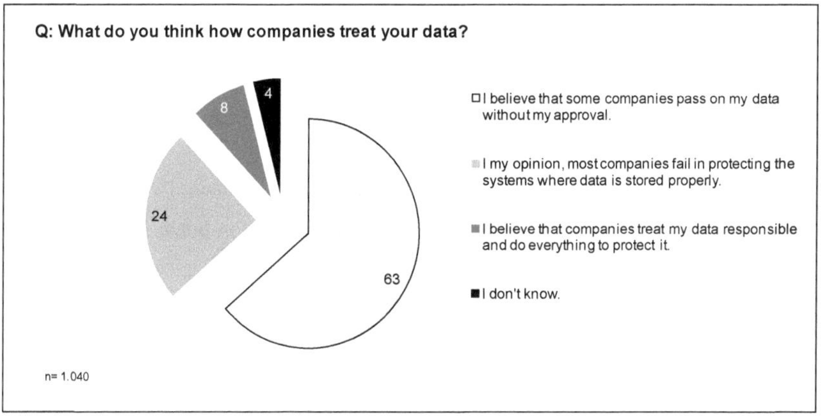

Figure 20: **Trust in handling of confidential data is low**
Source: Own illustration based on BURMANN/KLEINE-KALMER/HEMMANN (2014), p 63.

This development also has enormous impact for social networks.[683] Particularly Facebook has been criticised many time for collecting user data and for the lack if respect for privacy.[684] Consequently, this leads to people leaving Facebook. Among those who quit the social network, 48.3% say this is due to privacy concerns.[685] Young people are intensifying their usage of chat services (e.g. Snapchat, threema)

[683] Cf. SCHMUNDT (2013), p. 122.

[684] Cf. MUI (2011), cf. CBS (2013), cf. THE GUARDIAN (2013), cf. STÖCKER (2014).

[685] More than 600 people were surveyed by the University of Vienna. Cf. WOOLLASTON (2013).

that delete messages or pictures right after delivery to the recipient.[686] They are posting less in social networks because they do not want parents or teachers to read their status updates. Moreover, they are afraid of Facebook storing and saving embarrassing pictures for a lifetime.

XU ET AL. (2012) structure privacy concerns into three factors.[687] First, perceived surveillance[688] is an issue, especially in the case of mobile users. People are afraid that their activities are tracked, recorded or transmitted.[689] Second, perceived intrusion is triggered by programs that interrupt personal activities without authorisation.[690] And third, secondary use of information causes distrust.[691] This is confirmed in the research shown in Figure 20.

So, for brand pages this means that even attached users might not participate in the conversation in Facebook due to the fear of data abuse. Hence, a moderator relation can be phrased for this phenomenon.

H 3b	Privacy concerns are moderating the causal relation between brand page attachment and its behavioural consequences: (i) brand page participation (ii) WOM (iii) co-creation of value and meaning (iv) willingness to share personal data.

[686] Cf. SCHMUNDT (2013), p. 122.

[687] Cf. XU ET AL. (2012), pp. 4 et seqq.

[688] Perceived surveillance is defined as “the watching, listening to, or recording of an individual's activities.” SOLOVE (2006), p. 490.

[689] Cf. XU ET AL. (2012), p. 4.

[690] Cf. XU ET AL. (2012), pp. 4 et seq.

[691] Cf. XU ET AL. (2012), p. 5.

6 Summary and visualisation of research model

This chapter shall provide an overview on all hypotheses and summarise them into a visualisation of the overall research model (Figure 21). The hypotheses are subdivided into three sections: antecedents of brand page attachment, consequences of brand page attachment and moderators between brand page attachment and behavioural consequences.

H 1a	The benefit of information and service positively impacts brand page attachment.
H 1b	The benefit of entertainment positively impacts brand page attachment.
H 1c	The benefit of social value positively impacts brand page attachment.
H 1d	The benefit of economic incentives positively impacts brand page attachment.

Table 4: **Research hypotheses regarding antecedents of brand page attachment**
Source: Own illustration.

H 2a	Brand page attachment positively impacts the willingness to participate on the brand page.
H 2b	Brand page attachment positively impacts word-of-mouth or the willingness to recommend the brand page.
H 2c	Brand page attachment positively impacts co-creation of value and meaning.
H 2d	Brand page attachment positively impacts the willingness to share personal data with the brand.
H 2e	Brand page attachment positively impacts the intention to maintain the connection to the brand page.

Table 5: **Research hypotheses regarding consequences of brand page attachment**
Source: Own illustration.

H 3a	Users' propensity to interact is moderating the causal relation between brand page attachment and its behavioural consequences: (i) brand page participation (ii) WOM (iii) co-creation of value and meaning.
H 3b	Privacy concerns are moderating the causal relation between brand page attachment and its behavioural consequences: (i) brand page participation (ii) WOM (iii) co-creation of value and meaning (iv) willingness to share personal data.

Table 6: Research hypotheses regarding moderators between brand page attachment and behavioural consequences

Source: Own illustration.

To visualise the research project, all hypotheses and constructs are summarised into one illustration. The complete model is displayed in Figure 21.

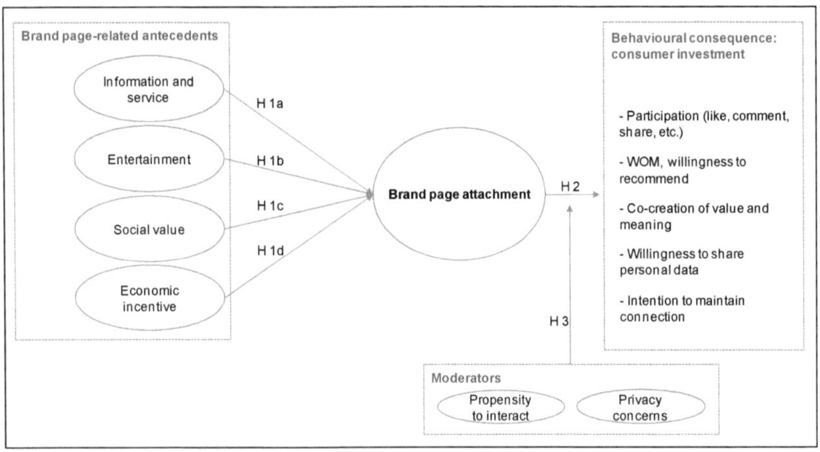

Figure 21: Research model

Source: Own illustration.

C Empirical validation of antecedents and consequences of brand page attachment

1 Research design

1.1 Structure of research process

The theoretical framework that has been elaborated in chapter B lays the ground for the empirical study. The research model illustrated in Figure 21 shall be validated empirically. In the following, the process and methods that are employed will be introduced.

The research process can be divided into two phases: first, in a pre-study, the antecedents for brand page attachment have been investigated in an explorative study and verified empirically.[692] For this purpose, an online-survey of 2,000 Facebook users has been accomplished.[693] The research project was presented at various international conferences and could be improved through valuable feedback from internationally renowned academics.[694] The discussion at the conferences was valuable for further insights on model and scale development. The scales that were tested in the pre-study are employed for hypothesis testing in the main study.

Second, in the main study, data will be collected to corroborate the causal effects that are hypothesised.

---

[692] The pre-test is explained in detail in chapter B 1.2.

[693] The study was executed in cooperation with a network of German food brands in Germany in February/March 2012 (BVE – Bundesvereinigung der deutschen Ernährungsindustrie), english: National union of German food industry.

[694] The international conferences were the 42nd European Marketing Academy (EMAC) Conference 2013 in Istanbul, the 12th International Conference on Research in Advertising (ICORIA) 2013 in Zagreb and the 2013 AMA summer educators' conference in Boston, Massachusetts. Cf. KLEINE-KALMER/BURMANN/SCHADE (2013), cf. KLEINE-KALMER/BURMANN (2013b), cf. KLEINE-KALMER/BURMANN (2013a).

1.2 Pre-study investigating relevant antecedents

Identifying antecedents that lead to positive evaluations of brand pages is a research project on its own. Therefore relevant factors that impact brand page evaluation have been deduced and empirically validated in a pre-study that was carried out in early 2012. The dependent variable was the user's attitude towards the brand page. The conceptualisation of the attitude construct is evaluative, meaning that emotional components are underlying but actively reviewed and therefore cognitive. Measuring brand page attachment should add further value to the measurement due to emotional components being dominant. The course of the research project was as follows:

First, a list of items was generated from a thorough literature review to explore factors that impact brand page evaluation. The items were reviewed in expert interviews. The list of items was then prepared for empirical validation.

Within the community research most empirical studies analyse products from categories that customers are highly involved with. Mass market products as fast moving consumer goods are only scarcely scrutinised yet.[695] However, in 2012 five of the top ten brand pages - ranked by their number of fans - were food and drink brands.[696] Thus, the pre-study was dedicated to examine brand pages in Facebook for food and beverage brands.

Second, in cooperation with a network of German food brands[697], an online-survey of 2,000 Facebook users has been accomplished. The study took place in Germany in February/March 2012. From the 2,000 Facebook users, only followers of food brands with an actual profile in the social network were included in the evaluation. To identify those followers, the respondents were asked to name food brands they recall being follower of. All further questions were asked referring to the brand that was mentioned in the first place. Respondents that only clicked through and answered the

---

[695] Cf. VELOUTSOU/MOUTINHO (2009), p. 314.

[696] Cf. SOCIALBAKERS (2012).

[697] BVE – Bundesvereinigung der deutschen Ernährungsindustrie, english: National union of German food industry.

questionnaire in less than half the time of the average respondent were disregarded. Also, cases that had more than 10% missing values were excluded. Finally, the cases of 313 respondents were used for the data analysis.

The motive structure was determined by an exploratory factor analysis. Based on Kaiser's eigenvalue criterion[698], five factors with eigenvalues greater than one were extracted.[699] All factors showed strong reliability with Cronbach's α bigger than 0.7.[700] Over 70% of the Variance could be explained.

The results of the structural model show that all indicator loadings are higher than 0.7, so the indicator reliability for all constructs is given. The internal consistency is measured by composite reliability, all values lie above 0.7. In literature, values bigger than 0.6 are considered supportive of internal consistency.[701] The average variance extracted is used as a measure for discriminant validity.[702] Since, the average variance extracted (AVE) of all constructs lies above 0.5, discriminant validity is also fulfilled.

The target construct displays a R^2 of 0.502 and thus, clearly exceeds the required minimum ratio of 0.19.[703] Moreover, Q^2 is greater than zero, so the predictive relevance of the structural model is given.[704]

Three factors were identified to be relevant for the attitude toward the brand page: *entertainment, information & service* and *support the brand.*[705] *Entertainment* had by far the highest impact (path coefficient 0.483).

---

[698] Cf. KAISER (1974), pp. 31 et seqq.

[699] Kaiser's eigenvalue criterion recommends to extract those factors whose eigenvalues are bigger than one. Cf. WEIBER/MÜHLHAUS (2010), p. 107.

[700] Cronbach's α is the commonly used reliability coefficient that measures the consistency of the scale. It is recommended to accept values above 0.7. Cf. HAIR ET AL. (2010), p. 123.

[701] Cf. BAGOZZI (1988), pp. 74 et seqq.

[702] Cf. FORNELL/LARCKER (1981), pp. 39 et seqq.

[703] Cf. CHIN (1998a), pp. 7 et seqq.

[704] Cf. GOETZ/LIEHR-GOBBERS (2004), pp. 714 et seqq.

[705] Cf. KLEINE-KALMER/BURMANN (2013a).

The path coefficients of the *social* factor and the factor *economic incentive* are not significant (t-value < 1.960). The effect size f^2 for these antecedents lies below the minimum level of 0.02 (Cohen 1998).[706] The *social value* factor was not significant although in the community research the social factor was proven to be of high relevance.[707] The *economic incentive* component was not significant either, which can be traced back to the relatively low financial risk of food and drink products. Because the pre-study was limited to food and drink brand pages, the two factors are integrated again for validation in other contexts.

1.3 Data collection and sample characteristics of main study

In the main study, data will be collected to corroborate the causal effects that are hypothesised. A cross-sectional[708] design is chosen for the study. The survey is conducted online. Given the digital nature of the subject investigated, respondents are highly familiar with this method. Further, there are several other advantages inherent to online surveys:

- Recruitment of Facebook users with the specific characteristic of following a brand from a certain product category is less difficult via online surveys[709]
- Speed of field research[710]
- Reduced bias of socially acceptable answers[711]
- No interviewer bias[712]
- No costs for postage[713]
- No costs for interviewers[714]

---

706 Cf. COHEN (1988), pp. 410 et seqq.

707 Cf. KLEINE-KALMER/BURMANN/SCHADE (2013).

708 "A cross-sectional study involves observations of a sample, or cross section, of a population or phenomenon that are made a tone point in a time." Cf. BABBIE (2013), p. 105.

709 Cf. SELM/JANKOWSKI (2006), p. 437.

710 Cf. COUPER/TRAUGOTT/LAMIAS (2001), p. 242.

711 Cf. SCHONLAU/FRICKER/ELLIOTT (2002), p. 17.

712 Cf. KUß/EISEND (2010), p. 117.

713 Cf. COMSCORE (2013), p. 123.

- Avoids coding errors[715].

To route the questionnaire to the participants, a panel management agency[716] was appointed for recruitment. As necessary condition, the respondents are required to have an active Facebook account. Moreover, they were asked if they follow ("like") one of 55 different brands from the three industries FMCG, automobile and restaurant chains (please see Table 8). If they do "like" at least one of the given brands, they were considered for further interviewing.

1.3.1 Questionnaire and pre-test

The design of the questionnaire for the online survey was accomplished following recommendations of the relevant literature.[717] AAKER ET AL. (2013) recommend following a sequence of logical steps[718]:

1) Plan what to measure.
2) Formulate questions to obtain the needed information.
3) Decide on the order and wording of questions and on the layout of the questionnaire.
4) Using a small sample, test the questionnaire for omissions and ambiguity.
5) Correct the problems (and pre-test again, if necessary).

The structure of the questionnaire shall be structured as shown in Figure 22.

---

714 Cf. SCHONLAU/FRICKER/ELLIOTT (2002), p. 11.

715 Cf. BUCKINGHAM/SAUNDERS (2004), p. 69.

716 Respondi AG, Köln, Germany.

717 Cf. KOTLER/ARMSTRONG (2014), pp. 139 et seqq., cf. AAKER ET AL. (2013), pp. 249 et seqq., cf. BUEHNER (2006), pp. 46 et seqq., cf. SEDLMEIER/RENKEWITZ (2013), pp. 90 et seqq., KUß/EISEND (2010), pp. 107 et seqq., cf. BEREKOVEN/ECKERT/ELLENRIEDER (2009), pp. 92 et seqq.

718 AAKER ET AL. (2013), p. 249.

Location	Type	Function
Starting questions	Broad, general questions	To break the ice and establish a rapport with the respondent
Next few questions	Simple and direct questions	To reassure the respondent that the survey is simple and easy to answer
Questions up to a third of the questionnaire	Focused questions	Relate more to the research objectives and convey to the respondent the area of research
Major portion of the questionnaire	Focused questions, some may be difficult	To obtain most of the information required for the research
Last few questions	Personal questions that my be perceived as sensitive by the respondent	To get classification and demographic information about the respondent

Figure 22: Structure of questions in a typical questionnaire
Source: Closely based on AAKER ET AL. (2013), p. 262.

When setting the order of questions, it should be considered to avoid the halo effect[719]. Hence, questions that aim at the overall evaluation of an object could influence the judgement of particular attributes if they are put upfront.[720] This would bias the individual evaluation.[721]

In addition, criteria that relate specifically to carrying out online surveys were taken into account:

- Provide welcome screen[722]
- Provide progress indicator[723]
- Allow respondents to pause the survey and return later[724]
- Offer detailed instructions[725]
- Place only few questions on one screen to avoid scrolling[726]

---

[719] "The halo effect is generally defined as the influence of a global evaluation on evaluations of individual attributes." NISBETT/WILSON (1977), p. 250.

[720] Cf. BECKWITH/KASSARJIAN/LEHMANN (1978), p. 465.

[721] Cf. BECKWITH/LEHMANN (1975), p. 265.

[722] Cf. SUE/RITTER (2012), p. 77.

[723] Cf. COUPER/TRAUGOTT/LAMIAS (2001), p. 243.

[724] Cf. SCHONLAU/FRICKER/ELLIOTT (2002), p. 48.

[725] Cf. SUE/RITTER (2012), p. 82.

- Offer a choice not to answer the question[727]
- For readability the text and background colours should contrast highly[728]
- Use radio buttons when only one answer is required, use check boxes for multiple choice[729]
- Ensure anonymity to respect respondent's privacy[730].

The questionnaire was pre-tested in two stages: first, experts from the background of social media, digital analytics within the FMCG industry and marketing as well as researchers from the University of Bremen were invited to review items from established scales.[731] They were also asked to review the questionnaire regarding comprehensiveness, adequacy of question design and questionnaire length.[732] Based on the feedback, few amendments and modifications were made. The second step included a test with students from the University of Bremen. After the second test, all questions were valued to be understandable and the time of completion was between 10 and 15 minutes which lie within acceptable boundaries with a maximum of 30 minutes.[733]

1.3.2 Data check and data cleansing

To secure the quality and validity of the data set, the data has to be checked and possibly cleansed. At first, it has to be confirmed that there are no "click-throughs".[734] These are participants that took part in the survey to get the incentive and therefore

[726] Cf. SCHONLAU/FRICKER/ELLIOTT (2002), p. 42.

[727] Cf. COUPER/TRAUGOTT/LAMIAS (2001), p. 240.

[728] Cf. SUE/RITTER (2012), p. 81.

[729] Cf. SUE/RITTER (2012), p. 84.

[730] Cf. SCHONLAU/FRICKER/ELLIOTT (2002), p. 46.

[731] In total there were 12 experts that reviewed the wording of the items regarding translation and appropriateness for the digital context.

[732] Cf. BEREKOVEN/ECKERT/ELLENRIEDER (2009), pp. 95 et seqq.

[733] Cf. BOEHLER (2004) p. 100.

[734] Cf. PIEHLER (2011), p. 369.

just clicked random answers rather than genuinely answering the questions.[735] Following the procedure recommended by PIEHLER (2011), there are two indicators that help identifying click-throughs: a) the duration time to complete the survey and b) the variance of the answers.[736] Regarding the duration time, respondents that needed less than half the average time of 10 minutes 12 seconds were eliminated. In such a case it can be concluded that the participant just ran through the questions without properly reading and evaluating the answer.[737] So, 620 completed questionnaires are left in total. With regard to the variance, respondents that just clicked through and always chose the same category as answer would have a variance of zero in their answering behaviour.[738] Hence, further 16 cases were deleted.

Further, cases as well as variables that contain a high percentage of missing values shall be excluded from the analysis. WIRTZ (2004) recommends excluding those cases and variables that have more than 30% missing values.[739] Accordingly, 14 cases were eliminated; there were no variables that had to be deleted regarding missing values. In summary, there were 590 cases used for the analysis. Per industry that leaves 199 cases for automobile, 194 for FMCG, 197 for restaurant chains. All samples exceed the required minimum for structural equation modelling of 120 cases.[740] The statistic on response rates and data cleansing is illustrated in Table 7.

---

[735] Cf. PIEHLER (2011), p. 369.

[736] Cf. PIEHLER (2011), p. 369, cf. HEGNER (2012), p. 165, cf. EILERS (2014), p. 93.

[737] Cf. PIEHLER (2011), p. 369.

[738] Cf. PIEHLER (2011), p. 369.

[739] Cf. WIRTZ (2004), pp. 109 et seqq.

[740] Cf. EILERS (2014), p. 94, cf. MUELLER (2006), p. 266, cf. GREFEN/STRAUB/BOUDREAU (2000), p. 9.

	Automobile	FMCG	Restaurant chains
Invited respondents		4548	
Fans of brands		763	
Elimination of incomplete questionnaires		130	
Net sample	210	210	213
Elimination of click-throughs	6	13	10
Elimination of missing values	5	3	6
Total sample	**199**	**194**	**197**

Table 7: Response rates and data cleansing
Source: Own illustration.

On the subject of missing values, there are several procedures to replace the remaining missing values in the data set.[741] Rather than elimination or mean substitution, the literature recommends more modern approaches as the Expectation-

[741] For a summary of the different possibilities, please read PIEHLER (2011) , pp. 373 et seqq., cf. WEIBER/MÜHLHAUS (2010), pp. 142 et seqq.

Maximisation-Algorithm (EM-Algorithm).[742] This method replaces the missing values under guarantee of maximum plausibility.[743]

1.3.3 Sample statistics

The adjusted research sample will be characterised by demographics and descriptive analysis in the following. The objective is to reveal differences in answer behaviour between the three industries. Table 8 shows the brand pages that have been investigated. These brand pages were chosen for the survey as in those categories they had the highest numbers of followers according to a ranking provided by SOCIALBAKERS (2012) and therefore the highest incidence in the sample.[744]

---

[742] Cf. PIEHLER (2011), p. 375, cf. WIRTZ (2004), pp. 109 et seqq.

[743] Cf. WIRTZ (2004), pp. 109 et seqq.

[744] Cf. SOCIALBAKERS (2012).

Automobile	# participants who like the brand page on Facebook	FMCG	# participants who like the brand page on Facebook	Restaurant chains	# participants who like the brand page on Facebook
Volkswagen Motorsport	10	kinder Riegel	12	McDonald's	18
Audi	15	nutella	14	Subway	16
BMW	13	Pringles	8	Burger King	13
Mercedes-Benz	10	HARIBO	12	Starbucks	15
Volkswagen	12	Pick up!	8	KFC	17
Opel	9	5 Gum	7	Pizza Hut	9
Ford	11	Ferrero Küss-chen	10	Vapiano	13
Harley-Davidson	9	Chocofresh	6	Petit Bistro	10
KIA Motors	8	Airwaves	9	Jim Block	9
Skoda	10	Milka	14	Nordsee	17
MINI	9	Leibniz	9	Cafe & Bar Celona	11
Hyundai	13	Ritter Sport	12	Ditsch	10
Alfa Romeo	9	Tic Tac	8	Block House	15
Ferrari	8	Monte	7	Dunkin' Donuts	17
Nissan	6	Ben & Jerry's	12	Domino's Pizza	7
Porsche	10	duplo	7		
Lamborghini	10	Wrigley's Extra	9		
Aston Martin	9	Babybel	9		
Jaguar	9	kinder Überra-schung	11		
Jeep	9	M&Ms	10		

Table 8: Investigated brand pages per category

Source: Own illustration.

The majority of the participants (43%) have been following the brand page for more than a year. For car brands, more than half of the respondents (56%) have liked the brand page more than a year ago (Figure 23).

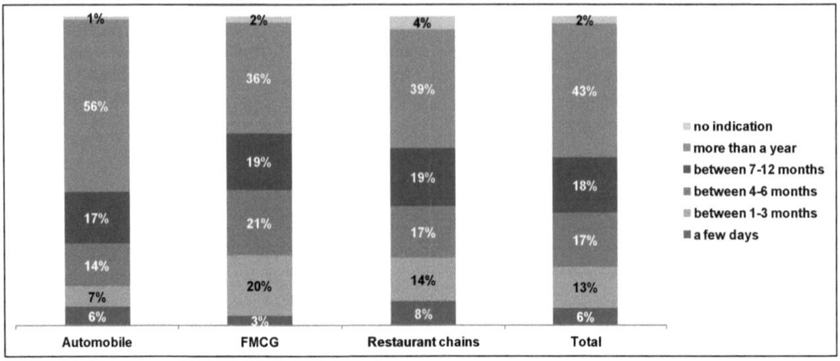

Figure 23: **Question: How long have you been following ("clicked like") the brand page of [BRAND]?**

Source: Own illustration.

The demographics of the sample are distributed as shown in Figure 24. Regarding gender the total sample contains equal numbers for male and female. Looking at different categories, equal gender distribution is only in the case of restaurant chains, there are 67% females that follow FMCG brands, on the contrary for automobile brands there are 65% males. Concerning age, the automobile sample has a tendency to be older than the average, while followers of restaurant chains tend to be younger.

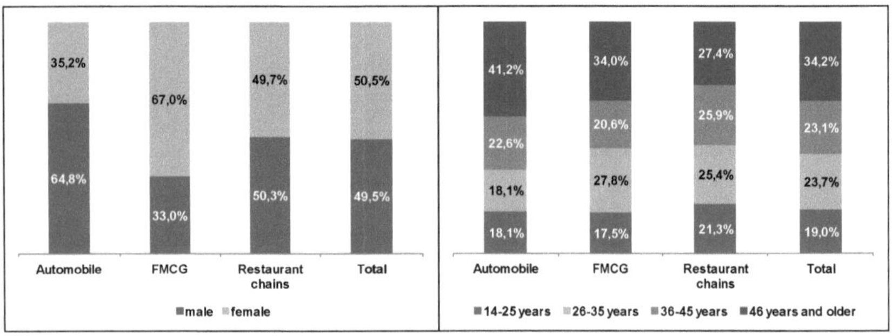

Figure 24: **Demographics by category**

Source: Own illustration.

The social media usage intensity is highest for Facebook with an average access between several times a day and once a day (Figure 25); followed by YouTube which is used between several times a week and once a week. The only other two channels that are of relevance are Google+ and Twitter, though neither is used on a daily or weekly basis.

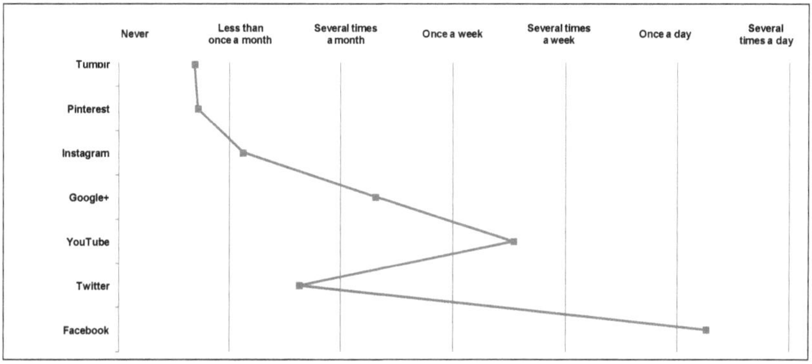

Figure 25: Social media usage intensity
Source: Own illustration

2 Methodological basis for the measurement of theoretical constructs

This chapter shall provide the foundation for the applied methodology. The relevant statistics will be outlined and recapitulated briefly. The summary makes no claim for completeness; it shall only extract important basics to ease the comprehension.

2.1 Structural equation modelling (SEM)

To test the deduced hypotheses and its underlying research model which has been introduced in chapter B 6, an adequate statistic approach needs to be detected. The hypotheses formulate cause-and-effect relationships, which form a causal model. For the empirical validation of causalities, structural equation modelling is employed.[745] Structural equation modelling enables quantifying complex causal effects between theoretical or latent constructs.[746] Latent constructs are unobserved concepts that cannot be measured directly (e.g. brand image or category involvement) but can be represented through indicating variables.[747] The terms manifest variables, items, in-

[745] Cf. BACKHAUS/ERICHSON/WEIBER (2011), p. 65.
[746] Cf. WEIBER/MÜHLHAUS (2010), p. 17.
[747] Cf. HAIR ET AL. (2010), pp. 634 et seq.

dicators or unobserved variables are used synonymously.[748] Latent constructs are predominantly measured through multi-item scales.[749]

There are two measurement models within structural equation models. One is the *structural* model or also called *inner* model. The inner model shows the relations among the theoretical constructs. Antecedence of the causative on the effected construct is required.[750] In other words, the relation between independent and dependent construct can only occur in one direction.[751] The direction needs to be hypothesised unmistakeably. If the directionality of effects is not clearly identifiable, a reciprocal effect can be assumed and the model becomes nonrecursive. This would add further complexity to the analysis.[752]

One distinguishes between exogenous and endogenous constructs.[753] Exogenous constructs consist of independent variables. Those are influenced by external factors. Endogenous constructs on the contrary are impacted through other constructs in the model. They are also labelled dependent or target constructs.[754] The relation between them is typically visualised by an arrow reaching from the independent to the dependent construct.

The second part of the structural equation model is the *outer* model or *measurement* model. The measurement model includes the latent constructs and its predictive indicators.[755] The indicators can be reflective or formative.[756] With reflective indicators, the causality direction is from construct to its manifest variables.[757] The observable variables are therefore consequential of the construct and highly correlated. If one

[748] Cf. TABACHNICK/FIDELL (2013), p. 682.

[749] Cf. HAIR ET AL. (2010), p. 637.

[750] Cf. TROPP (2011), p. 597.

[751] Cf. HAIR/RINGLE/SARSTEDT (2011), p. 141.

[752] Cf. KLINE (2005), pp. 99 et seq.

[753] Cf. HAIR ET AL. (2014a), p. 549.

[754] Cf. HAIR/RINGLE/SARSTEDT (2011), p. 141, cf. HAIR ET AL. (2014a), p. 549.

[755] Cf. HAIR/RINGLE/SARSTEDT (2011), p. 141.

[756] Cf. CHIN (1998a) , p. 9, cf. FASSOTT/EGGERT (2005), pp. 31-69.

[757] Cf. FASSOTT/EGGERT (2005), p. 36, cf. JARVIS/MACKENZIE/PODSAKOFF (2003), p. 201.

variable is removed from the scale, the meaning of the construct does not change.[758] Formative indicators on the contrary are causative for the construct.[759] The manifest variables can be independent an uncorrelated. Eliminating variables may change the connotation of the construct.[760] The difference between reflective and formative indicators is illustrated in Figure 26. The direction of the arrows is assigned accordingly.

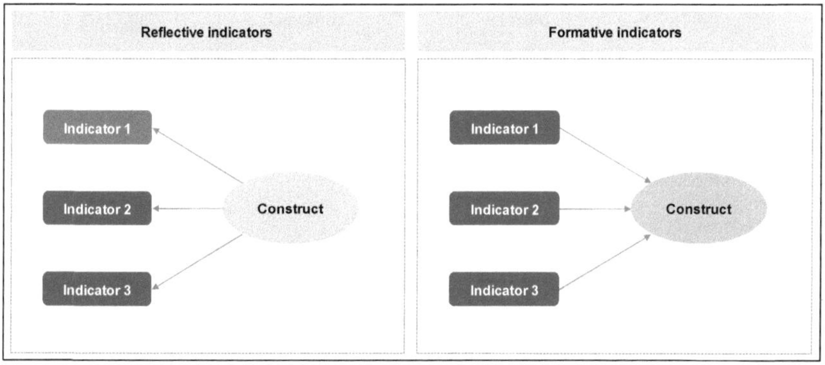

Figure 26: Reflective and formative measurement models with three indicators

Source: Own illustration based on FORNELL/BOOKSTEIN (1982) , p. 441, JARVIS/MACKENZIE/PODSAKOFF (2003), p. 201, FASSOTT/EGGERT (2005), pp. 37-39 and SCHADE (2012), p. 99.

For comprehension the structural equation model can be illustrated visually. Latent constructs are visualised through an ellipse or circle, the indicators are depicted through rectangles or squares. For differentiation between endogenous and exogenous variables, the endogenous are generally denoted as Y variables, whereas the exogenous variables are usually labelled with the letter X. Arrows signify the relation and direction of relation between constructs, leading from exogenous to endogenous.[761] The path coefficients are labelled λ for reflective indicators.

[758] Cf. JARVIS/MACKENZIE/PODSAKOFF (2003), p. 201.

[759] Cf. CHIN (1998a) , p. 9, cf. FASSOTT/EGGERT (2005), p. 38.

[760] Cf. JARVIS/MACKENZIE/PODSAKOFF (2003), p. 201.

[761] Cf. HAIR ET AL. (2014a), p. 550.

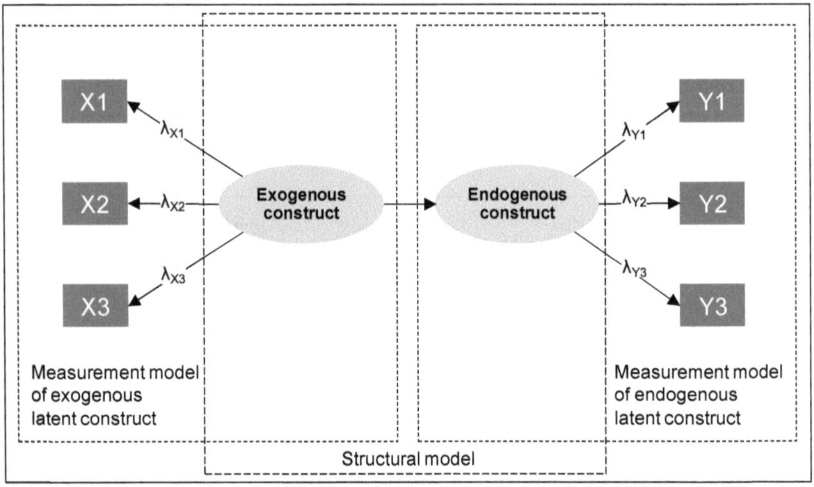

Figure 27: Simplified structural equation model with two constructs

Source: Own illustration based on HAIR ET AL. (2014a), p. 552, HAIR ET AL. (2014b), p. 11 and PIEHLER (2011), p. 389.

In general one can distinguish between two methods of structural equation modelling: covariance-based SEM (CB-SEM) and partial least squares SEM (PLS-SEM).[762] The former is based on the factor analysis theorem and estimates all parameters of the structural equation model on the basis of the variance-covariance matrix.[763] This approach is adequate for theory confirmation. PLS-SEM aims at "maximising the explained variance of the dependent latent constructs"[764], similar to multiple regression analysis.[765] It shall be employed for theory development, prediction or exploration.[766] The rationale for why the empirical investigation of this thesis shall be evaluated with the partial least squares method will be provided in the next chapter.

---

[762] Cf. HAIR/RINGLE/SARSTEDT (2011), p. 139, cf. WONG (2013), p. 2.

[763] Cf. WEIBER/MÜHLHAUS (2010), p. 47.

[764] HAIR/RINGLE/SARSTEDT (2011), p. 139.

[765] Cf. FORNELL/BOOKSTEIN (1982), p. 450, cf. ALGESHEIMER/DHOLAKIA/HERRMANN (2005), p. 140.

[766] Cf. HAIR/RINGLE/SARSTEDT (2011), p. 140.

2.2 Structural equation modelling with partial least squares (PLS-SEM)

There are several reasons that in the context of this dissertation project speak for the usage of partial least squares rather than covariance-based structural equation modelling. HAIR/RINGLE/SARSTEDT (2011) provide several rules of thumb for the decision which method to select.[767] Those are summarised in Figure 28.

In general, the choice of method should be based on the research objectives. If former theory is strong and the objective of the research is confirmation and validation, CB-SEM should be employed. The global goodness of fit measures help verifying if the model is suitable to reflect the developed theory. In the case of young research fields, where theory evolution is still in early stages, prediction and theory development are in focus. In this instance, PLS-SEM is more appropriate as it grants more predictive accuracy.[768] As social media is still a relatively young research area, PLS is the preferred method.[769] A further argument for PLS is the identification of key drivers. As the path model (Figure 21) shows, several drivers of brand page attachment are hypothesised. The key drivers shall be identified.

With many constructs and items in the structural model, it is recommended to use PLS.[770] Moreover, the variable scores are needed in further analyses.[771] In addition, PLS is more robust, even with smaller samples it delivers valid results.[772] It is also able to encompass reflective as well as formative constructs in contrast to CB-SEM.[773]

[767] Cf. HAIR/RINGLE/SARSTEDT (2011), p. 144.

[768] Cf. HAIR/RINGLE/SARSTEDT (2011), p. 144, cf. HAIR ET AL. (2011), p. 420, cf. GOODHUE/LEWIS/THOMPSON (2012), p. 999, cf. ROBINS (2012), p. 310.

[769] Cf. EILERS (2014), p. 114.

[770] Cf. FORNELL/BOOKSTEIN (1982), p. 450.

[771] Cf. HAIR/RINGLE/SARSTEDT (2011), p. 144.

[772] Cf. FORNELL/BOOKSTEIN (1982) , p. 450, cf. HAIR ET AL. (2011), p. 420, cf. MATEOS-APARICIO (2011), p. 2309, cf. WONG (2013), p. 3.

[773] Cf. CHIN (1998a), p. 9, cf. HAIR/RINGLE/SARSTEDT (2011), p. 144, cf. HAIR ET AL. (2011), p. 420.

The disadvantage of PLS-SEM is that there is no overall goodness of model fit measure with PLS.[774] But in summary most arguments speak for the usage of PLS in the case of this dissertation.

	PLS-SEM	CB-SEM
Research goals	- For predicting key target constructs or identifying key "driver" constructs - Research is exploratory or an extension of an existing structural theory	Theory testing, theory confirmation, or comparison of alternative theories
Measurement model specification	If formative constructs are part of the structural model. Note that formative measures can also be used with CB-SEM but to do so requires accounting for relatively complex and limiting specification rules.	If error terms require additional specification, such as covariation
Structural model	Complex structural model (many constructs and many indicators)	Nonrecursive model
Data characteristics and algorithm	- Sample size is relatively low - Minimum sample size should be: (1) ten times the largest number of formative indicators used to measure one construct or (2) ten times the largest number of structural paths directed at a particular latent construct in the structural model - Data is to some extent nonnormal	- Data meets the CB-SEM assumptions exactly, e.g. minimum sample size and distributional assumptions - Under normal data conditions, CB-SEM and PLS-SEM results are highly similar, with CB-SEM providing slightly more precise model estimates
Model evaluation	If latent variable scores are needed in subsequent analyses	- If your research requires a global goodness-of-fit criterion - If you need to test for measurement model invariance

Figure 28: Rules of thumb for SEM method decision

Source: Own illustration based on HAIR/RINGLE/SARSTEDT (2011), p. 144.

2.3 Second-order constructs

Theoretical constructs can be measured directly through a set of manifest variables as illustrated in Figure 26 and Figure 27. Alternatively, latent constructs can be conceptualised through multiple dimensions.[775] This is reasonable in case of high abstraction levels.[776] Rather than gathering a high amount of items into one construct

---

[774] Cf. HAIR/RINGLE/SARSTEDT (2011), p. 144.

[775] Cf. WEIBER/MÜHLHAUS (2010), p. 82.

[776] For example the construct brand love is conceptualised as higher-order construct due to its high level of abstractness. Its conceptual structure is built by the dimensions passion-driven behaviours, self-brand integration, positive emotional connection, long-term relationship, anticipated separation distress, overall attitude valence, attitude strength: certainty/confidence. The first three factors again are subdivided into three to four dimensions each. Cf. BATRA/AHUVIA/BAGOZZI (2012), p. 10.

that covers all facets, forming dimensions offers an opportunity to structure sublevels of a theoretical concept.[777] Constructs can be built up to n dimensions. This dissertation only contains second-order constructs, for reasons of simplicity the higher-order constructs will not be included in further debate.

For constructs that contain multiple levels, the discussion whether they are ordered formative or reflective need to be held for each abstraction level.[778] JARVIS/MACKENZIE/PODSAKOFF (2003) distinguish between four types of combinations for second-order models which are shown in Figure 29.

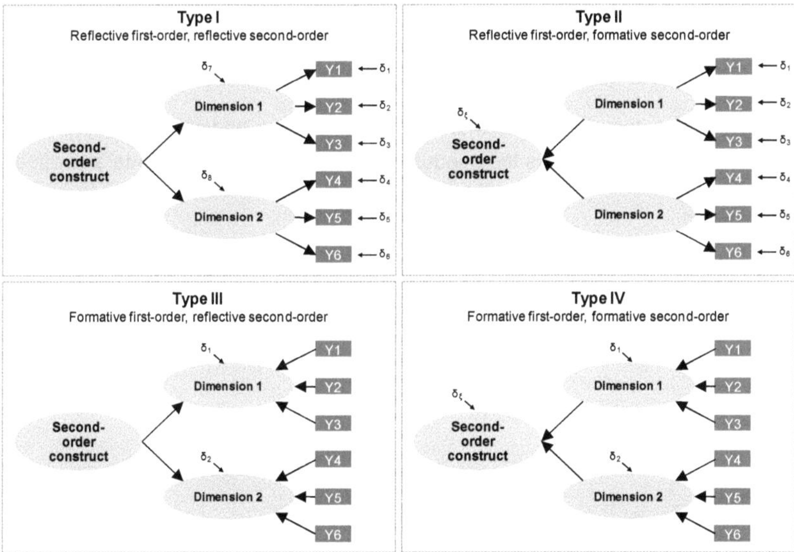

Figure 29: Second-order construct specifications

Source: Own illustration based on JARVIS/MACKENZIE/PODSAKOFF (2003), p. 205.

---

777 Cf. WETZELS/ODEKERKEN-SCHRÖDER/VAN OPPEN (2009), p. 178.

778 Cf. CHIN (1998a), p. 10.

Though ALBERS/GÖTZ (2006) argue that models of type I and III are pointless.[779] Modelling the second-order construct through reflective dimensions does not display the sovereignty of the dimensions. In the case of type I where the specification is reflective on both levels there is no justification for higher-order conceptualisation at all.[780] Reflective operationalisation implies high correlation, which basically means all indicators are interchangeable.[781]

Thus, if there is a raison d'être for autonomous dimensions, they need to be specified formative. Type IV is redundant because they indicators could form the second-order construct directly.[782] It can still be employed for reasons of structure simplification.[783]

2.4 Moderating effects

Moderators are external variables that impact the direction and/or intensity of a causal relation.[784] Figure 30 shows the adequate method for estimating moderator effects in PLS.[785]

---

[779] Cf. ALBERS/GÖTZ (2006), pp. 672 et seq.

[780] Cf. BECKER/KLEIN/WETZELS (2012), p. 363.

[781] Cf. ALBERS/GÖTZ (2006), pp. 672 et seq., cf. BECKER/KLEIN/WETZELS (2012), p. 363.

[782] Cf. ALBERS/GÖTZ (2006), p. 673, cf. PIEHLER (2011), p. 395.

[783] Cf. ALBERS/GÖTZ (2006), p. 673, cf. BECKER/KLEIN/WETZELS (2012), p. 364.

[784] Cf. CHIN/MARCOLIN/NEWSTED (2003), pp. 189 et seqq.

[785] For further details, please read CHIN/MARCOLIN/NEWSTED (2003), pp. 189 et seqq. or PIEHLER (2011), pp. 396 et seqq.

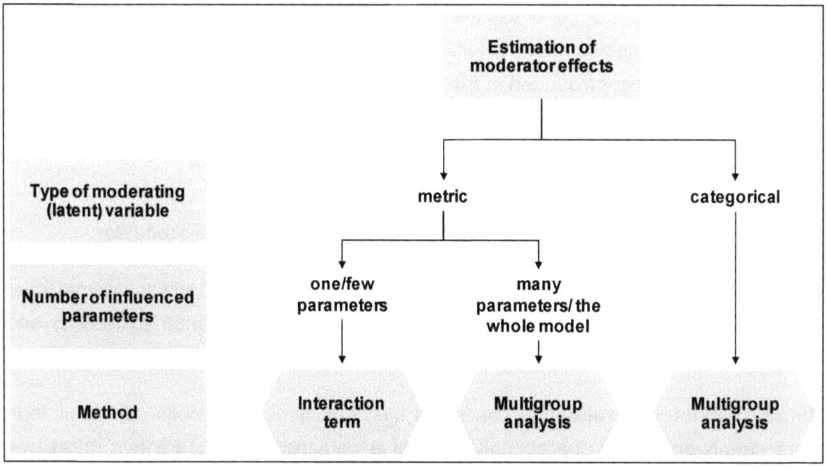

Figure 30: Methods for estimating moderator effects
Source: Based on BRAUNSTEIN (2001), p. 238.

2.5 Quality criteria for PLS structural equation modelling

For the evaluation of appropriateness of the structural equation model, at first it needs to be looked at reliability and validity of the measurement.[786] Reliability is given when independent measurements come to the same results, i.e. repeating measurements are consistent; given the circumstances do not change.[787] Validity is given if the model measures what it is supposed to measure.[788]

The systematic evaluation of the results requires two steps that have to be followed: first, the measurement models have to be assessed, second, the structural model needs to be evaluated.

---

[786] Cf. FINK (2013), p. 10, cf. HULLAND (1999), p. 198.

[787] Cf. HAIR ET AL. (2014b), pp. 96 et seqq.

[788] Cf. HAIR ET AL. (2014b), pp. 96 et seqq.

Within the assessment of the measurement models, the evaluation criteria for reflective and formative specifications differ. As both are used in this empirical study, the relevant criteria will be introduced in the next subchapters.

2.5.1 Evaluation of the measurement models

2.5.1.1 Quality criteria for the evaluation of reflective measurement models

There are four criteria for assessing reflective measurement models: internal consistency, indicator reliability, convergent validity (average variance extracted) and discriminant validity.[789]

Internal consistency reliability measures the consistency of results across all indicators employed in the operationalisation of a construct. There are two measures that express internal consistency: **Cronbach's alpha** and **composite reliability**. The former is traditionally accepted but sensitive to the number of items. For that reason, composite reliability has been introduced as more appropriate. Both measures vary between 0 and 1. Composite reliability values between 0.7 and 0.9 are generally seen as satisfactory[790]; in exploratory research values between 0.6 and 0.7 are within acceptable limits, too. Values above 0.95 show that the items are redundant, whereas below 0.6 indicates lack of internal consistency.[791]

To review the adequacy of each item that is used to measure a construct, **indicator reliability** shall be tested. This can be done by the **indicators' outer loadings**. In general they should lie above 0.7. Indicators with loadings under 0.4 should be eliminated. For those indicators whose outer loadings are between 0.4 and 0.7, it shall be checked whether their elimination improves composite reliability and average variance extracted. Overall, the indicators should be significant.[792]

---

[789] Cf. HAIR/RINGLE/SARSTEDT (2011), pp. 145 et seqq., cf. HAIR ET AL. (2014b), p. 97.

[790] Cf. NUNALLY/BERNSTEIN (1994).

[791] Cf. HAIR ET AL. (2014b), pp. 101 et seq., cf. DIAMANTOPOULOS (2005), pp. 1 et seqq., cf. ROSSITER (2002), pp. 326 et seqq.

[792] Cf. HULLAND (1999), p. 198, cf. HAIR ET AL. (2014b), p. 103; p. 107.

"**Convergent validity** is the extent to which a measure correlates positively with alternative measures of the same construct."[793] With PLS, indicators of a reflective construct are considered as alternative approaches for measuring the same construct. For that reason, indicators of a construct should share a high amount of variance. A measure that is commonly applied to examine convergent validity is **average variance extracted (AVE)**. It displays to which extent the latent construct explains the variance of its indicators. The average variance extracted should lie **above 0.5**. This implies that the construct explains more than half of the variance of its indicators.[794]

To prove the sovereignty of the construct, **discriminant validity** measures the distinction from other constructs in the model. There are two measures that are used to assess discriminant validity. The first is to look at the **cross loadings** of indicators. An indicator's outer loading on a construct should be higher than all its cross loadings on other constructs. Second is **Fornell-Larcker criterion**. The average variance extracted of each construct should be higher than the squared correlation with all other constructs. In other words, this means that a construct and indicators share more variance than with other constructs.[795]

---

[793] HAIR ET AL. (2014b) p. 102.

[794] Cf. HULLAND (1999), p. 199, cf. HAIR ET AL. (2014b), pp. 102 et seqq.

[795] Cf. HULLAND (1999), pp. 199 et seqq., cf. HAIR ET AL. (2014b), pp. 104 et seqq.

Criteria	Values
Internal consistency	Cronbach's alpha > 0.7 Composite reliability > 0.7; in exploratory research composite reliability values between 0.6 and 0.7 are acceptable
Indicator reliability	Outer loadings > 0.7 Indicators with outer loadings < 0.4 shall be eliminated Indicators whose outer loadings are between 0.4 and 0.7, it shall be checked whether their elimination improves composite reliability and average variance extracted Outer loadings should be significant: critical value for 95% significance level t>1.96
Convergent validity	Average variance extracted (AVE) > 0.5
Discriminant validity	An indicator's outer loading on a construct should be higher than all its cross loadings on other constructs. Fornell-Larcker criterion: AVE > max. correlation^2

Table 9: Quality criteria for the evaluation of reflective measurement models
Source: Own illustration based on HAIR ET AL. (2014b), pp. 97 et seqq.

2.5.1.2 Quality criteria for the evaluation of formative measurement models

There are three criteria for the examination of formative measurement models: convergent validity, collinearity among indicators, significance and relevance of outer weights.

In the context of formative measurement models, **convergent validity** is measured differently. In this case, it is examined whether the formatively measured construct is correlated with a reflective measure of the same construct.[796] This analysis is called **redundancy analysis**.[797] The formatively measured construct is used as exogenous construct predicting an endogenous construct measured through one or more reflective indicators.[798] Instead of employing multi-items scales, a global item can also be used as reflective indicator. This would be a compromise to not overstress the questionnaire length.[799] The strength of the path coefficient between exogenous and endogenous constructs is indicative. Ideally, the path coefficient lies above 0.8 with a minimum R^2 value of 0.64.[800]

The second criteria that needs to be checked, is **collinearity among indicators** of the formative construct.[801] With reflective constructs, indicators are expected to highly correlate. With regard to formative measurement models on the contrary, correlation between indicators is problematic. It impacts "the estimation of the weights and their statistical significance."[802] This is referred to as collinearity. If more than two indicators are correlated, it is called multicollinearity.[803] **Tolerance** and the **variance inflation factor (VIF)** show the level of (multi)collinearity. Tolerance values of 0.2 and below and VIF values of 5 or higher are indices for a collinearity issue.[804]

The outer weight delivers information on the contribution of a formative indicator. It is calculated by multiple regression analysis. The latent construct functions as dependent variable, the indicators as independent variables. Comparing the **outer weights** of the indicators delivers insight into which indicator offers most contribution (**relative**

---

[796] Cf. HAIR ET AL. (2014b), pp. 121 et seqq.

[797] Cf. CHIN (1998b), pp. 306 et seqq.

[798] Cf. HAIR ET AL. (2014b), p. 121.

[799] Cf. HAIR ET AL. (2014b), p. 122.

[800] Cf. HAIR ET AL. (2014b), p. 121.

[801] Cf. DIAMANTOPOULOS/WINKLHOFER (2001), p. 272, cf. GOETZ/LIEHR-GOBBERS (2004), p. 729.

[802] HAIR ET AL. (2014b), p. 123.

[803] Cf. HAIR ET AL. (2014b), pp. 123 et seqq.

[804] Cf. HAIR/RINGLE/SARSTEDT (2011), p. 145, cf. HAIR ET AL. (2014b), pp. 123 et seqq.

contribution). **Absolute contribution** of the indicators is represented by the **outer loadings**.[805] The decision process for keeping or deleting a formative indicator is illustrated in Figure 31.

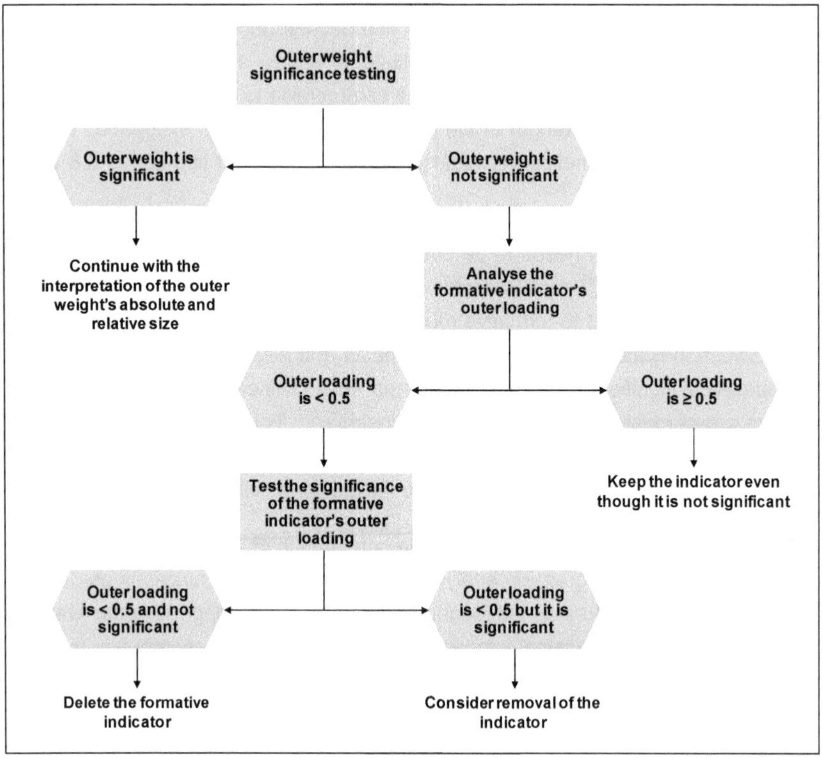

Figure 31: Process for a decision on keeping or deleting formative indicators
Source: Own illustration closely based on HAIR ET AL. (2014b), p. 131.

In summary all quality criteria that should be applied for formative measurement models are captured in Table 10.

---

[805] Cf. HAIR ET AL. (2014b), pp. 123 et seqq.

Criteria	Values
Convergent validity	Redundancy analysis: path coefficient > 0.8 and $R^2 > 0.64$
Collinearity among indicators	Tolerance > 0.2 VIF < 5
Significance and relevance of outer weights	**Keep** formative indicator, if: - Outer weight is significant - Outer weight is not significant, but outer loading ≥ 0.5 - Outer weight is not significant, outer loading < 0.5, but outer loading is significant **Delete** formative indicator, if: - Outer weight is not significant, outer loading < 0.5, outer loading is not significant

Table 10: Quality criteria for the evaluation of formative measurement models
Source: Own illustration based on HAIR ET AL. (2014b), pp. 118 et seqq.

2.5.2 Evaluation of the structural model

Similarly to the measurement models, the structural model needs to be assessed in terms of suitability. There are five relevant criteria: (Multi)collinearity, path coefficients, coefficient of determination R^2, effect size f^2, predictive relevance Q^2.

The assessment of **(multi)collinearity** is analogous to the evaluation of formative measurement models (chapter C 2.5.1.2). Only that in the structural model, the predictor constructs shall not be highly correlated. Again, **tolerance** and **VIF values** need to be considered.[806]

Path coefficients represent the relation between latent constructs in the model. They can have values between -1 and +1, with -1 indicating strong negative and +1 indicating strong positive relationships. The closer the value gets toward 0, the weaker the relation. With the **bootstrapping** routine the path coefficient can be examined regarding its significance. Through bootstrapping, the empirical t-value is computed.[807] If the empirical t-value is bigger than the critical value, the path coefficient is significant, on condition of a certain error probability or respectively significance level. The critical values are 1.65 (significance level = 10%), 1.96 (significance level = 5%), and 2.57 (significance level = 1%). In general, a significance level of 5% is applied in marketing research.[808]

The **coefficient of determination R^2** is a measure that accounts for the proportion of variance of an endogenous construct that is explained by the predictor constructs. The values of the coefficient lie between 0 and 1, whereas 1 is the highest accuracy of explained variance.[809] Generally in academia, R^2 values higher than 0.75 are considered as substantial, R^2 value between 0.5 and 0.75 as moderate, and R^2 value between 0.25 and 0.50 as weak.[810]

To determine the impact of each predictor construct on the endogenous construct, the **effect size f^2** shall be assessed. The relative impact of an exogenous construct can be calculated through the change of the R^2 value when one predictor construct is taken off. Hence, the effect size can be calculated as follows[811]:

---

[806] Cf. HAIR ET AL. (2014b), p. 170.

[807] Cf. GOETZ/LIEHR-GOBBERS (2004), p. 730.

[808] Cf. WEIBER/MÜHLHAUS (2010), p. 256, cf. HAIR ET AL. (2014b), pp. 170 et seqq.

[809] Cf. GOETZ/LIEHR-GOBBERS (2004), p. 730.

[810] Cf. HAIR ET AL. (2014b), pp. 174 et seqq.

[811] Cf. COHEN (1988), pp. 410-413.

$$f^2 = \frac{R^2_{\text{included}} - R^2_{\text{excluded}}}{1 - R^2_{\text{included}}},$$

with R^2_{included} representing the value when one certain predictor construct is included in the model and R^2_{excluded} representing the value when the predictor construct is taken from the model. Threshold values for the effect size are 0.35 for a large effect, f^2 values between 0.15 and 0.35 for a medium effect and values between 0.02 and 0.15 for a small effect.

In addition to R^2 values, the model's **predictive relevance** can be assessed by **Stone-Geisser's Q^2**.[812] Through the blindfolding procedure certain data points of reflective endogenous constructs' indicators are omitted and estimated through the remaining. The difference between true (i.e. omitted) and estimated data points is delivering input for Stone-Geisser's Q^2. Q^2 value shall lie above 0.

Criteria	Values
(Multi)collinearity	Tolerance > 0.2 VIF < 5
Path coefficients	Reach from -1 (strong negative relationship) to +1 (strong positive relationship) **Significant, if** t-value > 1.65 (significance level = 10%) t-value > 1.96 (significance level = 5%) t-value > 2.57 (significance level = 1%)

[812] For more information on the Stone-Geisser criterion, please see FORNELL/CHA (1994), pp. 71-73.

Coefficient of determination R^2	R^2 value ≥ 0.75 = substantial R^2 value ≥ 0.50 but < 0.75 = moderate R^2 value ≥ 0.25 but < 0.50 = weak
Effect size f^2	$0.02 \leq f^2 < 0.15$ = small effect $0.15 \leq f^2 < 0.35$ = medium effect $0.35 \leq f^2$ = large effect
Predictive relevance Q^2	$Q^2 > 0$

Table 11: Quality criteria for the evaluation of the structural model
Source: Own illustration based on HAIR ET AL. (2014b), pp. 167 et seqq.

3 Operationalisation and validation of constructs

3.1 Operationalisation procedure

The latent constructs in the model are unobservable concepts that cannot be measured directly but can be represented through indicating variables.[813] The process of choosing indicators for the latent constructs is called operationalisation. The operationalisation of the latent constructs will be executed as suggested in established academic literature.[814] For the majority of constructs in the model at hand, the generation and classification of potential indicators will be accomplished using established and validated scales from the marketing literature. Those scales are being reviewed regarding measurement conception, item specification and scaling.

---

[813] Cf. HAIR ET AL. (2010), pp. 634 et seq.

[814] Cf. CHURCHHILL (1979), pp. 64 et seqq., cf. STEENKAMP/BAUMGARTNER (2000), pp. 195 et seqq.,

First, the measurement conception has to be determined. For each construct there is an examination whether it is formative or reflective. This will be done following the decision rules by JARVIS/MACKENZIE/PODSAKOFF (2003).[815]

	Formative model	Reflective model
1. Direction of causality from construct to measure implied by the conceptual definition	**Direction of causality is from items to construct**	**Direction of causality is from construct to items**
Are indicators (items) (a) defining characteristics or (b) manifestations of the construct?	Indicators are defining characteristics of the construct	Indicators are manifestations of the construct
Would changes in the indicators/items cause changes in the construct or not?	Changes in the indicators should cause changes in the construct	Changes in the indicator should not cause changes in the construct
Would changes in the construct cause changes in the indicators?	Changes in the construct do not cause changes in the indicators	Changes in the construct do cause changes in the indicators
2. Interchangeability of the indicators/items	**Indicators need not be interchangeable**	**Indicators should be interchangeable**
Should the indicators have the same or similar content? Do the indicators share a common theme?	Indicators need not have the same or similar content / indicators need not share a common theme	Indicators should have the same or similar content / indicators should share a common theme
Would dropping one of the indicators alter the conceptual domain of the construct?	Dropping an indicator may alter the conceptual domain of the construct	Dropping an indicator should not alter the conceptual domain of the construct

[815] Cf. JARVIS/MACKENZIE/PODSAKOFF (2003), p. 203.

3. Covariation among the indicators Should a change in one of the indicators be associated with changes in the other indicators?	**Not necessary for indicators to covary with each other** Not necessarily	**Indicators are expected to covary with each other** Yes
4. Nomological net of the construct indicators Are the indicators/items expected to have the same antecedents and consequences?	**Nomological net for the indicators may differ** Indicators are not required to have the same antecedents and consequences	**Nomological net for the indicators should not differ** Indicators are required to have the same antecedents and consequences

Table 12: Decision rules for formative or reflective construct setup
Source: JARVIS/MACKENZIE/PODSAKOFF (2003), p. 203.

Second, the items respectively indicators for the constructs need to be specified. Constructs can be measured through single-item or multi-item scales.[816] As formative constructs are build on the premise of covering multiple aspects, single-item measurement would not make sense.[817] Therefore in the case of formative measurement models, multi-item scales are typically used. Likewise, in the case of reflective measurement, multi-item scales are more common than single-items.[818] The major advantage is, with providing several items in the questionnaire, random error through false phrasing can be avoided.[819] Further, the level of abstraction is diminished when several facets are not summarised but phrased into different sentences. But there can also be disadvantages, like the respondents fatigue when the questionnaire gets too long through too many items.[820] In this case single-items are useful.[821] Moreover,

[816] Cf. WEIBER/MÜHLHAUS (2010), p. 91.
[817] Cf. FUCHS/DIAMANTOPOULOS (2009), p. 199, cf. MACKENZIE/PODSAKOFF/JARVIS (2005), p. 727.
[818] Cf. WEIBER/MÜHLHAUS (2010), p. 93.
[819] Cf. MACKENZIE/PODSAKOFF/JARVIS (2005), p. 727, cf. WEIBER/MÜHLHAUS (2010), p. 93.
[820] Cf. FUCHS/DIAMANTOPOULOS (2009), p. 204.

when a construct can be reflected through one global item, single-item measurement should be applied.[822]

Third, the type of scale needs to be determined. In social science, four data types are distinguished[823]:

- Nominal data: values that cannot be assigned to any numbers and do not have a certain order, e.g. occupation, hair colour, country of residence.[824]
- Ordinal data: values can be ordered or ranked like a cycling race (first, second, third place and so on) but the distance between the values may vary.[825]
- Interval data: values provide information about the relative position; distance between values can be interpreted, e.g. age, size.[826]
- Ratio data: are the same as interval data, only that they have an interpretable zero point[827]. Examples are number of customers, amount of money spent.[828]

Rating scales[829] are most common in structural equation modelling. Often used is the Likert scale[830] which shall also be employed in this survey. Likert scales typically al-

---

[821] Cf. ROSSITER (2002), p. 313.

[822] Cf. DIAMANTOPOULOS/WINKLHOFER (2001), p. 272, cf. ROSSITER (2002), p. 313, cf. FUCHS/DIAMANTOPOULOS (2009), p. 200.

[823] Cf. SUE/RITTER (2012), p. 68.

[824] Cf. FOWLER (2002), p. 89, cf. SUE/RITTER (2012), p. 68, cf. OLSEN (2012), p. 143.

[825] Cf. FOWLER (2002), p. 89, cf. SUE/RITTER (2012), p. 68, cf. OLSEN (2012), pp. 144 et seq.

[826] Cf. FOWLER (2002), p. 90, cf. SUE/RITTER (2012), p. 68, cf. OLSEN (2012), p. 145.

[827] For example size does not have an interpretable zero point; there is no person that is zero meters tall. Cf. SUE/RITTER (2012), p. 68. Another example would be numbers of rooms in a house; a house without rooms does not exist. Cf. OLSEN (2012), p. 145.

[828] Cf. FOWLER (2002), p. 90, cf. SUE/RITTER (2012), p. 68, cf. OLSEN (2012), pp. 145 et seq.

[829] For structural equations, rating scales are predominantly used. They allow the respondent to subjectively rate the intensity or strength of the attributes regarded. Cf. GREEN/RAO (1970), p. 33, cf. WELLER/ROMNEY (1988), p. 38, cf. WEIBER/MÜHLHAUS (2010), p. 96.

[830] Cf. WEIBER/MÜHLHAUS (2010), p. 97, cf. FINK (2013), p. 45, cf. DAVINO/ROMANO (2013), p. 47.

low respondents to determine their attitude toward a statement.[831] The options provided range from strongly agree to strongly disagree.[832]

There is a discussion in social science whether scales should provide even or odd numbers and how many categories there should be.[833] Even scales have the advantage that respondents need to make a choice whether to take a negative or positive position.[834] They cannot avoid the decision by taking a neutral position. On the other hand, this forces people who are genuinely neutral to take on side and leads to a bias toward positive answers altogether.[835] As this leads to invalid data, the survey executed for this thesis will rely on uneven scales.

Further, a decision on the number of answer categories needs to made. Some researchers argue that 11-point scales provide more detail and greater granularity in information.[836] Others say it overexerts respondents; limited scales make it easier for respondents to choose an answer.[837] Most common are 5-point Likert scales which will be used in this thesis, they balance the granularity needed and at the same time reduce complexity for the respondent.[838]

The next passage will clarify how the statements that reflect the latent constructs will be phrased.

3.2 Operationalisation and evaluation of the construct brand page attachment

Brand page attachment is the central construct of the research model. Chapter B 2.4.2 delivers insights into the conceptualisation of brand page attachment. Analogue

---

[831] Cf. SUE/RITTER (2012), p. 63.

[832] Cf. FINK (2013), p. 45.

[833] Cf. FINK (2013), pp. 44 et seq., cf. SUE/RITTER (2012), pp. 64 et seq., cf. FOWLER (2002), pp.92 et seqq.

[834] Cf. FINK (2013), p. 44.

[835] Cf. SUE/RITTER (2012), p. 64.

[836] Cf. SUE/RITTER (2012), p. 64.

[837] Cf. SUE/RITTER (2012), p. 64.

[838] Cf. FINK (2013), p. 45.

to PARK ET AL. (2010) perception of brand attachment, brand page attachment also consists of two dimensions.[839] The dimensions that form brand page attachment are brand page connectedness and brand page prominence.

The operationalisation of brand page connectedness is inspired by PARK ET AL. (2010) conceptualisation. A few amendments were made to put a stronger focus on the emotional connection between a brand page and the user.[840] The amendments were induced by experts that reviewed the scales.[841] The operationalisation is shown in Table 13.

Label	Items	Source
Attach_1	The brand page of [BRAND] represents who I am.	PARK ET AL. (2010)
Attach_2	I feel emotionally bonded to the brand page of [BRAND].	PARK ET AL. (2010)
Attach_3	I feel personally connected to the brand page of [BRAND].	PARK ET AL. (2010)
Attach_4	There is a special bond that connects me to the brand page of [BRAND].	new
Attach_5	I feel closeness to the brand page of [BRAND].	new

Table 13: Operationalisation of the dimension brand page connectedness
Source: Own illustration.

The operationalisation of brand page prominence will be accomplished following the scale introduced by PARK ET AL. (2010).[842] This scale has been proven empirically in various other studies.[843] The operationalisation of items is provided in Table 14.

---

839 Cf. PARK ET AL. (2010), p. 2.

840 Cf. THOMSON/MACINNIS/PARK (2005), p. 80.

841 Please see chapter C **Fehler! Verweisquelle konnte nicht gefunden werden.**.

842 Cf. PARK ET AL. (2010), p. 6.

843 Cf. MERCHANT/ROSE (2013), cf. MUEHLING/SPROTT/SULTAN (2014), cf. LAM/SHANKAR (2014), cf. CHIOU/HSU/HSIEH (2013).

Label	Items	Source
Attach_6	The thoughts and feelings about the brand page of [BRAND] come to my mind naturally and instantly.	PARK ET AL. (2010)
Attach_7	I often think about the brand page of [BRAND] spontaneously.	Similar to PARK ET AL. (2010)
Attach_8	The thoughts and feelings about the brand page of [BRAND] come to my mind automatically, coming seemingly on their own.	PARK ET AL. (2010)
Attach_9	The brand page of [BRAND] evokes memories.	PARK ET AL. (2010)

Table 14: Operationalisation of the dimension brand page prominence
Source: Own illustration.

Brand page attachment is a second-order construct.[844] It consists of the two dimensions brand page connectedness and brand page prominence. This reflects the structure of the brand attachment construct introduced by PARK ET AL. (2010).[845] However, in the essay of PARK ET AL. (2010) there was no discussion as to whether to structure the construct formative or reflective, a reflective structure was just assumed. Applying the decision rules[846] for construct setup by JARVIS/MACKENZIE/PODSAKOFF (2003) onto the brand page attachment construct, it becomes clear, that the construct has to be conceptualised as a second-order construct Type II.[847] This is due to several reasons which will be debated in the following.

First, the direction of causality is from the two dimensions to the construct of brand page attachment. Both dimensions "form" the construct and are defining characteris-

---

[844] Please see chapter C 2.3 for second-order constructs.

[845] Cf. PARK ET AL. (2010), p. 9.

[846] Cf. JARVIS/MACKENZIE/PODSAKOFF (2003), p. 203, see also chapter C 3.1 where Table 12 illustrates the decision rules for construct setup.

[847] Please see chapter C 2.3 for second-order constructs where Figure 29 shows different types of second-order construct specifications. Type II represents reflective first-order and formative second-order constructs.

tics. Changes to brand page connectedness or brand page prominence will cause changes to brand page attachment.[848] Second, the dimensions are not interchangeable as it is the case with reflective models. The dimensions have dissimilar meanings. If one dimension is spared, it modifies the meaning of the construct brand page attachment altogether.[849] Further, covariation between dimensions of a formative construct is not required.[850]

For the assessment of the formative second-order construct, a global item for brand page attachment will be added to the questionnaire.[851] It is shown in Table 15.

Label	Items	Source
Attach_Glob	Overall, I feel attached to the brand page of [BRAND].	new development

Table 15: Global item to measure brand page attachment
Source: Own illustration.

To validate the two-dimensional formative operationalisation of the construct, an explorative factor analysis will be executed. To check the suitability of the data set for an explorative factor analysis, the KMO[852] criterion has to be bigger than 0.5.[853] With KMO value of 0.944, the data suitability is "marvellous"[854]. Bartlett's test of sphericity was also significant. Further, less than 25% of the non-diagonal values in the anti-image-covariance-matrix shall lie above 0.09.[855] All non-diagonal values are below 0.09, so the data set is suitable for explorative factor analysis.

---

[848] Cf. DIAMANTOPOULOS/WINKLHOFER (2001), pp. 269 et seqq., cf. JARVIS/MACKENZIE/PODSAKOFF (2003), p. 203.

[849] Cf. JARVIS/MACKENZIE/PODSAKOFF (2003), p. 203, cf. PIEHLER (2011), pp. 417 et seq.

[850] Cf. JARVIS/MACKENZIE/PODSAKOFF (2003), p. 203.

[851] Cf. PIEHLER (2011), p. 429.

[852] Kaiser-Meyer-Olkin Kriterium, also MSA which stands for "measure of sampling adequacy" BACKHAUS ET AL. (2011), p. 342.

[853] Cf. BACKHAUS ET AL. (2011), p. 342-343.

[854] BACKHAUS ET AL. (2011), p. 343.

[855] Cf. BACKHAUS ET AL. (2011), p. 342.

According to the literature review it is expected that the scale consists of two dimensions, which would lead to the extraction of two factors. In actual fact, based on the Kaiser criterion[856], there is only one factor that will be extracted; hence the construct brand page attachment is one-dimensional (see Table 16). The factor analysis was executed using the common factor analysis and promax rotation.[857]

Total Variance Explained

Factor	Initial Eigenvalues			Extraction Sums of Squared Loadings		
	Total	% of Variance	Cumulative %	Total	% of Variance	Cumulative %
1	7.140	79.335	79.335	6.917	76.861	76.861
2	.504	5.605	84.940			
3	.441	4.898	89.838			
4	.263	2.927	92.765			
5	.171	1.902	94.667			
6	.158	1.757	96.424			
7	.137	1.523	97.947			
8	.112	1.248	99.196			
9	.072	.804	100.000			

Table 16: **Total variance explained for the construct brand page attachment**
Source: Own illustration.

The factor matrix with factor loadings is shown in Table 17.

[856] According to the Kaiser criterion, factors with eigenvalues > 1 are extracted. Cf. BACKHAUS ET AL. (2011), p. 359.

[857] Cf. PIEHLER (2011), pp. 469 et seqq.

Factor Matrix

	Factor
	1
The brand page of [BRAND] represents who I am.	.839
I feel emotionally bonded to the brand page of [BRAND].	.912
I feel personally connected to the brand page of [BRAND].	.852
There is a special bond that connects me to the brand page of [BRAND].	.934
I feel closeness to the brand page of [BRAND].	.917
The thoughts and feelings about the brand page of [BRAND] come to my mind naturally and instantly.	.756
I often think about the brand page of [BRAND] spontaneously.	.878
The thoughts and feelings about the brand page of [BRAND] come to my mind automatically, coming seemingly on their own.	.889
The brand page of [BRAND] evokes memories.	.899

Table 17: Factor matrix for the construct brand page attachment
Source: Own illustration.

The question occurs why the construct of brand *page* attachment is one-dimensional in contrast to the two-dimensional brand attachment construct. In the context of brand pages, the two dimensions connectedness and prominence are linked closely to each other. The reason lies in the nature of brand pages and their usage intensity. On average people go on Facebook once or a few times every day (compare Figure 25). Therefore those brand pages that users are really fond of, are always prominent. Hence, high prominence of a brand page automatically means that a person is emotionally and mentally connected. Still, both facets are important for brand page attachment as prominence indicates the strength or intensity of connectedness. In contrast, for the construct of brand attachment, there can be a high connectedness to a brand without high the brand being highly prominent. This applies in the context of brands that are bought infrequently, like cars or luxury goods.

After determining the dimensionality of the construct, the quality criteria for measurement models as inferred in chapter C 2.5.1 will be checked. As shown in Table 18, all model evaluation criteria are fully met and provide support for the reliability and validity of the measurement.

Indicator	Item level (indicator reliability)		Construct level			
	Outer loadings > 0.4	Significance: t>1.96	Cronbach's alpha > 0.7	Internal consistency: composite reliability > 0.7	Convergent validity: AVE > 0.5	Discriminant validity: AVE > max correlation²
Attach_1	0.861	66.6789				
Attach_2	0.919	132.9987				
Attach_3	0.872	85.1268				
Attach_4	0.936	155.5650				
Attach_5	0.924	126.0983	0.9671	0.9718	0.7933	Yes
Attach_6	0.893	77.0771				
Attach_7	0.901	107.1323				
Attach_8	0.909	117.0851				
Attach_9	0.792	40.7995				

Table 18: Quality criteria for the reflective measurement model of the construct brand page attachment

Source: Own illustration.

3.3 Operationalisation and evaluation of the antecedent constructs

For most constructs validated scales will be employed. These are deduced from literature in chapter B.

The brand page-related antecedents have been investigated in a pre-study that was carried out in early 2012 as explained in chapter B 3.[858] For each construct, a list of items was generated from a thorough literature review.[859] Wherever possible, estab-

---

858 Cf. KLEINE-KALMER/BURMANN/SCHADE (2013), cf. KLEINE-KALMER/BURMANN (2013b), cf. [=195 - Kleine-Kalmer 2013 Uses and Gratificati...=].

859 Cf. KLEINE-KALMER/BURMANN/SCHADE (2013), cf. KLEINE-KALMER/BURMANN (2013b), cf. KLEINE-KALMER/BURMANN (2013a).

lished and validated scales were preferred over new scale development. The scales were reviewed in expert interviews and empirically validated through the pre-study.[860]

Construct	Label	Items	Source
Information and service	Info_1	The brand page of [BRAND] helps me to learn about unknown things.	based on KO/CHO/ROBERTS (2005)
	Info_2	Looking at the brand page of [BRAND] is a good way to do research.	based on KO/CHO/ROBERTS (2005)
	Info_3	The brand page of [BRAND] helps me to learn about useful things.	based on KO/CHO/ROBERTS (2005)
	Info_4	The brand page of [BRAND] lets me use the service that is provided by [BRAND].	KLEINE-KALMER/BURMANN (2013a)
Entertainment	Ent_1	The brand page of [BRAND] is fun to watch or read.	based on TAYLOR/LEWIN/STRUTTON (2011)
	Ent_2	The brand page of [BRAND] is clever and quite entertaining.	based on TAYLOR/LEWIN/STRUTTON (2011)
	Ent_3	The brand page of [BRAND] does not just sell – it also entertains me.	based on TAYLOR/LEWIN/STRUTTON (2011)
	Ent_4	The brand page of [BRAND] is often amusing.	based on TAYLOR/LEWIN/STRUTTON (2011)

[860] Please see chapter B **Fehler! Verweisquelle konnte nicht gefunden werden.**.

[861] BACKHAUS ET AL. (2011), p. 343.

Social value	Soc_1	I believe a chat among like-minded people on the brand page of [BRAND] is a nice thing.	based on HENNIG-THURAU ET AL. (2004)
	Soc_2	It is fun to communicate with other people on the brand page of [BRAND].	based on HENNIG-THURAU ET AL. (2004)
	Soc_3	I meet nice people on the brand page of [BRAND].	based on HENNIG-THURAU ET AL. (2004)
Economic incentive	Eco_1	I receive incentives through the brand page of [BRAND].	based on HENNIG-THURAU ET AL. (2004)
	Eco_2	I receive a reward through the brand page of [BRAND].	based on HENNIG-THURAU ET AL. (2004)
	Eco_3	The brand page of [BRAND] offers me advantages that others do not have.	KLEINE-KALMER/BURMANN (2013a)

Table 19: Operationalisation of antecedents
Source: Own illustration.

An explorative factor analysis will be executed to verify the discrimination of the determinants. Again, the suitability of the data set for an explorative factor analysis will be checked first. The KMO criterion lies at 0.931, so the data suitability is "marvellous"[861]. Bartlett's test of sphericity was also significant. Further, all non-diagonal values are below 0.09, so the data set is suitable for explorative factor analysis.[862]

---

[861] BACKHAUS ET AL. (2011), p. 343.

[862] Cf. BACKHAUS ET AL. (2011), p. 342.

The factor analysis was executed using the common factor analysis and promax rotation.[863] According to the Kaiser criterion[864] three factors are extracted (see Table 20).

Total Variance Explained

Factor	Initial Eigenvalues			Extraction Sums of Squared Loadings			Rotation Sums of Squared Loadings
	Total	% of Variance	Cumulative %	Total	% of Variance	Cumulative %	Total
1	8.329	59.494	59.494	8.066	57.611	57.611	7.234
2	1.551	11.079	70.573	1.326	9.475	67.086	5.410
3	1.048	7.488	78.062	.875	6.251	73.337	6.100
4	.788	5.628	83.689				
5	.383	2.736	86.425				
6	.358	2.555	88.980				
7	.281	2.004	90.984				
8	.263	1.875	92.859				
9	.224	1.597	94.457				
10	.215	1.533	95.990				
11	.182	1.299	97.290				
12	.155	1.108	98.398				
13	.144	1.027	99.425				
14	.081	.575	100.000				

Table 20: **Total variance explained for determinants factor analysis**
Source: Own illustration.

Unlike the pre-study and literature review, two factors are combined. Table 21 is showing the allocation of items. In the factor analysis, the two determinants information & service and entertainment merge. This can be justified as informational content on Facebook brand pages can often be amusing or entertaining. This delivers a reasonable explanation of why the two facets highly correlate and load onto one factor. For the structural model, the two facets will be merged into the determinant *infotainment*.

---

863 Cf. PIEHLER (2011), pp. 469 et seqq.

864 According to the Kaiser criterion, factors with eigenvalues > 1 are extracted. Cf. BACKHAUS ET AL. (2011), p. 359.

	Factor		
	1	2	3
Information_1	.656		
Information_2	.700		
Information_3	.700		
Information_4	.581		
Entertainment_1	.834		
Entertainment_2	.891		
Entertainment_3	.870		
Entertainment_4	.787		
Social Value_1			.894
Social Value_2			.990
Social Value_3			.824
Economic Incentive_1		.893	
Economic Incentive_1		.939	
Economic Incentive_1		.880	

Table 21: **Factor analysis for the determinants**
Source: Own illustration.

The quality criteria for the determinant constructs are fully met as shown in Table 22.

Indicator	Item level (indicator reliability)		Construct level			
	Outer loadings > 0.4	Significance: t>1.96	Cronbach's alpha > 0.7	Internal consistency: composite reliability > 0.7	Convergent validity: AVE > 0.5	Discriminant validity: AVE > max correlation²
Info_1	0.7568	38.4746	0.9310	0.9431	0.6747	Yes
Info_2	0.8396	62.4054				
Info_3	0.8444	61.1745				
Info_4	0.8189	54.1714				
Info_5	0.8202	55.6569				
Info_6	0.8491	63.3698				
Info_7	0.8145	42.5266				
Info_8	0.8245	53.9749				
Soc_1	0.9536	195.3088	0.9546	0.9706	0.9168	Yes
Soc_2	0.9709	306.4073				
Soc_3	0.9478	155.5387				
Eco_1	0.9295	127.4445	0.9347	0.9582	0.8843	Yes
Eco_2	0.9508	161.4694				
Eco_3	0.9407	120.9878				

Table 22: **Quality criteria for the reflective measurement models of the determinant constructs**
Source: Own illustration.

3.4 Operationalisation and evaluation of behavioural consequences

The behavioural consequences are deduced from literature. They all represent consumer sacrifices in favour of the brand. As the research field of social media is still in early stages[865], there are only few established scales.[866] Wherever possible, items that have been validated empirically in the context of social media are employed. If there are no established scales available, it is recommended to build on expert opinions.[867] For this purpose, experts from the background of social media, digital analytics within the FMCG industry as well as members of the Chair of innovative Brand Management were invited to review items from established scales and newly developed items.[868]

This procedure was applied to the constructs investing time reading and observing, brand page participation, co-creation of value and meaning and intention to maintain connection. The construct willingness to share personal data was validated by SMIT/BRONNER/TOLBOOM (2007).[869] The scale for word-of-mouth was adapted from JAHN/KUNZ (2012) who found that brand page participation would increase brand loyalty and eventually increase positive word-of-mouth.[870]

---

[865] Cf. TAYLOR/LEWIN/STRUTTON (2011), p. 271.

[866] Cf. EILERS (2014), p. 17.

[867] Cf. WEIBER (2010) , p. 88, cf. SCHLEGL (2010), p. 65.

[868] Cf. ROSSITER (2002), p. 319.

[869] Cf. SMIT/BRONNER/TOLBOOM (2007), p. 630.

[870] Cf. JAHN/KUNZ (2012), p. 353.

Construct	Label	Items	Source
Brand page participation	Partic_1	I often click "like" when I see posts [BRAND] publishes.	based on GUMMERUS ET AL. (2012), DARWELL (2012) and KLEINE-KALMER/BURMANN (2013a)
	Partic_2	I often "like" posts other users post on the brand page.	deduced from expert interviews
	Partic_3	I often comment on posts published by [BRAND].	based on GUMMERUS ET AL. (2012), DARWELL (2012) and KLEINE-KALMER/BURMANN (2013a)
	Partic_4	I comment on posts published by other users.	based on EILERS (2014)
	Partic_5	I share posts published by [BRAND] within my network of friends and acquaintances.	based on DARWELL (2012) and KLEINE-KALMER/BURMANN (2013a)
	Partic_6	I share posts published by other users about [BRAND] within my network of friends and acquaintances.	based on EILERS (2014)
	Partic_7	I often take part in raffles provided by [BRAND] on its brand page.	deduced from expert interviews
Co-creation of value and meaning	CoCre_1	I often write posts about [BRAND] on its brand page.	based on EILERS (2014)
	CoCre_2	I often provide pictures about [BRAND] on its brand page.	based on KLEINE-KALMER/BURMANN (2013a)
	CoCre_3	I often create videos about [BRAND].	based on KLEINE-KALMER/BURMANN (2013a)

Willingness to share personal data	DemoData_1-5 and PersData_1-5	How likely are you going to provide personal data on the brand page of [BRAND]? (Very likely=5, not likely at all=1) Categories: age, profession, education, family status, hobbies, e-mail, address, phone number, income, credit card details	based on SMIT/BRONNER/TOLBOOM (2007)
Intention to maintain connection	Maintain_1	I plan to continue using the brand page of [BRAND].	based on EISENBEISS ET AL. (2012) who cite DAVIS (1989) and LIN (2006)
	Maintain_2	I plan to continue read posts that [BRAND] publishes on its brand page.	deduced from expert interviews
	Maintain_3	In the future, I want to be informed of posts by [BRAND] in my newsfeed.	deduced from expert interviews
	Maintain_4	I intend to visit the brand page of [BRAND] in the future.	based on EISENBEISS ET AL. (2012) who cite DAVIS (1989) and LIN (2006)
	Maintain_5	I will not "dislike" the brand page of [BRAND].	deduced from expert interviews
Word-of-mouth	WOM_1	I recommend this brand page to my friends and acquaintances.	based on JAHN/KUNZ (2012)
	WOM_2	I introduce the brand page to other people.	based on JAHN/KUNZ (2012)
	WOM_3	I say positive things about this brand page to other people.	based on JAHN/KUNZ (2012)

Table 23: Operationalisation of behavioural consequences
Source: Own illustration.

An explorative factor analysis will be executed to verify the discrimination of the behavioural consequences. The suitability of the data set for an explorative factor analysis will be checked first. The KMO criterion lies at 0.944, so the data suitability is "marvellous"[871]. Bartlett's test of sphericity was also significant. Further, all non-diagonal values are below 0.09, so the data set is suitable for explorative factor analysis.[872]

The factor analysis was executed using the common factor analysis and promax rotation.[873] According to the Kaiser criterion[874] four factors are extracted (see Table 24).

871 BACKHAUS ET AL. (2011), p. 343.

872 Cf. BACKHAUS ET AL. (2011), p. 342.

873 Cf. PIEHLER (2011), pp. 469 et seqq.

874 According to the Kaiser criterion, factors with eigenvalues > 1 are extracted. Cf. BACKHAUS ET AL. (2011), p. 359.

Total Variance Explained

Factor	Initial Eigenvalues			Extraction Sums of Squared Loadings			Rotation Sums of Squared Loadings
	Total	% of Variance	Cumulative %	Total	% of Variance	Cumulative %	Total
1	13.251	47.324	47.324	12.991	46.397	46.397	11.530
2	3.500	12.502	59.826	3.259	11.639	58.035	7.709
3	3.132	11.185	71.011	2.867	10.240	68.275	7.667
4	1.516	5.416	76.426	1.271	4.541	72.816	6.410
5	.856	3.057	79.483				
6	.739	2.638	82.121				
7	.699	2.496	84.618				
8	.533	1.905	86.523				
9	.375	1.340	87.863				
10	.342	1.220	89.083				
11	.312	1.115	90.198				
12	.290	1.036	91.234				
13	.277	.989	92.224				
14	.223	.798	93.021				
15	.219	.781	93.802				
16	.205	.732	94.535				
17	.182	.651	95.186				
18	.175	.626	95.812				
19	.160	.571	96.383				
20	.158	.566	96.949				
21	.137	.491	97.440				
22	.129	.461	97.900				
23	.126	.451	98.351				
24	.111	.396	98.747				
25	.108	.387	99.134				
26	.103	.367	99.501				
27	.079	.281	99.782				
28	.061	.218	100.000				

Table 24: Total variance explained for behavioural consequences factor analysis
Source: Own illustration.

The initial five factors are diminished to four in the factor analysis. Table 25 illustrates the structure of item loadings onto the factors. The factor analysis reveals that the items that have been originally conceptualised to measure participation, co creation and WOM all load onto one factor (factor one). Looking at the content of the items, all statements commonly measure activities that users undertake in relation to or on the brand page. Hence, the three concepts can be summarised under the umbrella construct *user activity regarding brand page*.

The items for the factor intention to maintain connection load onto one factor as expected, so this construct is uni-dimensional.

Noteworthy is the division of the factor willingness to share data. This factor breaks up into two, so apparently there are two facets inherent. The first factor measures the willingness to share data like age, profession, education, family status, hobbies. These are all demographic data that cannot be traced back to a certain individual. The factor will be labelled *willingness to share demographic data*. On the other hand, the second factor measures the willingness to share data like e-mail, address, phone number, income, credit card details. These data are personalised and therefore highly private. According to the factor analysis, users differentiate between sharing individualised and non-individualised data. Hence, the second factor will be researched separately and labelled *willingness to share personal data.*

	Factor			
	1	2	3	4
Participation_1	.681			
Participation_2	.911			
Participation_3	.949			
Participation_4	.975			
Participation_5	.947			
Participation_6	.997			
Participation_7	.405			
CoCreation_1	.799			
CoCreation_2	.740			
CoCreation_3	.676			
WOM_1	.666			
WOM_2	.749			
WOM_3	.688			
Maintain connection_1		.914		
Maintain connection_2		.929		
Maintain connection_3		.819		
Maintain connection_4		.915		
Maintain connection_5		.878		
Share demographic data_1			.827	
Share demographic data_2			.885	
Share demographic data_3			.866	
Share demographic data_4			.884	
Share demographic data_5			.736	
Share personal data_1				.529
Share personal data_2				.814
Share personal data_3				.907
Share personal data_4				.752
Share personal data_5				.828

Table 25: Factor analysis for the behavioural consequences

Source: Own illustration.

All four constructs of the behavioural consequences fulfil the requirements of the quality criteria. This is demonstrated in Table 26.

Indicator	Item level (indicator reliability)		Construct level			
	Outer loadings > 0.4	Significance: t>1.96	Cronbach's alpha > 0.7	Internal consistency: composite reliability > 0.7	Convergent validity: AVE > 0.5	Discriminant validity: AVE > max correlation²
Activ_1	0.8002	47.8164	0.9626	0.9672	0.6964	Yes
Activ_2	0.8920	99.9177				
Activ_3	0.9059	103.0296				
Activ_4	0.9065	108.3452				
Activ_5	0.9009	102.4712				
Activ_6	0.9109	113.5708				
Activ_7	0.5922	18.7094				
Activ_8	0.8265	55.2602				
Activ_9	0.8032	45.4942				
Activ_10	0.7366	35.2613				
Activ_11	0.8193	51.5107				
Activ_12	0.8626	70.4423				
Activ_13	0.8345	55.8206				
Maintain_1	0.9178	95.1654	0.9497	0.9612	0.8323	Yes
Maintain_2	0.9491	169.6077				
Maintain_3	0.9089	110.6099				
Maintain_4	0.9379	138.6274				
Maintain_5	0.8440	39.3845				
DemoData_1	0.8525	50.2557	0.9353	0.9506	0.7940	Yes
DemoData_2	0.9074	87.926				
DemoData_3	0.9108	81.009				
DemoData_4	0.9160	100.4771				
DemoData_5	0.8667	69.2064				
PersData_1	0.7436	29.9365	0.9055	0.9300	0.7275	Yes
PersData_2	0.8610	41.6493				
PersData_3	0.9220	79.8097				
PersData_4	0.8778	44.8286				
PersData_5	0.8501	35.904				

Table 26: **Quality criteria for the reflective measurement models of the behavioural consequences constructs**

Source: Own illustration.

3.5 Operationalisation and evaluation of moderating constructs

Moderator scales were also deduced from the extensive literature review. Established scales are employed to measure the moderator constructs. Propensity to interact was validated by WIERTZ/DE RUYTER (2007) who identified online interaction propensity to be a significant moderator for community participation.[875] Privacy concerns have been researched in a social media context by TAYLOR/LEWIN/STRUTTON (2011). The authors proved a negative effect from privacy concern on the attitude toward advertisements in social media.[876]

Construct	Label	Items	Source
Propensity to interact	Int_1	In general, I like to get involved in online discussions.	based on WIERTZ/DE RUYTER (2007)
	Int_2	I am someone who enjoys interacting with like-minded others online.	based on WIERTZ/DE RUYTER (2007)
	Int_3	I am someone who likes actively participating in online discussions.	based on WIERTZ/DE RUYTER (2007)
	Int_4	In general, I thoroughly enjoy exchanging ideas with other people online.	based on WIERTZ/DE RUYTER (2007)

[875] Cf. WIERTZ/DE RUYTER (2007), p. 369.

[876] Cf. TAYLOR/LEWIN/STRUTTON (2011), p. 267.

Privacy concerns *items coded reversely*	Priv_1	I feel secure in providing sensitive information to the SNS Web site.*	based on TAYLOR/LEWIN/STRUTTON (2011) who cite WOLFINBARGER/GILLY (2003)
	Priv_2	I feel the SNS Web site will keep my personal details private.*	based on TAYLOR/LEWIN/STRUTTON (2011) who cite WOLFINBARGER/GILLY (2003)
	Priv_3	I feel secure in posting personal information on my SNS pages.*	based on TAYLOR/LEWIN/STRUTTON (2011) who cite WOLFINBARGER/GILLY (2003)

Table 27: Operationalisation of moderators
Source: Own illustration.

An explorative factor analysis will be executed to verify the discrimination of the moderator constructs. The suitability of the data set for an explorative factor analysis will be checked first. The KMO criterion lies at 0.851, so the data suitability is "meritorious"[877]. Bartlett's test of sphericity was also significant. Further, all non-diagonal values are below 0.09, so the data set is suitable for explorative factor analysis. [878]

The factor analysis was executed using the common factor analysis and promax rotation.[879] According to the Kaiser criterion[880] two factors are extracted (see Table 28).

---

[877] BACKHAUS ET AL. (2011), p. 343.

[878] Cf. BACKHAUS ET AL. (2011), p. 342.

[879] Cf. PIEHLER (2011), pp. 469 et seqq.

[880] According to the Kaiser criterion, factors with eigenvalues > 1 are extracted. Cf. BACKHAUS ET AL. (2011), p. 359.

Total Variance Explained

Factor	Initial Eigenvalues			Extraction Sums of Squared Loadings			Rotation Sums of Squared Loadings
	Total	% of Variance	Cumulative %	Total	% of Variance	Cumulative %	Total
1	4.333	61.904	61.904	4.142	59.171	59.171	3.706
2	1.695	24.209	86.113	1.503	21.470	80.642	3.072
3	.279	3.990	90.103				
4	.228	3.251	93.354				
5	.178	2.536	95.890				
6	.157	2.244	98.135				
7	.131	1.865	100.000				

Table 28: **Total variance explained for moderator factor analysis**
Source: Own illustration.

The two moderators privacy concerns and propensity to interact were inferred from literature.[881] Established scales that were validated empirically have been used for this study. The two moderators load on two factors which discriminates the construct privacy concerns from the construct propensity to interact.

	Factor	
	1	2
Interaction propensity_1	.850	
Interaction propensity_2	.923	
Interaction propensity_3	.930	
Interaction propensity_4	.877	
Privacy concerns_1		.858
Privacy concerns_2		.909
Privacy concerns_3		.924

Table 29: **Factor analysis for the moderators**
Source: Own illustration

The quality criteria for the moderator constructs are fully met. Table 30 shows the quality criteria for the two moderators.

[881] Cf. TAYLOR/LEWIN/STRUTTON (2011), p. 267, cf. WIERTZ/DE RUYTER (2007), p. 369.

Indicator	Item level (indicator reliability)		Construct level			
	Outer loadings > 0.4	Significance: t>1.96	Cronbach's alpha > 0.7	Internal consistency: composite reliability > 0.7	Convergent validity: AVE > 0.5	Discriminant validity: AVE > max correlation²
Int_1	0.9107	108.5354	0.9423	0.9586	0.8526	Yes
Int_2	0.9265	93.6432				
Int_3	0.9471	191.6245				
Int_4	0.9087	82.9352				
Priv_1	0.9247	96.9308	0.9258	0.9528	0.8707	Yes
Priv_2	0.9292	101.6577				
Priv_3	0.9457	150.3102				

Table 30: **Quality criteria for the reflective measurement models of the moderator constructs**
Source: Own illustration

On the basis of the factor analyses, amendments to the constructs and overall structural model are necessary. The final research model is illustrated in Figure 32.

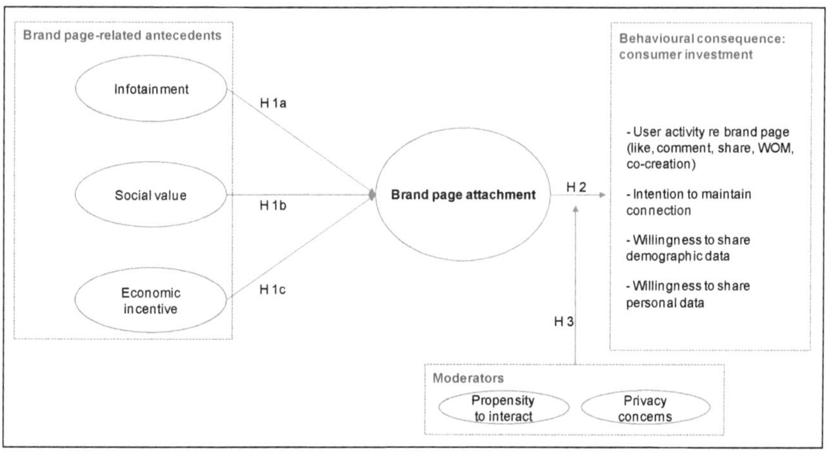

Figure 32: **Final research model**
Source: Own illustration.

According to the amendments in the model, the hypotheses have to be slightly amended. The hypotheses are subdivided into three sections: antecedents of brand page attachment, consequences of brand page attachment and moderators between brand page attachment and behavioural consequences.

H 1a	The benefit of infotainment positively impacts brand page attachment.
H 1b	The benefit of social value positively impacts brand page attachment.
H 1c	The benefit of economic incentives positively impacts brand page attachment.

Table 31: **Final research hypotheses regarding antecedents of brand page attachment**
Source: Own illustration.

H 2a	Brand page attachment positively impacts the user activity regarding the brand page.
H 2b	Brand page attachment positively impacts the willingness to share demographic data with the brand.
H 2c	Brand page attachment positively impacts the willingness to share personal data with the brand.
H 2d	Brand page attachment positively impacts the intention to maintain the connection to the brand page.

Table 32: **Final research hypotheses regarding consequences of brand page attachment**
Source: Own illustration.

H 3a	Users' propensity to interact is moderating the causal relation between brand page attachment and its behavioural consequences: (i) user activity regarding the brand page.
H 3b	Privacy concerns are moderating the causal relation between brand page attachment and its behavioural consequences: (ii) user activity regarding the brand page (iii) willingness to share demographic data (iv) willingness to share personal data.

Table 33: **Final research hypotheses regarding moderators between brand page attachment and behavioural consequences**
Source: Own illustration.

4 Analysis of the structural model

4.1 Evaluation of inner model

The aim of this chapter is to test the cause-effect relationships of the structural model. The path coefficients of the relations are displayed in Figure 33.

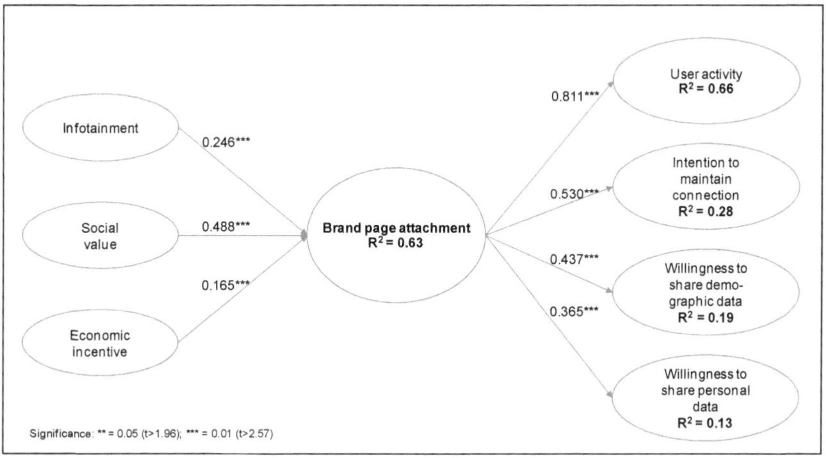

Figure 33: **Path coefficients and R^2 values for cause-effect relationships**
Source: Own illustration.

All path coefficients are significant on a 1% level and directed as postulated. The Q^2 values are bigger than zero and the quality criteria for f^2 statistics apply, too. There is no problem of (multi)collinearity as tolerance values are above 0.2 and VIF are less than 5. All quality criteria for the structural model are illustrated in Table 34.

Structural path	Path coefficient	Significance: t>1.96 (5%) t>2.57 (1%)	R^2>0.25	f^2>0.02	Q^2>0
Infotainment → Brand page attachment	0.2461	6.1534	0.6328	0.075	0.499
Social value → Brand page attachment	0.4884	12.1749	0.6328	0.302	0.499
Economic incentive → Brand page attachment	0.1648	5.0311	0.6328	0.046	0.499
Brand page attachment → User activity re brand page	0.8113	50.8282	0.6582	[a]	0.452
Brand page attachment → Maintain connection	0.5304	18.2419	0.2813	[a]	0.227
Brand page attachment → Willingness to share demographic data	0.4374	12.2041	0.1913	[a]	0.148
Brand page attachment → Willingness to share personal data	0.3650	11.1016	0.1332	[a]	0.094

[a] Measure can only be applied if there is more than one predictor

Table 34: Quality criteria for structural model

Source: Own illustration.

The weak R^2 values of the two constructs willingness to share demographic and personal data can be explained by brand page attachment being the only determinant of the constructs. Further, there are moderating effects postulated, which will be evaluated later. The R^2 value of the construct willingness to share demographic data is weak, but just about exceeds acceptable limits.[882] The only issue is the weak R^2 value of the construct willingness to share personal data. Hence, the hypothesis for this structural path can not be confirmed. It can neither be rejected due to the highly significant path coefficient. All other hypothesis that relate to the determinants and behavioural consequences of brand page attachment can be confirmed.

[882] CHIN (1998b) describes values above 0.19 as weak, above 0.33 as average and above 0.67 as substantial. Cf. CHIN (1998b), p. 316.

H 1a	The benefit of infotainment positively impacts brand page attachment.	confirmed
H 1b	The benefit of social value positively impacts brand page attachment.	confirmed
H 1c	The benefit of economic incentives positively impacts brand page attachment.	confirmed
H 2a	Brand page attachment positively impacts the user activity regarding the brand page.	confirmed
H 2b	Brand page attachment positively impacts the willingness to share demographic data with the brand.	confirmed
H 2c	Brand page attachment positively impacts the willingness to share personal data with the brand.	not rejected
H 2d	Brand page attachment positively impacts the intention to maintain the connection to the brand page.	confirmed

The overall explained variance of the brand attachment construct lies at 63% which is a solid value.[883] It is noteworthy to point out the different intensities of the determining effects on brand page attachment. The strongest effect from a determinant to brand page attachment is social value. This implies that users become most attached to the brand page if they enjoy communicating to others on the brand page. Other studies identified information or entertainment to have the strongest impact on the attitude toward a brand page.[884] The different findings results from the theoretical differences between the constructs attachment and attitude. While attitude is conceptualised as an evaluative construct, attachment contains more emotional components.[885] Hence, the relations to other people become more important when measuring the impact on brand page attachment. On the contrary, if a person is asked to evaluate the brand page, the functional content has a bigger impact. The rationale why brand page at-

[883] Cf. CHIN (1998b), p. 316.

[884] Cf. KLEINE-KALMER/BURMANN (2013b), cf. JAHN/KUNZ (2014), p. 353.

[885] Cf. PARK ET AL. (2010), p. 3, cf. MIKULINCER/SHAVER (2007).

tachment is superior to attitude has been provided theoretically in chapter B 2.3.1. The empiric proof will be delivered later in chapter C 4.4. The analysis in chapter C 4.4 will show that brand page attachment is a better predictor for behavioural consequences.

The postulated impact of brand page attachment on consumer behaviour can be verified in all cases except the willingness to share personal data which has to be re-examined with regard to the moderating effects. The construct user activity on brand pages which comprises the facets participation, WOM and recommendation of the brand page rises with an increase in brand page attachment. So if brand managers want to increase the activity on the brand page, they have to first work on the attachment to the brand page. Accordingly, higher attached users are more likely to maintain the connection to the brand via social media and are also willing to share demographic data within the brand page. In sum, brand page attachment is a valid predictor for consumer investments in favour of the brand.

4.2 Evaluation of moderating effects

The next step is the evaluation of moderating effects. Moderators are external variables that impact the direction and/or intensity of a causal relation.[886] In the case of this study, the intensity of the relation between brand page attachment and its consequences is hypothesised to be moderated by two constructs: privacy concerns and a user's propensity to interact. As per chapter C 2.4, the significance of the moderating effect will be computed via interaction term.

---

[886] Cf. CHIN/MARCOLIN/NEWSTED (2003), pp. 189 et seqq.

Exogenous construct	Endogenous construct	Path coefficient	Significance: t>1.96 (5%) t>2.57 (1%)	f^2>0.02	R^2
ATTACH*INT	ACT	0.098	4.147	0.112	0.740
ATTACH*PRIV	ACT	0.053	1.905	0.062	0.740
ATTACH*PRIV	DEMODATA	0.003	0.082	0.056	0.234
ATTACH*PRIV	PERSDATA	0.128	2.678	0.228	0.294

Table 35: Quality criteria for moderating effects
Source: Own illustration.

Table 35 shows the quality criteria for moderating effects. The t-values reveal that only two of the four postulated effects are significant. First, the effect of brand page attachment on activity on the brand page is moderated through a user's propensity to interact. Those followers of a brand page that are extrovert and outgoing are more likely to interact with the brand posts. They also tend to create content themselves and recommend the brand page to others. Consequently, hypothesis H 3a can be supported. Hence, this is an important insight into why rating the brand page on the basis of its engagement rate or the intensity of participation on a brand page might be misleading. The level of interactivity also depends on the user personality of the followers.

The second significant effect moderates the relation between brand page attachment and the willingness to share personal data. This relation is moderated through privacy concerns. Hypothesis H 3b(iii) is consequently validated. This implies that brand page attachment is a predictor for the willingness to share personal data on a brand page. But if the user is generally concerned about omitting her/his data, this effect is weakened.

The other two postulated moderating effects did not turn out to be significant. Users privacy concerns do not seem to affect the relation between brand page attachment and user activity. The level of user activity is more related to the interaction propensity rather than privacy concerns. This implies the rejection of hypothesis H 3b(i). The willingness to share demographic data on the brand page is determined through brand page attachment and not moderated at all. So H 3b (ii) is rejected, too. So here it can be concluded that the higher the attachment to a brand page, the more likely a user will share her/his demographic data. With personal data this is only the case, when users do not have a problem with giving away their personal details in general.

H 3a	Users' propensity to interact is moderating the causal relation between brand page attachment and its behavioural consequences: (i) user activity regarding the brand page.	 confirmed
H 3b	Privacy concerns are moderating the causal relation between brand page attachment and its behavioural consequences: (i) user activity regarding the brand page (ii) willingness to share demographic data (iii) willingness to share personal data.	 rejected rejected confirmed

4.3 Differences between industry types

For the evaluation of brand pages, currently the average page engagement rate functions as one of the key indicators for measuring the success of Facebook brand pages. The engagement rate is calculated as[887]:

$$Post\ engagement\ rate = \frac{\#\ of\ Likes + Comments + Shares\ on\ a\ given\ day}{Total\ \#\ of\ Fans\ on\ a\ given\ day}$$

High density of interaction is associated with success. Benchmarking this metric is difficult though, as the engagement rate varies immensely. While automotive pages have engagement rates of 0.86%, finance and electronics only generate an average engagement rate of 0.35% (see Figure 34).[888]

[887] Cf. SOCIALBAKERS (2013a).

[888] Cf. SOCIALBAKERS (2013b).

Industry	Average page engagement rate
Automotive	0.86 %
Alcohol	0.71 %
Airlines	0.64 %
FMCG	0.53 %
Telco	0.43 %
Fashion	0.41 %
Retail	0.38 %
Finance	0.35 %
Electronics	0.35 %

Figure 34: **Engagement rates by industry**
Source: Own illustration based on SOCIALBAKERS (2013b).

SOCIALBAKERS (2013b) are tracing this back to car manufacturers providing eye-catching visuals that find high acceptance within the audience.[889] Electronics and financial products are much more functional and therefore less appealing. EYL (2013) shares this view. He finds that brand pages from the sport sector have the highest engagement levels which in his opinion can be ascribed to the emotionality of the content.[890] With higher emotional topics, the likelihood of participation increases.

To check the validity of this assumption and whether the same applies to attachment to a brand page rather than engagement, a split of the industries will be carried out for the structural model. The results are presented in Figure 35.

[889] Cf. SOCIALBAKERS (2013b).

[890] Cf. EYL (2013).

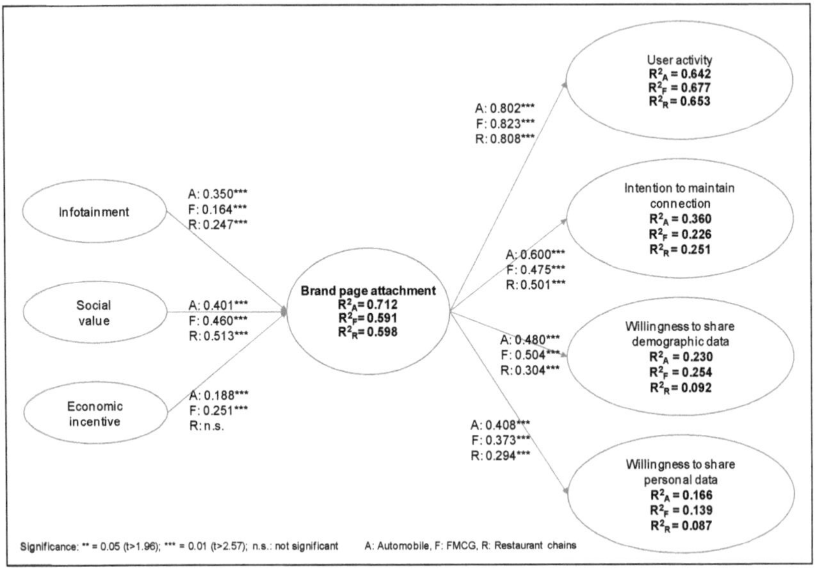

Figure 35: Evaluation of structural model by industry

Source: Own illustration.

Analysing each industry by itself, it can be seen that social value is the strongest determinant for all industries.

For automobile brands, infotainment is very strong, too. This is due to the reason of automobile brands being both visually attractive and technically complex. Manufactures often create a great variety of product ranges. Information is therefore highly valuable. Further, a person that is planning to buy a car will spend a lot of money and consequently gathers sufficient information before making a buying decision. Another reason can be related to the entertainment factor. Popular videos or pictures can be posted on the brand page, which are appreciated by users.[891] Automobile brands are status symbols. They enable individuals to demonstrate their position in society. Hence, they are closely connected to the self concept of an individual. Posting high

[891] Cf. SOCIALBAKERS (2013b).

appealing pictures and videos enhances the persons self perception and induces high attachment to the brand page.

Within the FMCG category, the economic incentive is the second strongest influence (after social value) of brand page attachment. So giving away hamper packages or regularly providing raffles and competitions fosters the users' attachment to the brand page.

Looking at restaurant chains, economic incentives are not significant for brand page attachment at all. This might be based on the fact that vouchers or discounts are often not distributed on the brand page solely but provided with loyalty cards, on the website or through sampling in the outlets. Further, the R^2 values for willingness to share demographic and personal data are very low for restaurant chains. Even after carrying out the moderating analysis, the R^2 values stay below the threshold value of 0.19.[892] The explanation can be based on the general low trust in restaurant chains. In addition, just before the survey started, there was a big scandal on hygiene in Burger King subsidiaries which received high media coverage in Germany.

To compare the findings from three distinct samples, a multi-group analysis will be executed. The multi-group analysis verifies whether the differences between the three industry types are statistically significant. For this purpose, the observed path coefficients of each function will be analysed. The PLS-MGA approach of HENSELER J. (2007) will be applied to test for differences between industries.[893] Table 36 provides the significance level of the group comparisons for each function.

---

[892] Cf. CHIN (1998b), p. 316.

[893] Cf. HENSELER J. (2007), pp. 104 et seqq.

	Automobile vs. FMCG	FMCG vs. Restaurant chains	Automobile vs. Restaurant chains
infotainment → brand page attachment	.04	.21	.13
social value → brand page attachment	.29	.31	.11
economic incentive → brand page attachment	.23	.06	.19
brand page attachment → user activity	.30	.34	.45
brand page attachment → intention to maintain connection	.04	.37	.07
brand page attachment → willingness to share demographic data	.38	**.01**	.02
brand page attachment → willingness to share personal data	.32	.16	.07

Table 36: Comparative results of the multi-group analysis represented by p-values
Source: Own illustration.

As the multi-group analysis per industry shows, the results merely differ slightly in relation to the industry. The only difference that is statistically significant on a 1% level is the path coefficient of brand page attachment on willingness to share demographic data which varies between the industries FMCG and restaurant chains. The reason here is, that restaurant chains in general suffer from lack of trust in the industry due to current developments. Therefore the impact of brand page attachment on willingness to share data is low. Strong attachment to a brand page can increase the willingness, as the model shows, but is not as strong as for other industries like FMCG or automobile (significant on 2% level).

In summary, the impact from brand page attachment on consumer behaviour for different categories only varies in very few cases. Hence, the industry impact is low and should not be over interpreted.

Yet, it should be mentioned that the *level* or *strength* of attachment can still vary, even if the impact on behaviour is not significant. Therefore, interaction on brand pages should not be benchmarked against other brand pages from different product categories.

4.4 Discrimination from competing constructs

Brand page attachment is competing against traditional attitude toward the ad constructs that are often used when evaluating social media stimuli.[894] As illustrated in chapter B 2.3.1, many arguments speak for the usage of the attachment construct in the context of evaluating brand pages. To prove its superiority, empirical evidence shall be delivered.

The aim of this dissertation is to establish a construct that best predicts behaviour in social media context and therefore that leads to higher user activity on brand pages. Hence, both rival constructs will be tested against each other in terms of their strength as a predictor for user activity. For this purpose a structural model as shown in Figure 36 will be computed.

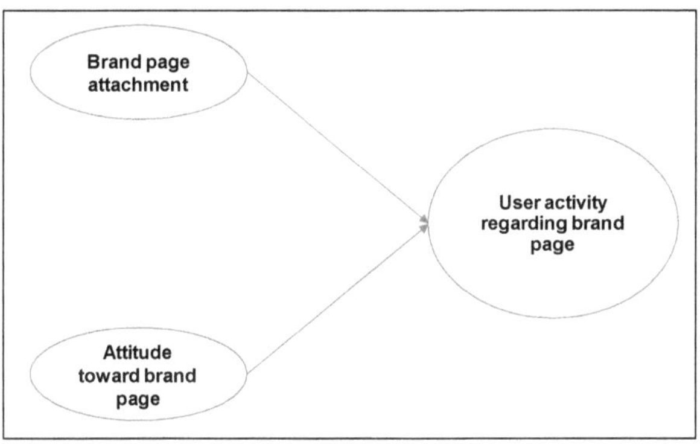

Figure 36: Discrimination of constructs
Source: Own illustration based.

[894] Cf. ARNHOLD (2010), p. 237, cf. EILERS (2014), p. 138.

A shortened standard scale from literature[895] is used that originally measured attitude toward the ad.[896] The items of the scale were phrased slightly different to adapt it to the context of brand pages (see Table 37).

Construct	Label	Items	Source
Attitude toward the brand page	Attitude_1	The brand page of [BRAND] delivers qualitatively valuable content.	Based on BURKE/EDELL (1986).
	Attitude_2	The brand page of [BRAND] offers content that is relevant/ meaningful to me.	
	Attitude_3	The brand page of [BRAND] convincingly employs different media (text, image, audio, and video).	
	Attitude_4	The brand page of [BRAND] offers interesting content.	
	Attitude_5	The posts published by [BRAND] are informative.	

Table 37: Scale for attitude toward the brand page based on BURKE/EDELL (1986)
Source: Own illustration.

The analysis shows that all quality criteria for the measurement models are fulfilled (see Table 38).

[895] The scale was taken from the Marketing Scales Handbook. Cf. BRUNER/HENSEL/JAMES (2005), pp. 87 et seqq.

[896] Cf. BURKE/EDELL (1986), p. 117, cf. WELLS/LEAVITT/MCCONVILLE (1971), pp. 11 et seqq.

Indicator	Item level (indicator reliability)		Construct level			
	Outer loadings > 0.4	**Significance: t>1.96**	**Cronbach's alpha > 0.7**	**Internal consistency: composite reliability > 0.7**	**Convergent validity: AVE > 0.5**	**Discriminant validity: AVE > max correlation²**
Attach_1	0.861	66.6789	0.9671	0.9718	0.7933	Yes
Attach_2	0.919	132.9987				
Attach_3	0.872	85.1268				
Attach_4	0.936	155.5650				
Attach_5	0.924	126.0983				
Attach_6	0.893	77.0771				
Attach_7	0.901	107.1323				
Attach_8	0.909	117.0851				
Attach_9	0.792	40.7995				
Attitude_1	0.881	75.7018	0.9168	0.9373	0.7494	Yes
Attitude_2	0.875	82.0638				
Attitude_3	0.864	60.3712				
Attitude_4	0.885	74.6013				
Attitude_5	0.823	43.4578				
Activ_1	0.800	47.8164	0.9626	0.9672	0.6964	Yes
Activ_2	0.892	99.9177				
Activ_3	0.906	103.0296				
Activ_4	0.907	108.3452				
Activ_5	0.901	102.4712				
Activ_6	0.911	113.5708				
Activ_7	0.592	18.7094				
Activ_8	0.827	55.2602				
Activ_9	0.803	45.4942				
Activ_10	0.737	35.2613				
Activ_11	0.819	51.5107				
Activ_12	0.863	70.4423				
Activ_13	0.835	55.8206				

Table 38: **Quality criteria for the reflective measurement models**

Source: Own illustration.

The quality criteria for the structural model reveal that the path coefficient from attitude toward brand page is not significant (Table 39). Therefore it can be concluded that the **construct brand page attachment is the better predictor** for participation, WOM and co-creation activities on the brand page. Highly attached users are more likely to actively participate. This analysis delivers a rationale for why brand page attachment is the key construct that should be managed by brand managers rather than the attitude construct. The emotionality that is reflected in the attachment construct is much more valid for explaining behaviour. While attitudes also contain underlying emotions, they are evaluated cognitively[897] and therefore not as strong as the emotions reflected in the attachment construct. Hence, again this highlights the importance of building emotional bonds between consumers and brands whether through brand pages or other media. This is central to the brand management.

Other competing constructs have already been excluded on a theoretical basis in chapter B 2.3. The determinants deliver useful insight how brand page attachment can be fostered.

Structural path	Path coefficient	Significance: t>1.96 (5%) t>2.57 (1%)	R^2>0.25	f^2>0.02	Q^2>0
Brand page attachment → User activity re brand page	0.799	31.798	0.661	1.024	0.781
Attitude toward brand page → User activity re brand page	0.021	0.758	0.661	0	0.739

Table 39: **Quality criteria for the structural model**
Source: Own illustration.

[897] Cf. BIELEFELD (2012), pp. 178 et seqq.

D Conclusion, reflection and outlook

1 Summary of the empirical results

The topic of branding in social networks has recently gained a lot of public attention due to the high reach[898] among existing and potential customers.[899] In Germany, nearly one quarter of all internet users like at least one brand page in a social network, a representative study conducted by BITKOM (2013) shows. This equals around 13 million internet users. Among the 14-29-year-olds nearly half of the internet users are "fan" of a brand page in a social network.[900]

Brand managers soon realised the importance of communicating with consumers via social networks. It opens up opportunities for building substantial bonds with actual customers and potential customers.[901] Today, social networks are an integral part of the day-to-day business in brand management.[902] However, branding in social networks (e.g. Facebook) is still a young research field in academia.[903] Because of the high reach, the impact of brand pages on consumer perception needs to be evaluated thoroughly.[904]

So far, the value of brand pages and their impact on consumer behaviour could not be specified further. Researchers are trying to evaluate the impact of brand pages through measuring the degree of user participation[905] also referred to as engagement.[906] Engagement measures the level of activity on a brand page[907] which has

---

[898] Cf. NELSON-FIELD/RIEBE/SHARP (2012), p. 262.

[899] Cf. JAHN/KUNZ (2012), p. 345.

[900] Cf. BITKOM (2013).

[901] Cf. JAHN/KUNZ (2012), p. 345.

[902] Cf. NAYLOR/LAMBERTON/WEST (2012), p. 105.

[903] Cf. SMITH/FISCHER/YONGJIAN (2012), p. 104.

[904] Cf. GUMMERUS ET AL. (2012), pp. 857 et seqq.

[905] Cf. PARENT/PLANGGER/BAL (2011), pp. 219 et seqq.

[906] Cf. GUMMERUS ET AL. (2012), pp. 857 et seqq.

[907] Cf. SCHOENFELD (2012).

been identified as crucial indicator for brand page performance.[908] Yet, **in social networks only very few people actively participate on brand pages**.[909] In fact, only 1.3% of users that follow a brand page are participating.[910] This raises the issue whether those behavioural constructs should be seen as key for brand page evaluation. In summary, the evaluation of brand page performance and its impact on consumer behaviour requires further attention in research.[911]

The thesis at hand addresses this matter and introduces the construct **attachment to measure users' bonds to brand pages** in social networks. The following research questions where identified to be relevant in this context:

1) What is attachment and why is it the best construct to measure the bond between user and brand page?
2) How can brand page attachment be conceptualised and measured in the context of social networks?
3) Which antecedents, consequences and moderators have to be considered?

To answer these questions a thorough literature review was conducted to lay out the theoretical basis for branding in social media. First, the attachment construct was valued to be the best concept for measuring the user's bond to a brand page in social networks (e.g. Facebook). For this purpose, academic research on the attachment construct was reflected in detail. Further, other relevant constructs that measure bonding were examined and discriminated from attachment. Again, evidence for the superiority of the attachment construct over other constructs was provided in the context of measuring users' bonds to brand pages.

---

[908] Cf. SOCIALBAKERS (2013a), cf. PARENT/PLANGGER/BAL (2011), pp. 219 et seqq.

[909] Cf. GUMMERUS ET AL. (2012), p. 870.

[910] The study conducted by the Ehrenberg-Bass Institute analysed the user engagement of 200 brand pages on Facebook during a time span of six weeks. To measure engagement, they used the publicly available metric "people talking about this" cf. HEDEMANN (2012), cf. FACEBOOK (2012), cf. DARWELL (2012).

[911] Cf. MUNTINGA/MOORMAN/SMIT (2011), p. 13, cf. SMITH/FISCHER/YONGJIAN (2012), pp. 102 et seqq.

Second, conceptualisation and operationalisation was inspired by the work of PARK ET AL. (2010), who identified two dimensions brand-self connection and brand prominence as relevant factors for brand attachment.[912] Transferred to brand pages in social networks, these dimensions were slightly amended to suit the context of brand pages and termed **brand page connectedness** and **brand page prominence**. The operationalisation was pursued accordingly. The empiric study revealed that in contrast to brand attachment, the brand *page* attachment construct is one-dimensional. All items load onto one factor.

Third, a model of antecedents, consequences and moderators related to brand page attachment was developed. The corresponding hypotheses were deduced through an intense review of social media and branding literature. An empirical study that surveyed Facebook users who follow at least one brand was carried out with the intention of testing the model and its hypotheses.

All antecedents identified are significant determinants of brand page attachment. Those were verified in the empirical study. The following constructs turned out to be relevant antecedents:

- Infotainment (merge of information and entertainment)
- Social value
- Economic incentive.

Social value has the strongest impact on brand page attachment. This was verified for all three industries: automobile, FMCG and restaurant chains. It implies that brand managers shall foster the communication among followers to strengthen brand page attachment. In the case of automobile brands, the infotainment factor also proved to be of high relevance. For FMCG brands on the contrary, raffles and giveaway hampers help promoting brand page attachment. The latter was not relevant at all for restaurant chains.

The study results demonstrate that brand page attachment is a reliable predictor for consumer behaviour on brand pages. The impact on user activity regarding the brand

---

[912] Cf. PARK ET AL. (2010), pp. 1 et seqq.

page (including the facets participation, WOM and co-creation of value and meaning), on intention to maintain the connection to the brand via social networks and on the willingness to share demographic as well as personal data was verified through structural equation modelling. The relation between brand page attachment and user activity is moderated through a user's propensity to interact. This implies that higher brand page attachment does stimulate interaction on brand pages but it does depend on the users' personalities and whether they are sociable and jovial individuals online. The impact brand page attachment has on willingness to share personal data is moderated through privacy concerns.

In the case of restaurant chains, the effect brand page attachment causes on willingness to share demographic and personal data could not be validated. The R^2 values are below the threshold value. This can be related to the fact that overall trust in restaurant chains due to current food and hygiene scandals is low and therefore the willingness to share data is impacted through external variables.

The superiority of brand page attachment over other constructs has been demonstrated in the theoretical part of this thesis. But it could also be validated empirically. For this purpose, the often employed scale for attitude toward the ad in the context of social media[913] was compared to the brand page attachment construct regarding their ability to predict consumer behaviour on the brand page. As postulated in theory (see chapter B 2.3), the attachment construct was validated to be the superior option. This evidence shows the importance of emotions towards brands as attachment is a construct highly reflecting emotional bonding. The research backs up the findings of BIELEFELD (2012) who emphasises the importance of emotions as underlying cause for behaviour.[914]

2 Managerial implications

So far, brand managers are not content with the options of assessing activities on brand pages in social networks (e.g. Facebook). The tools and scales that are pro-

---

[913] Cf. ARNHOLD (2010), p. 237, cf. EILERS (2014), p. 138.

[914] Cf. BIELEFELD (2012), pp. 178 et seqq.

vided to date are not sufficient according to ROSSMANN (2013).[915] The construct brand page attachment offers brand managers an instrument that evaluates the performance of their brand pages continually. The concept of brand page attachment can be integrated into a controlling system, i.e. a scorecard or cockpit of metrics that evaluate the activities in social media.

To date, researchers and consultants have structured metrics employing advertising effectiveness measurement models or following the logic of the customer journey.

BILGRAM/FUELLER/RAPP (2013) draw on the established AIDA (attention-interest-desire-action) model that has been used for measuring media effectiveness and was modified many times.[916] They augment the AIDA model integrating three more levels into the sequence: awareness, interest, desire, *engagement*, action, *loyalty, and advocacy*. This model bears several shortcomings. The different levels cannot be demarcated; the process steps of engagement, actions, loyalty and advocacy overlap. It is neither clear which impact they have on another, nor which relation can be presumed between them. Moreover, performance indicators for each level cannot be assigned precisely.

Among many, WAGENFÜHRER (2013) structures his set of performance indicators along the customer journey. In this logic, the sequence consists of the modules: social campaigns, awareness, recognition, experience, ambassadors. Similar, but more simple is the system developed by HOFFMAN/FODOR (2010). They categorise performance indicators into brand awareness, brand engagement, word-of-mouth.[917] The list of metric systems can be continued ad infinitum. Corresponding to the advertising effectiveness models, these KPI systems too have limitations. There is no integration of goals. It is not clear how the metrics fit with the purpose of the campaign. Further, there is no validation or benchmark of the measures. There is no indication for managerial implications.

---

[915] Cf. ROSSMANN (2013), p. 10.

[916] Cf. TROPP (2011), pp. 601-603.

[917] Cf. HOFFMAN/FODOR (2010), p. 44.

In summary, both ways have been criticised much for deficiencies and for the lack of ability to meet the requirements of new media. Psychographic metrics are neglected completely. Likewise, goals are ignored. Plus, there is no direction for managerial action; it is not clear how implications should be inferred. Evidently, there is a need for new solutions in measurement systems. For this reason, a **cockpit of brand page performance indicators** that meets the shortcomings outlined above and integrated a psychographic measure in the evaluation will be developed in the following. Beforehand, the goals of brand page activities need to be clarified. The cockpit can be employed by brand managers, consultants, media agencies or creative agencies.

2.1 Definition of brand page objectives

Like every marketing activity, plans for brand pages in social networks should start with the definition of a purpose. The phrasing of the aims should be operational. This basically means that they should contain which content, scope, time and segment are pertained.[918] Brand page goals can be

a) Generate awareness[919]
b) Obtain consumer insights[920] for new product development
c) Reach out to new target groups (through multiplicators or ambassadors)[921]
d) Strengthen the consumer relation through user experience[922]
e) Social sales (e-commerce)

Ultimately, all goals lead to attachment to the brand page. Hence, this key construct is the heart of the performance cockpit. But, depending on the purpose, other performance indicators should be assembled, too.

The logic of the brand page performance cockpit is illustrated in Figure 37.

---

[918] Cf. BURMANN/HALASZOVICH/HEMMANN (2012), p. 97.

[919] Cf. WAGENFÜHRER (2013), p. 28.

[920] Cf. MURDOUGH (2009), p. 95.

[921] Cf. WAGENFÜHRER (2013), p. 30.

[922] Cf. HEMMANN (2014).

Figure 37: **Cockpit for brand page performance indicators**
Source: Own illustration.

2.2 Deducing brand page key performance indicators

Depending on the goal, indicators for campaign performance are deduced. First, **raising awareness** is one option of setting a target for a social media campaign. It pays off on the infotainment but also on the social value gratification which have been validated highly significant and therefore ultimately lead to attachment to the brand page. Awareness can be created for a specific topic or campaign, for a new product or for the brand on the whole. In the UK and Ireland, a viral social media campaign raised awareness for breast cancer.[923] Women took selfies[924] wearing no

---

[923] Cf. DOCKTERMAN (2014).

make-up, whilst men put on mascara and lipstick and posted the pictures to Facebook or Twitter with a plea for donation.[925] They then nominated their friends and acquaintances to do the same, consequently social value became very high in this incident. The campaign rapidly went viral and raised over 8 million £ in the UK within six days.[926] This example shows how social value increased brand page attachment and consequently lead to user participation.

Awareness can also be raised for new product development. Launches can be supported through social media. Followers of Facebook brand pages see the information on new products in their newsfeed. Further, awareness for the brand in general can be generated. Volvo for example filmed a video with Jean-Claude Van Damme that went viral under the headline "the epic split"[927]. It shows the actor performing his famous split between two trucks (see Figure 38).[928] It is meant to "demonstrate the stability and precision of Volvo Dynamic Steering"[929]. The video got 73 million clicks on YouTube. The campaign was highly entertaining which in the case of automobile brands impacts brand page attachment.

---

[924] A selfie is "a photograph that one has taken of oneself, typically one taken with a smartphone or webcam and uploaded to a social media website." OXFORD DICTIONARIES (2014e).

[925] Cf. BREAST CANCER CAMPAIGN (2014).

[926] Cf. THE GUARDIAN (2014).

[927] VOLVO TRUCKS (2013).

[928] Cf. AMBASSADOR (2013).

[929] VOLVO TRUCKS (2013).

Figure 38: **The Epic Split feat. Van Damme**
Source: VOLVO TRUCKS (2013).

These campaigns are created to enlarge the reach of a brand. Hence, performance indicators are those that mirror the size of the brand exposure like number of followers, clicks, likes, leads or social share of voice[930] and sentiment[931] which are measured in brand mentions[932] in social web and can be compared to competitors.[933]

Second, generating **consumer insights** is another opportunity that can be taken up through social media. Through listening the social media chatter, consumer needs and problems can be identified, analysed and tailored solutions can be composed.[934] Real-time and authentic feedback from consumers regarding products and services

---

[930] Cf. ZENN (2012).
[931] Cf. BENDROR (2013).
[932] Cf. SOCIALMENTION (2014).
[933] Cf. WAGENFÜHRER (2013), p. 29.
[934] Cf. IBM (2011), p. 6.

are provided at low costs.[935] Further, new product development can be implemented using the knowledge of the crowd.[936]

One example is provided by Lay's potato chips who invited their audience to "Do Us A Flavor"[937]. Consumer had the option of entering different flavours on the Facebook brand page. The three best flavours were produced and sold in store.[938] The users could then vote for their favourite which would get a permanent position in the Lay's assortment (see Figure 39). Overall the campaign generated 3.8 million submissions, over 1 billion Facebook impressions and a 12% increase in sales.[939]

This example demonstrates how brand page attachment impacts co-creation of value and meaning. The brand page activated a high amount of users to actively take part in brand building measures.

Figure 39: **Lay's "Do Us A Flavor"**
Source: SCHUPP (2013).

[935] Cf. WHITLER (2013).

[936] Also known as crowdsourcing which means "obtain information or input into a particular task or project by enlisting the services of a number of people, either paid or unpaid, typically via the Internet." OXFORD DICTIONARIES (2014f).

[937] Cf. LAY'S (2014).

[938] Cf. AMBASSADOR (2013).

[939] Cf. AMBASSADOR (2013).

Consumer insights that are generated through social media can be evaluated either by the quality of the input. The campaign above was produced not only to gain insights but also to raise awareness for new products. Hence, this campaign should also be evaluated by the impact it had on improving entertainment value and strengthening brand page attachment.

Third, accessing **new target groups** is a goal that can be pursued through social media. Mostly, this happens through acquisition campaigns like raffles or competitions which are advertised with eye catching banners. Once, users go onto the brand page, they are exposed to the brand and its products. Cross selling products can help acquiring consumers for new or less known products. But also, consumers that are no buyers or lights buyers can be targeted. If the brand is able to strengthen their brand page attachment, it is likely they will act in favour of the brand in future.

The chocolate brand Cadbury delivers a successful example of reaching out to new target groups. To thank their Facebook audience that they have reached the one million mark of people following the brand page, they build a gigantic "thumbs up"[940] from chocolate bards of Cadbury Dairy Milk (see Figure 40). The studio was decorated with content sent in by users during the live event that was filmed and publicly visible via live stream.[941] They obtained 40,000 new followers who were reached through influencers and friends of followers.[942]

---

[940] Cf. TOBESOCIAL (2013).

[941] Cf. CADBURY (2012).

[942] Cf. TOBESOCIAL (2013).

Figure 40: **Cadbury: Thanks A Million**
Source: CADBURY (2012).

Fourth, consumer relations are strengthened by creating **consumer experience** through social media. There are several cases of campaigns that are published via social media. One is the Real Beauty campaign by Dove. The brand hired a FBI forensic artist that drew sketches of women by their own instructions without the artist actually seeing the women.[943] The differences of how they view and describe themselves and what they actually look like were remarkable (see Figure 41). The video gained nearly 60 million impressions within the first 60 days of launch.[944]

[943] Cf. CASSINELLI (2013).

[944] Cf. AMBASSADOR (2013).

Figure 41: Dove Real Beauty Sketches
Source: DOVE (2013).

Fifth, **social sales** can be generated through shops within social networks. Eventim for examples uses a completely integrated Facebook shop system.[945] As this is a special case of social e-commerce, the findings for brand pages cannot completely be transferred. Brand page attachment is still important for these cases as the managers of social shops are depending on the users' willingness to share their data.

To sum up, the study delivers many insights into how brand managers can foster brand page attachment which ultimately encourages users to act in favour of the brand and thus become brand ambassadors online. The implications have to be considered on an industry level as they vary across different product categories. It is

945 Cf. PROJECTOR ONLINE MARKETING BLOG (2013).

recommended to monitor the development of the brand page attachment values over time and initiate marketing activities to constantly improve brand page attachment.

3 Implications for further research

The thesis contributes to a better understanding of the concept of brand pages in social networks. The conceptual differentiation from brand communities has closed a highly relevant gap in current research. Further, it contributes to the research on the construct of attachment. While the thesis is able to build on further approaches of THOMSON/MACINNIS/PARK (2005) and PARK ET AL. (2010) it discriminates the construct of brand *page* attachment and establishes its own one-dimensional scale which was validated empirically. The differentiation from competing constructs is executed both, conceptually and empirically and overall leads to a better understanding on constructs that measure the bonds between consumers and their brands.

There are limitations of this thesis that leave room for further research. First, the focus of this thesis is set on brand pages in social networks which are investigated using Facebook brand pages. The theory can be extended to other social networks like Instagram, Twitter, Pinterest, YouTube and many others. Hence, to establish the construct of brand page attachment in social media practice, further research shall verify the adaptability to other social networks.

Second, the empiric study was conducted in Germany only. Future studies shall incorporate research in other countries to validate if the concept can be generalised.

Third, to illustrate differences between industries, three industries were chosen and compared to each other in the study, namely automobile, FMCG and restaurant chains. Though this builds a good basis, further industries have to be investigated in future.

Appendix

Appendix A: Questionnaire

The original German wording of each item is available upon request from the author.

Dear respondent,
thank you for taking part in this survey about brand pages on Facebook. We would highly apreciate if you would spare 15 minutes of your time and support our research at the University of Bremen by responding to the following questions. Your information and personal data will only be used anonymously, will not be passed to third parties and kept strictly confidential!

Question	Scale
Screening: Which brand pages are you fan of on Facebook?	55 brands of the three categories automobile, FMCG and restaurant chains

How long have you been fan of the (brand)?	a few days	1-3 months	4-6 months	7-12 months	more than a year	n/a		

The following questions relate to your usage of social media (e.g. Facebook).

	never	less than once a month	several times a month	once a week	several times a week	once a day	several times a day	n/a
How often do you use the following social media:								
Facebook	☐	☐	☐	☐	☐	☐	☐	☐
Twitter	☐	☐	☐	☐	☐	☐	☐	☐
YouTube	☐	☐	☐	☐	☐	☐	☐	☐
Google+	☐	☐	☐	☐	☐	☐	☐	☐
Instagram	☐	☐	☐	☐	☐	☐	☐	☐
Pinterest	...	...	...	...	...	...	...	...
Tumblr								
others:								

Please think about the brand page of (brand). To what extent do you agree with the following statements?

	Completely disagree (1)	2	3	4	Completely agree (5)	n/a
The brand page of [BRAND] helps me to learn about unknown things.	☐	☐	☐	☐	☐	☐
Looking at the brand page of [BRAND] is a good way to do research.	☐	☐	☐	☐	☐	☐
The brand page of [BRAND] helps me to learn about useful things.	☐	☐	☐	☐	☐	☐
The brand page of [BRAND] lets me use the service that is provided by [BRAND].	☐	☐	☐	☐	☐	☐

	Completely disagree (1)	2	3	4	Completely agree (5)	n/a
The brand page of [BRAND] is fun to watch or read.	☐	☐	☐	☐	☐	☐
The brand page of [BRAND] is clever and quite entertaining.	☐	☐	☐	☐	☐	☐
The brand page of [BRAND] does not just sell – it also entertains me.	☐	☐	☐	☐	☐	☐
The brand page of [BRAND] is often amusing.	☐	☐	☐	☐	☐	☐

	Completely disagree (1)	2	3	4	Completely agree (5)	n/a
I believe a chat among like-minded people on the brand page of [BRAND] is a nice thing.	☐	☐	☐	☐	☐	☐
It is fun to communicate with other people on the brand page of [BRAND].	☐	☐	☐	☐	☐	☐
I meet nice people on the brand page of [BRAND].	☐	☐	☐	☐	☐	☐

	Completely disagree (1)	2	3	4	Completely agree (5)	n/a
I receive incentives through the brand page of [BRAND].	☐	☐	☐	☐	☐	☐
I receive a reward through the brand page of [BRAND].	☐	☐	☐	☐	☐	☐
The brand page of [BRAND] offers me advantages that others do not have.	☐	☐	☐	☐	☐	☐

	Completely disagree (1)	2	3	4	Completely agree (5)	n/a
The brand page of [BRAND] represents who I am.						
I feel emotionally bonded to the brand page of [BRAND].	☐	☐	☐	☐	☐	☐
I feel personally connected to the brand page of [BRAND].	☐	☐	☐	☐	☐	☐
There is a special bond that connects me to the brand page of [BRAND].	☐	☐	☐	☐	☐	☐
I feel closeness to the brand page of [BRAND].	☐	☐	☐	☐	☐	☐
The thoughts and feelings about the brand page of [BRAND] come to my mind naturally and instantly.	☐	☐	☐	☐	☐	☐
I often think about the brand page of [BRAND] spontaneously.	☐	☐	☐	☐	☐	☐
The thoughts and feelings about the brand page of [BRAND] come to my mind automatically, coming seemingly on their own.	☐	☐	☐	☐	☐	☐
The brand page of [BRAND] evokes memories.	☐	☐	☐	☐	☐	☐
Overall, I feel attached to the brand page of [BRAND].	☐	☐	☐	☐	☐	☐

	Completely disagree (1)	2	3	4	Completely agree (5)	n/a
The brand page of [BRAND] delivers qualitatively valuable content.	☐	☐	☐	☐	☐	☐
The brand page of [BRAND] offers content that is relevant/ meaningful to me.	☐	☐	☐	☐	☐	☐
The brand page of [BRAND] convincingly employs different media (text, image, audio, and video).	☐	☐	☐	☐	☐	☐
The brand page of [BRAND] offers interesting content.	☐	☐	☐	☐	☐	☐
The posts published by [BRAND] are informative.	☐	☐	☐	☐	☐	☐

	Completely disagree (1)	2	3	4	Completely agree (5)	n/a
I often click "like" when I see posts [BRAND] publishes.	☐	☐	☐	☐	☐	☐
I often "like" posts other users post on the brand page.	☐	☐	☐	☐	☐	☐
I often comment on posts published by [BRAND].	☐	☐	☐	☐	☐	☐
I comment on posts published by other users.	☐	☐	☐	☐	☐	☐
I share posts published by [BRAND] within my network of friends and acquaintances.	☐	☐	☐	☐	☐	☐
I share posts published by other users about [BRAND] within my network of friends and acquaintances.	☐	☐	☐	☐	☐	☐
I often take part in raffles provided by [BRAND] on its brand page.	☐	☐	☐	☐	☐	☐

	Completely disagree (1)	2	3	4	Completely agree (5)	n/a
I often write posts about [BRAND] on its brand page.	☐	☐	☐	☐	☐	☐
I often provide pictures about [BRAND] on its brand page.	☐	☐	☐	☐	☐	☐
I often create videos about [BRAND].	☐	☐	☐	☐	☐	☐

How likely are you going to provide personal data on the brand page of [BRAND]?	Not likely at all (1)	2	3	4	Very likely (5)	n/a
age	☐	☐	☐	☐	☐	☐
profession	☐	☐	☐	☐	☐	☐
education	☐	☐	☐	☐	☐	☐
family status	☐	☐	☐	☐	☐	☐
hobbies	☐	☐	☐	☐	☐	☐
e-mail	☐	☐	☐	☐	☐	☐
address	☐	☐	☐	☐	☐	☐
phone number	☐	☐	☐	☐	☐	☐
income	☐	☐	☐	☐	☐	☐
credit card details	☐	☐	☐	☐	☐	☐

	Completely disagree (1)	2	3	4	Completely agree (5)	n/a
I plan to continue using the brand page of [BRAND].	☐	☐	☐	☐	☐	☐
I plan to continue read posts that [BRAND] publishes on its brand page.	☐	☐	☐	☐	☐	☐
In the future, I want to be informed of posts by [BRAND] in my newsfeed.	☐	☐	☐	☐	☐	☐
I intend to visit the brand page of [BRAND] in the future.	☐	☐	☐	☐	☐	☐
I will not "dislike" the brand page of [BRAND].	☐	☐	☐	☐	☐	☐

	Completely disagree (1)	2	3	4	Completely agree (5)	n/a
I recommend this brand page to my friends and acquaintances.	☐	☐	☐	☐	☐	☐
I introduce the brand page to other people.	☐	☐	☐	☐	☐	☐
I say positive things about this brand page to other people.	☐	☐	☐	☐	☐	☐

	Completely disagree (1)	2	3	4	Completely agree (5)	n/a
In general, I like to get involved in online discussions.	☐	☐	☐	☐	☐	☐
I am someone who enjoys interacting with like-minded others online.	☐	☐	☐	☐	☐	☐
I am someone who likes actively participating in online discussions.	☐	☐	☐	☐	☐	☐
In general, I thoroughly enjoy exchanging ideas with other people online.	☐	☐	☐	☐	☐	☐

	Completely disagree (1)	2	3	4	Completely agree (5)	n/a
I feel secure in providing sensitive information to the SNS Web site. (r)	☐	☐	☐	☐	☐	☐
I feel the SNS Web site will keep my personal details private. (r)	☐	☐	☐	☐	☐	☐
I feel secure in posting personal information on my SNS pages. (r)	☐	☐	☐	☐	☐	☐

Sociodemographics:

Sex
Age
Profession
Income

References

AAKER, D. A. (1996), Building strong brands, New York.

AAKER, D./JACOBSON, R. (2001), The Value Relevance of Brand Attitude in High-Technology Markets, in: Journal of Marketing Research, Vol. 38 (4), pp. 485-493.

AAKER, D./KUMAR, V./LEONE, R./DAY, G. (2013), Marketing research, 11. ed., internat. student versionEd., Hoboken, NJ.

AAKER, J. (1997), Dimensions of brand personality, in: Journal of Marketing Research, Vol. 34 (3), pp. 347-356.

AAKER, J. (1999), The malleable self: The role of self-expression in persuasion, in: Journal of Marketing Research, Vol. 36 pp. 45-57.

AHUVIA, A./BATRA, R./BAGOZZI, R. (2009), Love, desire and identity: A theory of the love of things, in: MACINNIS, D./PARK, C./PRIESTER, J. (Ed.), The Handbook of Brand Relationships, New York, pp. 342-357.

ALBA, J./CHATTOPADHYAY, A. (1986), Salience Effects in Brand Recall, in: Journal of Marketing Research, Vol. 23 (4), pp. 363-369.

ALBERS, S./GÖTZ, O. (2006), Messmodelle mit Konstrukten zweiter Ordnung in der betriebswirtschaftlichen Forschung, in: Die Betriebswirtschaft, Vol. 66 (6), pp. 669-677.

ALBERT, N./MERUNKA, D./VALETTE-FLORENCE, P. (2008), When consumers love their brands: Exploring the concept and its dimensions, in: Journal of Business Research, Vol. 61 (10), pp. 1062-1075.

ALBERT, N./MERUNKA, D./VALETTE-FLORENCE, P. (2013), Brand passion: antecedents and consequences, in: Journal of Business Research, Vol. 66 (7), pp. 904-909.

ALBERT, N./MERUNKA, D. (2013), The role of brand love in consumer-brand relationships, in: Journal of Consumer Marketing, Vol. 30 (3), pp. 258-266.

ALGESHEIMER, R./DHOLAKIA, U./HERRMANN, A. (2005), The social influence of brand community: evidence from european car clubs, in: Journal of Marketing, Vol. 69 (3), pp. 19-34.

ALLARD, S. (2012), Why The Current Facebook Engagement Rate Calculation Is Inaccurate, http://blog.wisemetrics.com/why-your-analytics-engagement-rate-is-not-measuring-your-pages-engagement/ (accessed: 02.07.2012).

ALLPORT, G., *Attitudes,* Worcester, Mass.: 1935.

AMBASSADOR (2013), The 16 best social media campaigns from 2013, http://blog.getambassador.com/best-social-media-campaigns/.

AMBLER, T./ROBERTS, J. (2008), Assessing marketing performance: don't settle for a silver metric, in: Journal of Marketing Management, Vol. 24 (7-8), pp. 733-750.

ARNHOLD, U. (2010), User generated branding, Wiesbaden.

ASHFORTH, B./MAEL, F. (1989), Social identity theory and the organization, in: The Academy of Management Review, Vol. 14 (2), pp. 20-39.

BABAD, E. (1987), Wishful thinking and objectivity among sports fans, in: Social Behavior, Vol. 2 pp. 231-240.

BABBIE, E. (2013), The practice of social research, 13Ed., Belmont, California.

BACKHAUS, K./ERICHSON, B./PLINKE, W./WEIBER, R. (2011), Multivariate Analysemethoden, 13., überarb. AuflEd., Berlin.

BACKHAUS, K./ERICHSON, B./WEIBER, R. (2011), Fortgeschrittene multivariate Analysemethoden, Berlin [u.a.].

BAGOZZI, R. Y. Y. (1988), On the Evaluation of Structural Equation Models, in: Journal of the Academy of Marketing Science, Vol. 16 pp. 74-94.

BALL, A. D./TASAKI, L. (1992), The Role and Measurement of Attachment in Consumer Behavior, in: Journal of Consumer Psychology, Vol. 1 (2), pp. 155-172.

BATRA, R./AHUVIA, A./BAGOZZI, R. (2012), Brand Love, in: Journal of Marketing, Vol. 76 (2), pp. 1-16.

BECKER, C. (2012), Einfluss der räumlichen Markenherkunft auf das Markenimage: Kausalanalytische Untersuchung am Beispiel Indiens, Wiesbaden.

BECKER, J./KLEIN, K./WETZELS, M. (2012), Hierarchical Latent Variable Models in PLS-SEM: Guidelines for Using Reflective-Formative Type Models, in: Long Range Planning, Vol. 45 (5-6), pp. 359-394.

BECKWITH, N./KASSARJIAN, H./LEHMANN, D. (1978), Halo effects in marketing research: review and prognosis, in: Advances in Consumer Research, Vol. 5 (1), pp. 465-

467.

BECKWITH, N./LEHMANN, D. (1975), The Importance of Halo Effects in Multi-Attribute Attitude Models, in: Journal of Marketing Research, Vol. 12 (3), pp. 265-275.

BENDROR, J. (2013), 6 Ways to Measure Social Media, http://webmarketingtoday.com/articles/6-ways-to-measure-social-media/ (accessed: 15.02.2013).

BEREKOVEN, L./ECKERT, W./ELLENRIEDER, P. (2009), Marktforschung, 12., überarbeitete und erweiterte AuflageEd., Wiesbaden.

BERGAMI, M./BAGOZZI, R. P. (2000), Self-categorization, affective commitment and group self-esteem as distinct aspects of social identity in the organization, in: The British journal of social psychology, Vol. 39 (4), pp. 555-577.

BERRY, L. (2014), Facebook Engagement Rate: How One Little Metric Got So Tough To Nail Down, http://simplymeasured.com/blog/2014/02/19/facebook-engagement-rate/ (accessed: 19.02.2014).

BHARADWAJ, A./EL SAWY, O./PAVLOU, P./VENKATRAMAN, N. (2013), Digital business strategy: toward a next generation of insights, in: MIS Quarterly, Vol. 37 (2), pp. 471-482.

BHATTACHARYA, C. B./SEN, S. (2003a), Consumer-company identification : A framework for understanding consumers' relationships with companies, in: Journal of Marketing, Vol. 67 (2), pp. 76-88.

BHATTACHARYA, C./SEN, S. (2003b), Consumer-Company Identification: A Framework for Understanding Consumers' Relationships with Companies, in: Journal of Marketing, Vol. 67 (2), pp. 76-88.

BIELEFELD, K. (2012), Consumer Neuroscience, Wiesbaden.

BIJMOLT, T./LEEFLANG, P./BLOCK, F./EISENBEISS, M./HARDIE, B./LEMMENS, A./SAFFERT, P. (2010), Analytics for customer engagement, in: Journal of Service Research, Vol. 13 (3), pp. 341-356.

BILGRAM, V./FUELLER, J. K. G./RAPP, M. (2013), The potential of crowdsourcing for co-marketing: How consumers may be turned into brand ambassadors, in: transfer Werbeforschung & Praxis, Vol. 59 (4), pp. 42-48.

BITKOM (2013), 13 Millionen sind in sozialen Netzwerken Fan einer Marke,.

BLANCHARD, O. (2009), Basics of social media ROI,.

BLINDA, L. (2007), Markenführungskompetenzen eines identitätsbasierten Markenmanagements, 1. AuflEd., Wiesbaden.

BLOEMER, J./KASPER, H. (1995), The complex relationship between consumer satisfaction and brand loyalty, in: Journal of Economic Psychology, Vol. 16 (2), pp. 311-329.

BOEHLER, H. (2004), Marktforschung, Stuttgart.

BOWLBY, J. (1979), The making and breaking of affectional bonds, London.

BOWLBY, J. (1980), Attachment and Loss: Vol. 3. Loss, New York.

BOWLBY, J. (1997), Attachment, Pimlico edEd., London.

BRAKUS, J./SCHMITT, B./ZARANTONELLO, L. (2009), Brand Experience: What Is It? How Is It Measured? Does It Affect Loyalty? in: Journal of Marketing, Vol. 73 (3), pp. 52-68.

BRAUNSTEIN, C. (2001), Einstellungsforschung und Kundenbindung, Wiesbaden.

BREAST CANCER CAMPAIGN (2014), Comment on 'no makeup selfie' viral campaign for cancer awareness, http://www.breastcancercampaign.org/articles/comment-on-no-makeup-selfie-viral-campaign-for-cancer-awareness (accessed: 19.03.2014).

BRODIE, R. J./HOLLEBEEK, L. D./JURIC, B./ILIC, A. (2011), Customer engagement: conceptual domain, fundamental propositions, and implications for research, in: Journal of Service Research, Vol. 14 (3), pp. 252-271.

BRODIE, R./ILIC, A./JURIC, B./HOLLEBEEK, L. (2013), Consumer engagement in a virtual brand community: An exploratory analysis, in: Journal of Business Research, Vol. 66 (1), pp. 105-114.

BRUHN, M./SCHOENMUELLER, V./SCHÄFER, D. (2012), Are social media replacing traditional media in terms of brand equity creation? in: Management Research Review, Vol. 35 (9), pp. 770-790.

BRUHN, M./SCHWARZ, J./SCHÄFER, D. B./AHLERS, G. M. (2011), Wie Social Media im Vergleich zur klassischen Marketingkommunikation die Marke stärken, in: Marketing Review St. Gallen, Vol. 28 (2), pp. 40-46.

BRUNER, G./HENSEL, P./JAMES, K. (2005), Marketing scales handbook, Chicago, Ill.

BUCKINGHAM, A./SAUNDERS, P. (2004), The survey methods workbook, Cambridge, UK.

BUEHNER, M. (2006), Einführung in die Test- und Fragebogenkonstruktion, 2., aktualisierte und erw. AuflEd., München.

BUILDING BRAND SALIENCE FOR COMMODITY-BASED WINE REGIONS (2009), Remaud, H.; Lockshin, L, in: International Journal of Wine Business Research, Vol. 21 (1), pp. 79-92.

BURKE, M./EDELL, J. (1986), Ad Reactions Over Time: Capturing Changes in the Real World, in: Journal of Consumer Research, Vol. 13 (June), pp. 114-118.

BURMANN, C./BLINDA, L./NITSCHKE, A. (2003), Konzeptionelle Grundlagen des identitätsbasierten Markenmanagements, in: BURMANN, C. (Ed.), Working Paper No. 1, Lehrstuhl für innovatives Markenmanagement (LiM), Universität Bremen, Bremen,.

BURMANN, C./HALASZOVICH, T./HEMMANN, F. (2012), Identitätsbasierte Markenführung, Wiesbaden.

BURMANN, C./KLEINE-KALMER, B./HEMMANN, F. (2013), Big Data, Big Impact? Anspruch und Wirklichkeit für die marktorientierte Unternehmensführung,.

BURMANN, C./KLEINE-KALMER, B./HEMMANN, F. (2014), Vermittlung von Markenerlebnissen durch die Nutzung von Big Data, in: Marketing Review St. Gallen, Vol. 1 pp. 56-67.

BURMANN, C./KLEINE-KALMER, B. (2013), Professionell im Netz, in: Markenartikel, Vol. 4 pp. 100-102.

BURMANN, C./ULBRICHT, A. (2013), Brand Delivery - Erfolgsfaktor der Markenführung, in: Vol. 6 pp. 12-21.

CADBURY (2012), Cadbury Dairy Milk: Thanks A Million - How did we do it? http://www.youtube.com/watch?v=uHtDRw4ujYw (accessed: 18.01.2012).

CARLSON, B. D./SUTER, T. A./BROWN, T. J. (2008), Social versus psychological brand community: The role of psychological sense of brand community, in: Journal of Business Research, Vol. 61 (4), pp. 284-291.

CARROLL, B./AHUVIA, A. (2006), Some antecedents and outcomes of brand love, in: Marketing Letters, Vol. 17 (2), pp. 79-89.

CASALÓ, L. V./CARLOS F.; GUINALÍU,/GUINALÍU, M. (2010), Antecedents and consequences of consumer participation in on-line communities: The case of the travel sector, in: International Journal of Electronic Commerce, Vol. 15 (2), pp. 137-167.

CASSINELLI, A. (2013), 13 best social media campaigns of 2013, http://www.postano.com/blog/13-best-social-media-campaigns-of-2013 (accessed: 31.12.2013).

CASTELEYN, J./MOTTART, A./RUTTEN, K. (2009), How to use Facebook in your market research, in: International Journal of Market Research, Vol. 51 (4), pp. 439-447.

CBS (2013), Facebook gets rid of privacy setting for Timeline searches, http://www.cbsnews.com/news/facebook-gets-rid-of-privacy-setting-for-timeline-searches/ (accessed: 11.10.2013).

CHADWICK MARTIN BAILEY (2011), 10 Quick Facts You Should Know About Consumers Behavior on Facebook, http://www.brandchannel.com/images/papers/530_chadwick_martin_bailey_ppt_fb_consumer_behavior_0911.pdf (accessed: 23.01.2014).

CHAUDHURI, A./HOLBROOK, M. (2001), The chain of effects from brand trust and brand affect to brand performance: The role of brand loyalty, in: Journal of Marketing, Vol. 65 (2), pp. 81-93.

CHAUHAN, K./PILLAI, A. (2013), Role of content strategy in social media brand communities: a case of higher education institutes in India, in: Journal of Product & Brand Management, Vol. 22 (1), pp. 40-51.

CHIN, W./MARCOLIN, B./NEWSTED, P. (2003), A Partial Least Squares Latent Variable Modeling Approach for Measuring Interaction Effects, in: Information Systems Research, Vol. 14 (2), pp. 189-217.

CHIN, W. (1998a), Issues and opinion on structural equation modeling, in: MIS Quarterly, Vol. March pp. 7-16.

CHIN, W. (1998b), The partial least squares approach to structural equation modeling, in: MARCOULIDES, G. (Ed.), Modern methods for business research, Mahwah, NJ, pp. 295-358.

CHIOU, J./HSU, A./HSIEH, C. (2013), How negative online information affects consumers' brand evaluation, in: Online Information Review, Vol. 37 (6), pp. 910-926.

CHU, S. (2011), Viral advertising in social media: participation in Facebook groups and responses among college-aged users, in: Journal of Interactive Advertising, Vol. 12 (1), pp. 30-43.

CHURCHHILL, G. (1979), A Paradigm for Developing Better Measures of Marketing Constructs, in: Journal of Marketing Research, Vol. 16 (1), pp. 64-73.

CIAO! (2014), What is Ciao? http://www.ciao.co.uk/faq/what-is-ciao,92 (accessed: 11.03.2014).

COHEN, J. (1988), Statistical Power Analysis for the Behavioral Sciences, 2nd ed.Ed., Hillsdale.

COLLINS, N. (1996), Working models of attachment: implications for explanation, emotion and behavior, in: Journal of Personality and Social Psychology, Vol. 71 (4), pp. 810-832.

COMSCORE (2013), Nutzerzahlen sozialer Netzwerke, zitiert nach de.statista.com, http://de.statista.com/statistik/daten/studie/170467/umfrage/besucherzahlen-sozialer-netzwerke-in-deutschland/ (accessed: März 2013).

CORSTJENS, M./UMBLIJS, A. (2013), The power of evil: The damage of negative social media strongly outweigh positive contributions, in: Journal of Advertising Research, Vol. 52 (4), pp. 433-449.

COUPER, M./TRAUGOTT, M./LAMIAS, M. (2001), Web survey design and administration, in: Vol. 65 (2), pp. 230-253.

COVA, B./COVA, V. (2002), Tribal marketing: The tribalism of society and its impact on the conduct of marketing, in: European Journal of Marketing, Vol. 36 (5), pp. 595-620.

COVA, B./PACE, S. (2006), Brand community of convenience products: new forms of customer empowerment, in: European Journal of Marketing, Vol. 40 (9-10), pp. 1087-1105.

COVA, B. (1997), Community and consumption: Towards a definition of the "linking value" of product or services, in: European Journal of Marketing, Vol. 31 (3), pp. 297-316.

DARWELL, B. (2012), 'People Talking About This' defined, http://www.insidefacebook.com/2012/01/10/people-talking-about-this-defined/ (accessed: 23.01.2014).

DAVINO, C./ROMANO, R. (2013), Assessing multi-item scales for subjective measurement, Berlin.

DAVIS, F. (1989), Perceived Usefulness, Perceived Ease of Use, and User Acceptance of Information Technology, in: MIS Quarterly, Vol. 13 (3), pp. 319-340.

DAY, G. (1976), A two-dimensional concept of brand loyalty, in: Journal of Advertising Research, Vol. 9 (3), pp. 29-35.

DAY, G. (2011), Closing the marketing capabilities gap, in: Journal of Marketing, Vol. 75 (4), pp. 183-195.

DEVRIES, L./GENSLER, S./LEEFLANG, P. (2012), Popularity of brand posts on brand fan pages: an investigation of the effects of social media marketing, in: Journal of Interactive Marketing, Vol. 26 (2), pp. 83-91.

DHOLAKIA, U. M./BAGOZZI, R. P./KLEIN PEARO, L. (2004), A social influence model of consumer participation in network- and small-group-based virtual communities, in: International Journal of Research in Marketing, Vol. 21 (3), pp. 241-263.

DIAMANTOPOULOS, A./WINKLHOFER, H. (2001), Index construction with formative indicators: an alternative to scale development, in: Journal of Marketing Research, Vol. 38 pp. 269-277.

DIAMANTOPOULOS, A. (2005), The C-OAR-SE procedure for scale development in marketing: a comment, in: International Journal of Research in Marketing, Vol. 22 (1), pp. 1-9.

DICHTER, E. (1966), How word-of-mouth advertising works, in: Harvard Business Review, Vol. 44 (November-December), pp. 147-166.

DOCKTERMAN, E. (2014), NoMakeupSelfie Brings Out the Worst of the Internet for a Good Cause, http://time.com/40506/nomakeupselfie-brings-out-the-worst-of-the-internet-for-a-good-cause/ (accessed: 27.03.2014).

DOVE (2013), Dove Real Beauty Sketches, http://realbeautysketches.dove.com/ (accessed: 19.05.2014).

DUBOFF, R./WILKERSON, S. (2010), Social Media ROI, in: Marketing Management, Vol. Winter 2010 pp. 32-37.

EBSCO INDUSTRIES, I. (2013), About EBSCO, http://www.ebsco.com/about (accessed: 25.11.2013).

EICHEN, F. (2010), Messung und Steuerung der Markenbeziehungsqualität, Wiesbaden.

EILERS, D. (2014), Wirkung von Social Media auf Marken, Wiesbaden.

EISENBEISS, M./BLECHSCHMIDT, B./BACKHAUS, K./FREUND, P. (2012), "The (Real) World Is Not Enough:" Motivational Drivers and User Behavior in Virtual Worlds, in: Journal of Interactive Marketing, Vol. 26 (1), pp. 4-20.

EPINIONS (2014), About Epinions, http://www.epinions.com/about/show_~about (accessed: 11.03.2014).

EPROFESSIONAL (2013), 40 Prozent der Marketing-Budgets sind nicht sinnvoll investiert, http://www.eprofessional.de/pr-und-news/meldungen/20130814-40-prozent-der-marketing-budgets-sind-nicht-sinnvoll-investiert.html (accessed: 14.08.2013).

ESCH, F./LANGNER, T./SCHMITT, B./GEUS, P. (2006), Are brands forever? How brand knowledge and relationships affect current and future purchases, in: Journal of Product & Brand Management, Vol. 15 (2), pp. 98-105.

EYL, S. (2013), Study on Facebook engagement and interaction rates, http://blog.fanpagekarma.com/2013/02/13/facebook-engagement-interaction-rates/?sw=1 (accessed: 13.02.2013).

FACEBOOK (2012), Facebook "LIKES" vs "TALKING ABOUT THIS" numbers. TALKING ABOUT is the number that matters most, https://www.facebook.com/notes/art-jonak/facebook-likes-vs-talking-about-this-numbers-talking-about-is-the-number-that-ma/10151465281555517 (accessed: 23.01.2014).

FACEBOOK (2013), Key facts, http://newsroom.fb.com/content/default.aspx?NewsAreaId=22 (accessed: 07.10.2013).

FACEBOOK (2014), Facebook Basics, http://en-gb.facebook.com/business/overview/ (accessed: 08.04.2014).

FASSOTT, G./EGGERT, A. (2005), Zur Verwendung formativer und reflektiver Indikatoren in Strukturgleichungsmodellen: Bestandsaufnahme und Anwendungsempfehlungen, in: BLIEMEL, F./EGGERT, A./FASSOTT, G./HENSELER, J. (Ed.), Handbuch PLS-Pfadmodellierung: Methode, Anwendung, Praxisbeispiele, Stuttgart, pp. 31-69.

FETSCHERIN, M./CONWAY-DATO-ON, M. (2010), Brand Love: Interpersonal or Parasocial Love Relationship,.

FETSCHERIN, M./HEINRICH, D. (2014b), Consumer brand relationships: A research landscape, in: Journal of Brand Management, Vol. 21 (5), pp. 366-371.

FETSCHERIN, M./HEINRICH, D. (2014a), Consumer brand relationships research: A bibliometric citationmeta-analysis, in: Journal of Business Research, Vol. 6 pp. 1-11.

FILISKO, G. (2011), Social media or snake oil: Does social media measure up to the hype? http://www.abajournal.com/magazine/article/social_media_or_snake_oil/ (accessed: 01.01.2011).

FINK, A. (2013), How to conduct surveys, 5. edEd., Los Angeles.

FISHER, T. (2009), ROI in social media: A look at the arguments, in: Journal of Database Marketing & Customer Strategy Managment, Vol. 16 (3), pp. 189-195.

FORNELL, C./BOOKSTEIN, F. (1982), Two structural equation models: LISREL and PLS applied to consumer exit-voice theory, in: Journal of Marketing Research, Vol. 19 (4), pp. 440-452.

FORNELL, C./CHA, J. (1994), Partial Least Squares, in: BAGOZZI, R. (Ed.), Advanced Methods of Marketing Research, Cambridge, pp. 52-78.

FORNELL, C./LARCKER, D. (1981), Evaluating Structural Equation Models with Unobservable Variables and Measurement Errors,.

FOURNIER, S./DOBSCHA, S./MICK, D. (1998), Preventing the premature death of relationship marketing, in: Harvard Business Review, Vol. 76 (1), pp. 42-51.

FOURNIER, S./MICK, D. (1999), Rediscovering satisfaction, in: Journal of Marketing, Vol. 63 (4), pp. 5-23.

FOURNIER, S./YAO, J. L. (1997), Reviving brand loyalty: A reconceptualization within the framework of consumer-brand relationships, in: International Journal of Research in Marketing, Vol. 14 (5), pp. 451-472.

FOURNIER, S. (1998), Consumers and their brands: developing relationship theory in consumer research, in: Journal of Consumer Research, Vol. 24 (4), pp. 343-373.

FOWLER, F. J. (2002), Survey research methods, 3rd edEd., Thousand Oaks, California.

FREILING, J./GERSCH, M./GOEKE, C. (2008), On the path towards a competence-based theory of the firm, in: Organization Studies, Vol. 29 (8-9), pp. 1143-1164.

FUCHS, C./DIAMANTOPOULOS, A. (2009), Using single-item measures for construct measurement in management research, in: Die Betriebswirtschaft, Vol. 69 (2), pp. 195-210.

GARDNER, M. (1985), Does Attitude Toward the Ad Affect Brand Attitude Under a Brand Evaluation Set? in: Journal of Marketing Research, Vol. 22 (2), pp. 192-198.

GERMANN, F./GREWAL, R./ROSS, W./SRIVASTAVA, R. (2013), Product recalls and the moderating role of brand commitment, in: Marketing Letters,.

GFK (2014), GfK Experience Effects, http://www.gfk.com/solutions/brand-and-customer-experience/Pages/experience-effects.aspx (accessed: 03.10.2014).

GILFOIL, D./JOBS, C. (2012), Return on Investment For Social Media, in: Journal of Business & Economics Research, Vol. 10 (11), pp. 637-650.

GILMORE, G. (1919), Animism or thought currents of primtive peoples, Boston.

GILMORE; G.W. (1919), Animism, Boston.

GOEBEL, V. (2014), Ansprüche an Social-Media-Monitoring-Tools steigen, http://www.markenartikel-magazin.de/no_cache/medien-werbung/artikel/details/1007325-ansprueche-an-social-media-monitoring-tools-steigen/ (accessed: 28.01.2014).

GOETZ, O./LIEHR-GOBBERS, K. (2004), Analyse von Strukturgleichungsmodellen mit Hilfe der Partial-Least-Squares (PLS)-Methode, in: Die Betriebswirtschaft, Vol. 64 (6), pp. 714-738.

GOODHUE, D./LEWIS, W./THOMPSON, R. (2012), Does PLS have advantages for small sample size or non-normal data? in: MIS Quarterly, Vol. 36 (3), pp. 981-1001.

GOOGLE SCHOLAR (2014), web search, http://scholar.google.de/ (accessed: 30.01.2014).

GREEN, P./RAO, V. (1970), Rating scales and information recovery, in: Journal of Marketing, Vol. 34 pp. 33-39.

GREFEN, S./STRAUB, D./BOUDREAU, M. (2000), Structural Equation Modelling and Regression, in: Communications of Association for Information Systems, Vol. 4 pp.

1-78.

GUARINI, D. (2013), Hold your gasps, Facebook is under fire for its privacy policy again, http://www.huffingtonpost.com/2013/09/05/facebook-privacy-ftc_n_3873764.html (accessed: 09.05.2013).

GUMMERUS, J./LILJANDER, V./WEMAN, E./PIHLSTRÖM, M. (2012), Customer engagement in a Facebook brand community, in: Management Research Review, Vol. 35 (9), pp. 857-877.

HAIR, J./BLACK, W./BABIN, B./ANDERSON, R. (2010), Multivariate data analysis, 7. ed., global edEd., Upper Saddle River, NJ.

HAIR, J./BLACK, W./BABIN, B./ANDERSON, R. (2014a), Multivariate data analysis, 7. ed., Pearson new internat. edEd., Harlow.

HAIR, J./HULT, G./RINGLE, C./SARSTEDT, M. (2014b), A primer on partial least squares structural equation modeling (PLS-SEM), Los Angeles, Calif. [u.a.].

HAIR, J./RINGLE, C./SARSTEDT, M. (2011), PLS-SEM: Indeed a Silver Bullet, in: The Journal of Marketing Theory and Practice, Vol. 19 (2), pp. 139-152.

HAIR, J./SARSTEDT, M./RINGLE, C./MENA, J. (2011), An assessment of the use of partial least squares structural equation modeling in marketing research, in: Journal of the Academy of Marketing Science, Vol. 40 (3), pp. 414-433.

HAZAN, C./SHAVER, P. (1994), Attachment as an organizational framework for research on close relationships, in: Psychological Inquiry, Vol. 5 (1), pp. 1-22.

HAZAN, C./ZEIFMAN, D. (1999), Pair bonds as attachments, in: CASSIDY, J./SHAVER, P. (Ed.), Handbook of Attachment, New York, pp. 336-354.

HEDEMANN, F. (2012), Facebook-Fans: Interagieren wirklich nur 1 Prozent mit Marken? http://t3n.de/news/facebook-fans-interagieren-363255/ (accessed: 23.01.2014).

HEGNER, S. (2012), Die Relevanz des Vertrauens für das identitätsbasierte Management globaler Marken, Wiesbaden.

HEMMANN, F. (2014), Einfluss des Social Media Markenerlebnisses auf Markenimage und Kaufverhalten, im Druck.

HENNIG-THURAU, T./GWINNER, K./WALSH, G./GREMLER, D. (2004), Electronic word-of-mouth via consumer-opinion platforms: What motivates consumers to articulate themselves on the internet? in: Journal of Interactive Marketing, Vol. 18 (1), pp. 38-52.

HENNIG-THURAU, T./MALTHOUSE, E./FRIEGE, C./GENSLER, S./LOBSCHAT, L./RANGASWAMY, A./SKIERA, B. (2010), The Impact of New Media on Customer Relationships, in: Journal of Service Research, Vol. 13 (3), pp. 311-330.

HENSELER J. (2007), A new and simple approach to multi-group analysis in partial least squares path modeling, in: MARTENS, H./NÆS T., (Ed.), Causalities explored by indirect observation: Proceedings of the 5th international symposium on PLS and related methods, Oslo, 2007., pp. 104-107.

HILL, R./STAMEY, M. (1990), The homeless in America: an examination of posessions and consumption behaviours, in: Journal of Consumer Research, Vol. 17 (3), pp. 303-321.

HOFFMAN, D./FODOR, M. (2010), Can you measure the ROI of your social media marketing? in: MIT Sloan Management Review, Vol. 52 (1), pp. 40-49.

HOLIDAYCHECK (2014), About HolidayCheck, http://www.holidaycheck.com/aboutus.php (accessed: 11.03.2014).

HOMBURG, C./ARTZ, M./WIESEKE, J. (2012), Marketing performance measurement systems: does comprehensiveness really improve performance? in: Journal of Marketing, Vol. 76 (3), pp. 56-77.

HONG, S./WANG, Y./DE LOS SANTOS, G. (2008), The Effective Product Placement: Finding Appropriate Methods and Contexts for Higher Brand Salience, in: Journal of Promotion Management, Vol. 14 (1-2), pp. 103-120.

HUANG, C./SHEN, Y./LIN, H./CHANG, S. (2007), Blogger's motivations and behaviors: A model, in: Journal of Advertising Research, Vol. 47 (4), pp. 472-484.

HULLAND, J. (1999), Use of partial least squares (PLS) in strategic management research: a review of four recent studies, in: Strategic Management Journal, Vol. 20 (2), pp. 195-204.

IBM INSTITUTE FOR BUSINESS AND VALUE ANALYSIS (2011), From social media to Social CRM - What customers want, http://www-935.ibm.com/services/us/gbs/thoughtleadership/ibv-social-crm-whitepaper.html (accessed: 23.08.2012).

IBM (2011), Social Media Analytics, Makting Customer Insights Actionable,.

IHNENFELDT, E. (2013), BITKOM Studie 2013: Social Media Manager schon in 16% der Unternehmen, http://www.steadynews.de/allgemein/bitkom-studie-2013-social-media-manager-schon-in-16-der-unternehmen-ausbildung-und-weiterbildungen (accessed: 20.03.2013).

INTERBRAND (2012), Best global brands 2012, http://www.interbrand.com/de/best-global-brands/2012/Best-Global-Brands-2012-Brand-View.aspx (accessed: 27.02.2013).

JACOBY, J./CHESTNUT, R. (1978), Brand loyalty: measurement and management, New York.

JACOBY, J./KYNER, D. (1973), Brand loyalty vs. repeat purchasing behavior, in: Journal of Marketing Research, Vol. 10 (1), pp. 1-9.

JAHN, B./KUNZ, W. (2012), How to transform consumers into fans of your brand, in: Journal of Service Management, Vol. 23 (3), pp. 344-361.

JAHN, B./KUNZ, W. (2014), A Brand Like a Friend -The Influence of Customer Engagement with Social Media Brand Pages on Brand Relationships and Loyalty Intentions,.

JANG, H./OLFMAN, L./KO, I./KOH, J./KIM, K. (2008), The Influence of on-line brand community characteristics on community commitment and brand loyalty, in: International Journal of Electronic Commerce, Vol. 12 (3), pp. 57-80.

JARVIS, C./MACKENZIE, S./PODSAKOFF, P. (2003), A critical review of construct indicators and measurement model misspecification in marketing and consumer research, in: Journal of Consumer Research, Vol. 30 (2), pp. 199-218.

JOHNSON, Z./MASSIAH, C./ALLAN, J. (2013), Community identification increases consumer-to-consumer helping, but not always, in: Journal of Consumer Marketing, Vol. 30 (2), pp. 121-129.

JOHNSTONE, E./DODD, C. (2000), Placements as mediators of brand salience within a UK cinema audience, in: Journal of Marketing Communications, Vol. 6 (3), pp. 141-158.

JOINSON, A. (2008), Looking at, looking up or keeping up with people? Motives and uses of Facebook, New York, NY.

KAISER, H. (1974), An index of factoral simplicity, in: Psychometrika, Vol. 39 (1), pp. 31-36.

KAPFERER, J. N. (1992), Die Marke. Kapital des Unternehmens, Landsberg/Lech.

KAPLAN, A./HAENLEIN, M. (2010), Users of the world, unite! The challenges and opportunities of social media,.

KELLER, E./FAY, B. (2013), Word-of-mouth advocacy: A new key to advertising effectiveness, in: Journal of Advertising Research, Vol. 52 (4), pp. 459-464.

KELLER, K. L. (1993), Conceptualizing, measuring, and managing customer-based brand equity, in: Journal of Marketing, Vol. 57 pp. 1-22.

KIM, J. W./CHOI, J./QUALLS, W./HAN, K. (2008), It takes a marketplace community to raise brand commitment: the role of online communities, in: Journal of Marketing Management, Vol. 24 (3-4), pp. 409-431.

KLEINE, S./BAKER, S. (2004), An integrative review of material possession attachment, in: Academy of Marketing Science Review, Vol. 1 pp. 1-39.

KLEINE, S./KLEINE, R./ALLEN, C. (1995), How is a possession "me" or "not me"? Characterizing types and an antecedent of material possession attachment, in: Journal of Consumer Research, Vol. 22 (3), pp. 327-343.

KLEINE-KALMER, B./BURMANN, C./SCHADE, M. (2013), What Makes Brand Fan Pages in Social Networks Successful? Istanbul.

KLEINE-KALMER, B./BURMANN, C. (2013a), Uses and Gratifications of Brand Fan Pages in Social Networks, Boston, MA.

KLEINE-KALMER, B./BURMANN, C. (2013b), Determinants of the attitude toward brand fan pages in social networks, Zagreb.

KLINE, R. (2005), Principles and practice of structural equation modeling, 2. edEd., New York, NY.

KNOX, S. W. D. (2003), Empirical developments in the measurement of involvement, brand loyalty and their relationship in grocery markets, in: Journal of Strategic Marketing, Vol. 11 (4), pp. 271-286.

KO, H./CHO, C./ROBERTS, M. (2005), Internet uses and gratifications: A Structural Equation Model of Interactive Advertising, in: Journal of Advertising, Vol. 34 (2), pp. 57-70.

KOTLER, P./ARMSTRONG, G. (2014), Principles of marketing, 15. ed., global edEd., Boston, MA.

KOZINETS, R./DE VALCK, K./WOJNICKI, A./WILNER, S. (2010), Networked narratives: Understanding word-of-mouth marketing in online communities, in: Journal of Marketing, Vol. 74 (2), pp. 71-89.

KOZINETS, R. (2002), The field behind the screen: using netnography for marketing research in online communities, in: Journal of Marketing Research, Vol. 39 (1), pp. 61-72.

KROEBER-RIEL, W./WEINBERG, P./GRÖPPEL-KLEIN, A. (2009), Konsumentenverhalten, 9Ed., München.

KUß, A./EISEND, M. (2010), Marktforschung, 3., überarbeitete und erweiterte AuflageEd., Wiesbaden.

LACOEUILHE, J. (2000), L'attachement à la marque : Proposition d'une échelle de mesure, in: Recherche et Applications en Marketing, Vol. 15 (4), pp. 61-77.

LAM, S./SHANKAR, V. (2014), Asymmetries in the Effects of Drivers of Brand Loyalty Between Early and Late Adopters and Across Technology Generations, in: Journal of Interactive Marketing, Vol. 28 (1), pp. 26-42.

LAMBERT-PANDRAUD, R./LAURENT, G. (2010), Why do older consumers buy older brands? The role of attachment and declining innovativeness, in: Journal of Marketing, Vol. 74 pp. 104-121.

LANGE, M. (2008), Social Media Monitoring, in: TORSTEN SCHWARZ (Ed.), Leitfaden Online Marketing, Waghäusel, pp. 655-659.

LANGNER, T./BRUNS, D./FISCHER, A./ROSSITER, J. (2014), Falling in love with brands: a dynamic analysis of the trajectories of brand love, in: Marketing Letters, pp. 1-12.

LANGNER, T./KÜHN, J./BRUNS, D. (2013), All you need is love, in: Markenartikel, Vol. 7 pp. 32-34.

LANGNER, T./MÜLLER, J. (2013), Marketing im Netz: Herausforderungen der digitalen Markenkommunikation, in: transfer Werbeforschung & Praxis, Vol. 59 (4), pp. 19-22.

LAURENT, G./KAPFERER, J. (1985), Measuring consumer involvement profiles, in: Journal of Marketing Research, Vol. 22 (1), pp. 41-53.

LAY'S (2014), Do us a flavor, https://www.dousaflavor.com/ (accessed: 19.05.2014).

LEE, H. J./LEE, D./TAYLOR, C. R./LEE, J. (2011), Do online brand communities help build and maintain relationships with consumers? A network theory approach, in: Journal of Brand Management, Vol. 19 (3), pp. 213-227.

LIM (2013), Facebook accounts of the top 100 global brands, Bremen.

LIN, H. (2006), Understanding Behavioral Intention to Participate in Virtual Communities, in: CyberPsychology & Behavior, Vol. 9 (5), pp. 540-547.

LOUIS, D./LOMBART, C. (2010), Impact of brand personality on three major relational consequences (trust, attachment, and commitment to the brand), in: Journal of Product & Brand Management, Vol. 19 (2), pp. 114-130.

MACKENZIE, S./PODSAKOFF, P./JARVIS, C. (2005), The problem of measurement model misspecification in behavioral and organizational research and some recommended solutions, in: The Journal of Applied Psychology, Vol. 90 (4), pp. 710-30.

MALÄR, L./KROHMER, H./HOYER, W./NYFFENEGGER, B. (2011), Emotional brand attachment and brand personality: the relative importance of the actual and the ideal self, in: Journal of Marketing, Vol. 75 pp. 35-52.

MALHOTRA, A./MALHOTRA, C./SEE, A. (2013), How to create brand engagement on Facebook, in: MIT Sloan Management Review, Vol. 54 (2), pp. 17-20.

MARKETING SCIENCE INSTITUTE (2010), Research Priorities 2010-2012, Cambridge, MA.

MATEOS-APARICIO, G. (2011), Partial Least Squares (PLS) Methods: Origins, Evolution, and Application to Social Sciences, in: Communications in Statistics - Theory and Methods, Vol. 40 (13), pp. 2305-2317.

MATHWICK, C. (2002), Understanding the online consumer: A typology of online relational norms and behavior, in: Journal of Interactive Marketing, Vol. 16 (1), pp. 40-55.

MATZLER, K./PICHLER, E./FÜLLER, J./MOORADIAN, T. A. (2011), Personality, person-brand fit, and brand community: An investigation of individuals, brands, and brand communities, in: Journal of Marketing Management, Vol. 27 (9-10), pp. 874-890.

MCALEXANDER, J./SCHOUTEN, J./KOENIG, H. (2002), Building brand community,.

MEFFERT, H./BURMANN, C./KIRCHGEORG, M. (2012), Marketing, 11. AuflEd., s.l.

MEFFERT, H./BURMANN, C. (1996), Identitätsorientierte Markenführung, Grundlagen für das Management von Markenportfolios,.

MENDE, M./BOLTON, R./BITNER, M. (2013), Decoding Customer-Firm Relationships: How Attachment Styles Help Explain Customers' Preferences for Closeness, Repurchase Intentions, and Changes in Relationship Breadth, in: Journal of Marketing Research, Vol. L pp. 125-142.

MERCHANT, A./ROSE, G. (2013), Effects of advertising-evoked vicarious nostalgia on brand heritage, in: Journal of Business Research, Vol. 66 (12), pp. 2619-2625.

MEYER, J./ALLEN, N. (1997), Commitment in the workplace, Thousand Oaks, California.

MEYER, J./ALLEN, N. (1991), A three-component conceptualization of organizational commitment, in: Human Resource Management Review, Vol. 1 (1), pp. 61-89.

MICK, D./DEMOSS, M. (1990), Self-gifts: Phenomenological insights from four contexts, in: Journal of Consumer Research, Vol. 17 (3), pp. 322-332.

MIKULINCER, M./SHAVER, P. (2007), Attachment in adulthood, New York.

MILLAN, A./DIAZ, E. (2014), Analysis of consumers' response to brand community integration and brand identification, in: Journal of Brand Management, Vol. 21 (3), pp. 254-272.

MILLER, S./BERRY, L. (1998), Brand salience versus brand image: two theories of advertising effectiveness, in: Journal of Advertising Research, Vol. 38 (5), pp. 77-82.

MILLWARDBROWN (2014), CrossMedia Research, https://www.millwardbrown.com/solutions/slick-sheets/millwardbrown_CrossMedia.aspx (accessed: 03.10.2014).

MOONEY, C. (2010), Theories of attachment, St. Paul, MN, USA.

MOORMAN, C./ZALTMANN, G./DESHPANDE, R. (1992), Relationships between providers and users of market research: the dynamics of trust within and between organizations, in: Journal of Marketing Research, Vol. 29 (3), pp. 314-328.

MORGAN, R./HUNT, S. (1994), The commitment-trust theory of relationship marketing, in: Journal of Marketing, Vol. 58 (3), pp. 20-38.

MOWDAY, R./STEERS, R./PORTER, L. (1979), The measurement of organizational commitment, in: Journal of Vocational Behavior, Vol. 14 (2), pp. 224-247.

MOZART, F. (2013), Immer mehr Unternehmen beschäftigen Social Media Manager, http://www.wuv.de/digital/immer_mehr_unternehmen_beschaeftigen_social_media_manager (accessed: 19.03.2013).

MUEHLING, D./SPROTT, D./SULTAN, A. (2014), Exploring the Boundaries of Nostalgic Advertising Effects: A Consideration of Childhood Brand Exposure and Attachment on Consumers' Responses to Nostalgia-Themed Advertisements, in: Journal of Advertising, Vol. 43 (1), pp. 73-84.

MUELLER, D. (2006), Moderatoren und Mediatoren in Regressionen, in: ALBERS, S./KLAPPER, D./KONRADT, U./WALTER, A./WOLF, J. (Ed.), Methodik der empirischen Forschung, Wiesbaden, pp. 257-274.

MUI, C. (2011), Facebook's Privacy Issues Are Even Deeper Than We Knew, http://www.forbes.com/sites/chunkamui/2011/08/08/facebooks-privacy-issues-are-even-deeper-than-we-knew/ (accessed: 08.08.2011).

MUNIZ, A. J./O'GUINN, T. (2001), Brand Community, in: Journal of Consumer Research, Vol. 27 (4), pp. 412-432.

MUNTINGA, D./MOORMAN, M./SMIT, E. (2011), Introducing COBRAs, in: International Journal of Advertising, Vol. 30 (1), pp. 13-46.

MURDOUGH, C. (2009), Social Media Measurement: it's not impossible, in: Journal of Interactive Advertising, Vol. 10 (1), pp. 94-100.

NAYLOR, R./LAMBERTON, C./WEST, P. (2012), Beyond the "Like" button: The impact of mere virtual presence on brand evaluations and purchase intentions in social media settings, in: Journal of Marketing, Vol. 76 (6), pp. 105-120.

NEDUNGADI, P./HUTCHINSON, J. (1985), The Prototypicality of Brands: Relationships With Brand Awareness, Preference and Usage, in: Advances in Consumer Research, Vol. 12 pp. 498-503.

NELSON-FIELD, K./RIEBE, E./SHARP, B. (2012), What's not to “like”? Can a Facebook fan base give a brand the advertising reach it needs? in: Journal of Advertising Research, Vol. 52 (2), pp. 262-269.

NISBETT, R./WILSON, T. (1977), The halo effect: Evidence for unconscious alteration of judgments, in: Journal of Personality and Social Psychology, Vol. 35 (4), pp. 250-256.

NÖCKER, R. (2014), Ökonomie der Werbung, Wiesbaden.

NUNALLY, J./BERNSTEIN, I. (1994), Psychometric theory, New York.

NUTELLA UK & IRELAND (2014), 50 years full of stories, https://www.facebook.com/nutellauk?fref=ts (accessed: 24.02.2014).

O'REILLY, C./CHATMAN, J. (1986), Organizational commitment and psychological attachment: The effects of compliance, identification, and internalization on prosocial behavior, in: Journal of Applied Psychology, Vol. 71 (3), pp. 492-499.

OLSEN, W. (2012), Data collection, Los Angeles.

OREO COOKIE (2013), Power out? No problem, https://twitter.com/Oreo/status/298246571718483968 (accessed: 03.02.2013).

OXFORD DICTIONARIES (2013a), Definition of attachment in English, http://www.oxforddictionaries.com/definition/english/attachment?q=attachment (accessed: 13.12.2013).

OXFORD DICTIONARIES (2013b), Definition of commitment in English, http://www.oxforddictionaries.com/definition/english/commitment?q=commitment (accessed: 13.12.2013).

OXFORD DICTIONARIES (2014a), Defintion of fan in English, http://www.oxforddictionaries.com/definition/american_english/fan?q=fans#fan-2 (accessed: 12.03.2014).

OXFORD DICTIONARIES (2014b), Definition of closeness in English, http://www.oxforddictionaries.com/definition/english/close?q=closeness#close__54 (accessed: 03.08.2014).

OXFORD DICTIONARIES (2014c), Definition of proximity in English, http://www.oxforddictionaries.com/definition/english/proximity (accessed: 03.08.2014).

OXFORD DICTIONARIES (2014d), Defintion of relationship in English, http://www.oxforddictionaries.com/definition/english/relationship?q=relationship (accessed: 11.02.2014).

OXFORD DICTIONARIES (2014e), Definition of selfie in English, http://www.oxforddictionaries.com/definition/english/selfie.

OXFORD DICTIONARIES (2014f), Definition of crowdsource in English, http://www.oxforddictionaries.com/definition/english/crowdsource?q=crowdsourci

ng (accessed: 19.05.2014).

Pai, P./Tsai, H. (2011), How virtual community participation influences consumer loyalty intentions in online shopping contexts: an investigation of mediating factors, in: Behaviour & Information Technology, Vol. 30 (5), pp. 603-615.

Parent, M./Plangger, K./Bal, A. (2011), The new WTP: Willingness to participate, in: Business Horizons, Vol. 54 (3), pp. 219-229.

Park, C./Eisingerich, A./Park, J. (2013), Attachment-aversion (AA) model of customer-brand relationships, in: Journal of Consumer Psychology, Vol. 23 (2), pp. 229-248.

Park, C./MacInnis, D. J./Priester, J./Eisingerich, A. B./Iacobucci, D. (2010), Brand attachment and brand attitude strength: conceptual and empirical differentiation of two critical brand equity drivers, in: Journal of Marketing, Vol. 74 (6), pp. 1-17.

Park, C./MacInnis, D./Priester, J. (2006a), Beyond attitudes: Attachment and consumer behavior, in: Seoul Journal of Business, Vol. 12 (2), pp. 3-35.

Park, C./MacInnis, D./Priester, J. (2006b), Brand attachment: constructs, consequences, and causes, in: Foundations and Trends in Marketing, Vol. 1 (3), pp. 191-230.

Park, C./MacInnis, D. (2006), What's in and what's out; Questions on the boundaries of the attitude construct, in: Journal of Consumer Research, Vol. 33 (1), pp. 16-18.

Park, C./Young, S. (1983), Types and levels of involvement and brand attitude formation, in: Advances in Consumer Research, Vol. 10 (1), pp. 320-324.

Park, H./Cho, H. (2012), Social network online communities: information sources for apparel shopping, in: Journal of Consumer Marketing, Vol. 29 (6), pp. 400-411.

Park, N./Kee, K./Valenzuela, S. (2009), Being immersed in social networking environment: Facebook groups, uses and gratifications, and social outcomes, in: CyberPsychology & Behavior, Vol. 12 (6), pp. 729-733.

Patterson, A. (2012), Social-networkers of the world, unite and take over: A meta-introspective perspective on the Facebook brand, in: Journal of Business Research, Vol. 65 (4), pp. 527-534.

Pentina, I./Gammoh, B./Zhang, L./Mallin, M. (2013), Drivers and outcomes of brand relationship quality in the context of online social networks, in: International Journal of Electronic Commerce, Vol. 17 (3), pp. 63-86.

PHILLIPS, M. (2013), Why your engagement rate is low and how you can fix it, https://econsultancy.com/blog/62694-why-your-engagement-rate-is-low-and-how-you-can-fix-it (accessed: 09.05.2013).

PIEHLER, R. (2011), Interne Markenführung, 1. AuflEd., Wiesbaden.

PORSCHE (2014), Porsche Facebook brand page, https://www.facebook.com/porsche (accessed: 08.04.2014).

PORTER, C. E. (2004), A typology of virtual communities: a multi-disciplinary foundation for future research, in: Journal of Computer-Mediated Communication, Vol. 10 (1),.

PRAHALAD, C./RAMASWAMY, V. (2004), Co-creation experiences: The next practice in value creation, in: Journal of Interactive Marketing, Vol. 18 (3), pp. 5-14.

PROJECTOR ONLINE MARKETING BLOG (2013), Top 10 der deutschen Facebook-Shops, http://www.projecter.de/blog/social-media/top-10-der-deutschen-facebook-shops.html (accessed: 22.01.2013).

RAUSCHNABEL, P./AHUVIA, A. (2014), You're so lovable: Anthropomorphism and brand love, in: Journal of Brand Management, Vol. 21 (5), pp. 372-395.

REN, Y./HARPER, F./DRENNER, S./TERVEEN, L./KIESLER, S./RIEDL, J./KRAUT, R. (2012), Building member attachment in online communities: applying theories of group identity and interpersonal bonds, in: MIS Quarterly, Vol. 36 (3), pp. 841-864.

RICHINS, M. (1994), Special possessions and the expression of material values, in: Journal of Consumer Research, Vol. 21 (3), pp. 522-533.

ROBINS, J. (2012), Partial Least Squares, in: Long Range Planning, Vol. 45 (5-6), pp. 309-311.

ROMANIUK, J./SHARP, B. (2003), Brand Salience and Customer Defection in Subscription Markets, in: Journal of Marketing Manangement, Vol. 19 (1-2), pp. 25-44.

ROMANIUK, J./SHARP, B. (2004), Conceptualizing and measuring brand salience, in: Marketing Theory, Vol. 4 (4), pp. 327-342.

ROSSITER, J. (2002), The C-OAR-SE procedure for scale development in marketing, in: International Journal of Research in Marketing, Vol. 19 (4), pp. 305-335.

ROSSMANN, A. (2013), Auf der Suche nach dem Return on Social Media, St. Gallen.

RUGGIERO, T. (2000), Uses and gratifications theory in the 21st century, in: Mass communication and society, Vol. 3 (1), pp. 3-37.

SASHI, C. (2012), Customer engagement, buyer-seller relationships, and social media, in: Management Decision, Vol. 50 (2), pp. 253-272.

SCHADE, M. (2012), Identitätsbasierte Markenführung professioneller Sportvereine, 1. AuflEd., Wiesbaden.

SCHALLEHN, M./BURMANN, C./RILEY, N. (2014), Brand authenticity: model development and empirical testing, in: Journal of Product & Brand Management, Vol. 23 (3), pp. 192-199.

SCHALLEHN, M. (2012), Marken-Authentizität, Wiesbaden.

SCHAU, H./MUNIZ, A./ARNOULD, E. (2009), How brand community practices create value, in: Journal of Marketing, Vol. 73 (5), pp. 30-51.

SCHLEGL, S. (2010), Schätzung und Beurteilung von Strukturgleichungsmodellen mit dem PLS-Verfahren, in: transfer Werbeforschung & Praxis, Vol. 3 pp. 64-65.

SCHMALZ, S./ORTH, U. (2012), Brand attachment and consumer emotional response to unethical firm behavior, in: Psychology & Marketing, Vol. 29 (11), pp. 869-884.

SCHMUNDT, H. (2013), Facebook ist für Opa, in: Der Spiegel, Vol. 52 pp. 122.

SCHOENFELD, A. (2012), Google+ Brand Page Adoption and Engagement Are on the Rise, http://simplymeasured.com/blog/2012/05/09/google-brand-page-adoption-and-engagement-are-on-the-rise-study/ (accessed: 09.05.2012).

SCHONLAU, M./FRICKER, R./ELLIOTT, M. (2002), Conducting research surveys via e-mail and the Web, Santa Monica, California.

SCHOUTEN, J./MCALEXANDER, J. (1995), Subcultures of consumption: An ethnography of the new bikers, in: Journal of Consumer Research, Vol. 22 (1), pp. 43-61.

SCHULTZ, D./BARNES, B./SCHULTZ, H./AZZARO, M. (2009), Building customer-brand relationships, Armonk, NY.

SCHULTZ, S./KLEINE, R. K. J. (1989), "These Are A Few of My Favorite Things", in: Advances in Consumer Research, Vol. 16 pp. 359-366.

SCHUPP (2013), Lay's "Do Us A Flavor" and Let Me Try Your Flavors, http://www.schuppco.com/blog/?p=3990.

SEDLMEIER, P./RENKEWITZ, F. (2013), Forschungsmethoden und Statistik für Psychologen und Sozialwissenschaftler, 2., aktualisierte und erw. AuflEd., München.

SELM, M./JANKOWSKI, N. (2006), Conducting online surveys, in: Quality & Quantity, Vol. 40 (3), pp. 435-456.

SIRGY, M. (1982), Self-concept in consumer behavior: a critical review, in: Journal of Consumer Research, Vol. 9 (3), pp. 287-300.

SIRGY, M. (1985), Using self-congruity and ideal congruity to predict purchase motivation, in: Journal of Business Research, Vol. 13 (3), pp. 195-206.

SMIT, E./BRONNER, F./TOLBOOM, M. (2007), Brand relationship quality and its value for personal contact, in: Journal of Business Research, Vol. 60 (6), pp. 627-633.

SMIT, E./NEIJENS, P. (2011), The march to reliable metrics: A half-century of coming closer to the truth, in: Journal of Advertising Research, Vol. 51 (124-135),.

SMITH, A./FISCHER, E./YONGJIAN, C. (2012), How does brand-related user-generated content differ across YouTube, Facebook and Twitter? in: Journal of Interactive Marketing, Vol. 26 (2), pp. 102-113.

SMITH, S. (2013), Conceptualising and evaluating experiences with brands on Facebook, in: International Journal of Market Research, Vol. 55 (3), pp. 357-374.

SOCIALBAKERS (2012), Ranking Facebook pages, http://www.socialbakers.com/facebook-pages/brands/ (accessed: 24.02.2012).

SOCIALBAKERS (2013a), Formulas revealed: The Facebook and Twitter engagement rate, http://www.socialbakers.com/blog/467-formulas-revealed-the-facebook-and-twitter-engagement-rate (accessed: 16.10.2013).

SOCIALBAKERS (2013b), Is your business benchmarking its engagement rate? http://www.socialbakers.com/blog/1525-is-your-business-benchmarking-its-engagement-rate (accessed: 16.10.2013).

SOCIALMENTION (2014), Real-time social media search and analysis, http://www.socialmention.com/ (accessed: 19.05.2014).

SOLOVE, D. (2006), A taxonomy of privacy, in: University of Pennsylvania Law Review, Vol. 154 (3), pp. 477-564.

STAFFORD, T./STAFFORD, M./SCHKADE, L. (2004), Determining uses and gratifications for the internet, in: Decision Sciences, Vol. 35 (2), pp. 259-288.

STEENKAMP, J./BAUMGARTNER, H. (2000), On the use of structural equation models for marketing modeling, in: International Journal of Research in Marketing, Vol. 17 (2-3), pp. 195-202.

STEPHEN, A./GALAK, J. (2012), The effects of traditional and social earned media on sales: A study of a microlending marketplace, in: Journal of Marketing Research, Vol. 49 (5), pp. 624-639.

STERNBERG, R. (1986), A triangular theory of love, in: Psychological Review, Vol. 93 (2), pp. 119-135.

STERNBERG, R. (1997), Construct validation of a triangular love scale, in: European Journal of Social Psychology, Vol. 27 pp. 313-335.

STÖCKER, C. (2014), Übernahme durch Facebook: Viele WhatsApp-Nutzer erwägen Wechsel, http://www.spiegel.de/netzwelt/apps/whatsapp-nach-facebook-uebernahme-erwaegen-viele-nutzer-wechsel-a-955440.html (accessed: 25.02.2014).

STONE, M./WOODCOCK, N. (2013), Social intelligence in customer engagement, in: Journal of Strategic Marketing, Vol. 21 (5), pp. 394-401.

SUE, V./RITTER, L. (2012), Conducting online surveys, 2. edEd., Los Angeles.

SWAMINATHAN, V./STILLEY, K./AHLUWALIA, R. (2009), When Brand Personality Matters: The Moderating Role of Attachment Styles, in: Journal of Consumer Research, Vol. 35 (6), pp. 985-1002.

TABACHNICK, B./FIDELL, L. (2013), Using multivariate statistics, 6. ed., internat. edEd., Boston, MA.

TAJFEL, H./TURNER, J. (1986), The social identity theory of intergroup behaviour, in: WORCHEL, S./AUSTIN, W. (Ed.), Psychology of intergroup relations, Chicago, IL, pp. 7-24.

TALKWALKER (2014), Social Media Monitoring, http://www.talkwalker.com/de/about-us/unternehmen/ (accessed: 31.01.2014).

TAYLOR, D./LEWIN, J./STRUTTON, D. (2011), Friends, fans, and followers: Do ads work on social networks? How gender and age shape receptivity, in: Journal of Advertising Research, Vol. 51 (1), pp. 258-275.

THE GUARDIAN (2013), You think Facebook is free? Well, it'll only cost you your private life, http://www.theguardian.com/commentisfree/2013/dec/29/observer-editorial-digital-privacy (accessed: 29.12.2013).

THE GUARDIAN (2014), No-makeup selfies raise £8m for Cancer Research UK in six days, http://www.theguardian.com/society/2014/mar/25/no-makeup-selfies-cancer-charity (accessed: 25.03.2014).

THELEN, E./WOODSIDE, A. (1997), What evokes the brand or store? Consumer research on accessibility theory applied to modeling primary choice, in: International Journal of Research in Marketing, Vol. 14 (2), pp. 125-145.

THOMPSON, S./SINHA, R. (2008), Brand communities and new product adoption: the influence and limits of oppositional loyalty, in: Journal of Marketing, Vol. 72 (6), pp. 65-80.

THOMSON, M./JOHNSON, A. (2006), Marketplace and personal space: investigating the differential effects of attachment style across relationship contexts, in: Psychology & Marketing, Vol. 23 (8), pp. 711-726.

THOMSON, M./MACINNIS, D./PARK, C. W. (2005), The ties that bind: Measuring the strength of consumers' emotional attachments to brands, in: Journal of Consumer Psychology, Vol. 15 (1), pp. 77-91.

THOMSON, M. (2006), Human brands: investigating antecedents to consumers' strong attachments to celebrities, in: Journal of Marketing, Vol. 79 (3), pp. 104-119.

TNS (2012), Auch Gutverdiener in sozialen Netzwerken aktiv, http://www.tns-infratest.com/presse/presseinformation.asp?prID=843 (accessed: 01.10.2012).

TOBESOCIAL (2013), Beste Social Media Kampagnen - Die Top 10 von tobesocial, http://tobesocial.de/blog/beste-social-media-kampagnen-2012-social-media-marketing-erfolg (accessed: 19.04.2013).

TROMMSDORFF, V./TEICHERT, T. (2011), Konsumentenverhalten, 8., vollst. überarb. und erw. AuflEd., Stuttgart.

TROPP, J. (2011), Moderne Marketing-Kommunikation, 1. AuflEd., Wiesbaden.

TRUSOV, M./BODAPATI, A./BUCKLIN, R. (2010), Determining influential users in internet social networks, in: Journal of Marketing Research, Vol. 47 (4), pp. 643-658.

TSAI, S. (2011), Fostering international brand loyalty through committed and attached relationships, in: International Business Review, Vol. 20 (5), pp. 521-534.

TUCKER, W. (1964), The development of brand loyalty, in: Journal of Marketing Research, Vol. 1 (3), pp. 32-35.

TUTEN, T./SOLOMON, M. (2013), Social media marketing, International edEd., Boston, MA.

VAN DER LANS, R./PIETERS, R./WEDEL, M. (2008), Competitive Brand Salience, in: Marketing Science, Vol. 27 (5), pp. 922-931.

VAN DOORN, J./LEMON, K. N./MITTAL, V./NASS, S./PICK, D./PIRNER, P./VERHOEF, P. C. (2010), Customer engagement behavior: Theoretical foundations and research directions, in: Journal of Service Research, Vol. 13 (3), pp. 253-266.

VAN DOORN, J. (2011), Customer engagement: Essence, dimensionality, and boundaries, in: Journal of Service Research, Vol. 14 (3), pp. 280-282.

VAN LANGE, P./RUSBULT, C./DRIGOTAS, S./ARRIAGA, X./WITCHER, B./COX, C. (1997), Willingness to sacrifice in close relationships, in: Journal of Personality and Social Psychology, Vol. 72 (6), pp. 1373-1395.

VELOUTSOU, C./MOUTINHO, L. (2009), Brand relationships through brand reputation and brand tribalism, in: Journal of Business Research, Vol. 62 (3), pp. 314-322.

VOLVO TRUCKS (2013), The Epic Split feat. Van Damme (Live Test 6), http://www.youtube.com/watch?v=M7FIvfx5J10 (accessed: 13.11.2013).

WAGENFÜHRER, D. (2013), Social Media-Monitoring 2.0: Die Bedeutung von Anwendungsszenarien zur Messung des Social Media-Erfolgs, in: transfer Werbeforschung & Praxis, Vol. 59 (4), pp. 28-33.

WALLACE, E./BUIL, I./DE CHERNATONY, L. (2012), Facebook "friendship" and brand advocacy, in: Journal of Brand Management, Vol. 20 (2), pp. 128-146.

WALLENDORF, M. A. E. (1988), "My Favorite Things": A Cross-Cultural Inquiry into Object Attachment, Possessiveness, and Social Linkage, in: Journal of Consumer Research, Vol. 14 (4), pp. 531-547.

WEIBER, R./MÜHLHAUS, D. (2010), Strukturgleichungsmodellierung, Heidelberg [u.a.].

WEIBER, R. (2010), Strukturgleichungsmodellierung - Eine anwendungsorientierte Einführung in die Kausalanalyse mit Hilfe von AMOS, SmartPLS und SPSS, Berlin.

WELLER, S./ROMNEY, A. (1988), Systematic data collection, Newbury Park, California.

WELLS, W./LEAVITT, C./MCCONVILLE, M. (1971), A reaction profile for TV commercials, in: Journal of Advertising Research, Vol. 11 (6), pp. 11-18.

WENSKE, A. V. (2008), Management und Wirkungen von Marke-Kunden-Beziehungen im Konsumgüterbereich, Wiesbaden.

WETZELS, M./ODEKERKEN-SCHRÖDER, G./VAN OPPEN, C. (2009), Using PLS path modeling for assessing hierarchical construct models: guidelines and empirical illustration, in: MIS Quarterly, Vol. 33 (1), pp. 177-195.

WHANG, Y./ALLEN, J./SAHOURY, N./ZHANG, H. (2004), Falling in love with a product: the structure of a romantic consumer-product relationship, in: Advances in Consumer Research, Vol. 31 pp. 320-327.

WHITLER, K. (2013), Leveraging social media to drive superior consumer insight, http://www.cmo.com/articles/2013/5/7/leveraging_social_me.html (accessed: 13.05.2013).

WIERTZ, C./DE RUYTER, K. (2007), Beyond the call of duty: Why customers contribute to firm-hosted commercial online communities, in: Organization Studies, Vol. 28 (3), pp. 347-376.

WILCOX, G./KIM, K. (2012), Multivariate time series use for the measurement of social media effects, in: The Marketing Management Journal, Vol. 22 (2), pp. 90-101.

WIRTZ, J./DEN AMBTMAN, A./BLOEMER, J./HORVATH, C./RAMASESHAN, B./VAN DE KLUNDERT, J./CANLI, Z. G./KANDAMPULLY, J. (2013), Managing brands and customer engagement in online brand communities, in: Journal of Service Management, Vol. 24 (3), pp. 223-244.

WIRTZ, M. (2004), Über das Problem fehlender Werte, in: Vol. 43 (2), pp. 109-115.

WOISETSCHLÄGER, D./HARTLEB, V./BLUT, M. (2008), How to make brand communities work: Antecedents and consequences of consumer participation, in: Journal of Relationship Marketing, Vol. 7 (3), pp. 237-256.

WOLFINBARGER, M./GILLY, M. (2003), EtailQ: Dimensionalizing, Measuring, and Predicting Etail Quality, in: Journal of Retailing, Vol. 79 (3), pp. 183-198.

WONG, K. (2013), Partial Least Squares Structural Equation Modeling (PLS-SEM)

Techniques Using SmartPLS, in: Marketing Bulletin, Vol. 24 pp. 1-32.

WOOLLASTON, V. (2013), Facebook users are committing 'virtual identity suicide' in droves and quitting the site over privacy and addiction fears Read more: http://www.dailymail.co.uk/sciencetech/article-2423713/Facebook-users-committing-virtual-identity-suicide-quitting-sit, http://www.dailymail.co.uk/sciencetech/article-2423713/Facebook-users-committing-virtual-identity-suicide-quitting-site-droves-privacy-addiction-fears.html (accessed: 17.09.2013).

XU, H./GUPTA, S./ROSSON, M./CARROLL, J. (2012), Measuring Mobile Users' Concerns for Information Privacy, Orlando.

YEH, Y./CHOI, S. M. (2011), Mini-lovers, maxi-mouths: An investigation of antecedents to eWOM intention among brand community members, in: Journal of Marketing Communications, Vol. 17 (3), pp. 145-162.

ZAGLIA, M. E. (2013), Brand communities embedded in social networks, in: Journal of Business Research, Vol. 66 (2), pp. 216-223.

ZENN, J. (2012), 9 Ways to Measure Your Brand's Social Media Health, http://mashable.com/2012/06/11/social-media-brand-data/ (accessed: 11.06.2012).

ZHOU, Z./ZHANG, Q./SU, C./ZHOU, N. (2012), How do brand communities generate brand relationships? Intermediate mechanisms, in: Journal of Business Research, Vol. 65 pp. 890-895.

FSC www.fsc.org
MIX
Papier aus verantwortungsvollen Quellen
Paper from responsible sources
FSC® C105338

If you have any concerns about our products,
you can contact us on
ProductSafety@springernature.com

In case Publisher is established outside the EU,
the EU authorized representative is:
Springer Nature Customer Service Center GmbH
Europaplatz 3, 69115 Heidelberg, Germany

Printed by Libri Plureos GmbH
in Hamburg, Germany